TECHTV'S GUIDE TO CREATING DIGITAL VIDEO LIKE A PRO

Deras Flynn

CONTENTS
AT A GLANCE

techtv

650 Townsend Street
San Francisco, California 94103

TECHTV'S GUIDE TO CREATING DIGITAL VIDEO LIKE A PRO

Copyright © 2002 by Pearson Education

Published by TechTV Press, in association with New Riders Publishing, a division of Pearson Education.

New Riders Publishing
201 West 103rd Street, Indianapolis IN 46290

International Standard Book Number: 0-7897-2656-4

Library of Congress Catalog Card Number: 2002101825

Printed in the United States of America

First Printing: March 2002

05   04   03   4   3   2

(handwritten: 778.59 0285 Flyn)

Trademarks

Warning and Disclaimer

ASSOCIATE PUBLISHERS
Dean Miller
Greg Wiegand

ACQUISITIONS EDITOR
Angelina Ward

DEVELOPMENT EDITOR
Maureen A. McDaniel

TECHNICAL EDITOR
James Kim

MANAGING EDITOR
Thomas F. Hayes

PROJECT EDITOR
Tricia Liebig

PRODUCTION EDITOR
Benjamin Berg

INDEXER
Chris Barrick

PROOFREADERS
Bob LaRoche
Plan-it Publishing

COPY EDITOR
Casey Flynn

TEAM COORDINATOR
Cindy Teeters

MEDIA DEVELOPER
Michael Hunter

INTERIOR DESIGNER
Anne Jones

COVER PHOTOGRAPHER
Shawn Roche

COVER DESIGNERS
Anne Jones
Planet 10

PAGE LAYOUT
Ayanna Lacey

TECHTV MANAGING EDITOR
Andrew Guest

TECHTV EXECUTIVE EDITOR, BOOKS
Regina Lynn Preciado

TECHTV TECHNICAL EDITOR
Robert Heron

TECHTV VICE PRESIDENT, EDITORIAL DIRECTOR
Jim Louderback

TECHTV VICE PRESIDENT, STRATEGIC PARTNERSHIPS
Glenn Farrell

CONTENTS

CONTENTS

CONTENTS

ABOUT THE AUTHOR

Deras Flynn has been a freelance videographer and amateur filmmaker for more than 10 years. He has followed the evolution of video and computer technology, with a keen interest on the closing gap between professional and consumer quality. He began editing video on computers in 1995. He is the founder of the tech webzine Multimedian.com (www.multimedian.com), which covers all facets of multimedia production on a computer.

TELL US WHAT YOU THINK!

As the reader of this book, *you* are our most important critic and commentator. We value your opinion and want to know what we're doing right, what we could do better, what areas you'd like to see us publish in, and any other words of wisdom you're willing to pass our way.

As the Associate Publisher for New Riders Publishing, I welcome your comments. You can fax, e-mail, or write me directly to let me know what you did or didn't like about this book—as well as what we can do to make our books stronger.

Please note that I cannot help you with technical problems related to the topic of this book, and that due to the high volume of mail I receive, I might not be able to reply to every message.

When you write, please be sure to include this book's title and author as well as your name and phone or fax number. I will carefully review your comments and share them with the author and editors who worked on the book.

Fax: 317-581-4663

E-mail: stephanie.wall@newriders.com

Mail: Stephanie Wall
           Associate Publisher
           New Riders Publishing
           201 West 103rd Street
           Indianapolis, IN 46290 USA

PRODUCT SUPPORT

If you need support for this or any other TechTV Press product, visit www.newriders.com and select the type of support you are looking for from the Contact Us menu. This menu will lead you to a product support form and other relevant contact information.

INTRODUCTION

The DV camcorder used to be a luxury item and computer editing used to be a complicated mess. However, digital camcorders and computer video editing have become very mature and easy-to-use technologies in the last year. Computer video editing is now well within the learning curve of any consumer. Prices have also significantly fallen. A digital camcorder can now be purchased for as little as $500. A computer capable of editing video can be obtained for under $1,000.

WHAT IS SO GOOD ABOUT DIGITAL VIDEO, AND WHY SHOULD I CARE?

If you ever watched blurry family home movies or an amateur film, digital video technology significantly raises the quality level you can achieve and requires much less effort on your part.

November 2001 was the first month that DVD players outsold VCRs, and recordable DVD technology is just starting to roll out. You now have the ability to create your own DVDs to send to friends and family. A homemade DVD can last for around 100 years (before the internal dye starts to degrade).

This book is written to address the concerns of the digital video novice, prosumer, and even the amateur filmmaker. This book keeps things as simple as possible for the novice who is new to most of this technology, while still covering all the best hardware and software on the market for the discerning prosumer. For the amateur filmmaker, the future of digital video as a bona fide replacement of film is addressed.

This book will illustrate every facet of digital video technology, with an emphasis on digital video camcorders and computer video editing. I will go over what is worth buying today and what will be rolling out into the marketplace in the near future. In these pages you will find the answers to all of the following (and more):

- Why is a digital camcorder better than an analog camcorder?
- What is the best digital camcorder for my needs?
- How do you operate a camcorder?
- What is the best computer for my needs?
- How do you edit video on a computer?
- What is the best way to distribute your digital movie?
- Is digital video good enough to shoot an independent movie?
- What is HDTV?
- How do I create my own DVD?

In Part I of this book, I will take you through a short history of video technology, followed by an overview of current and future digital video technology. This history is important because, as you will learn, not every good technology ends up on top.

In Part II, I will dissect the digital camcorder so you understand how it works. I will address its technological advantage over older analog camcorder technology, and we will even look into the weaknesses of digital video. I will go over the different digital video formats currently available (miniDV, Digital8, DVCAM, DVC PRO), addressing which format is appropriate for each type of user.

More importantly, we will look at the best currently available camcorders, including recommendations for different types of users. I will address the differences between a good digital camcorder and a shoddy one. You will also learn about all the different camcorder accessories. I will help you sort out which ones you might need and which ones you don't (depending on your application).

You will also find out how to get the best deal on your camcorder purchase by shopping online and at your local electronics store. I will also answer the high-pressure question—extended warranty or no extended warranty?

Finally, I will cover proper camcorder maintenance—how to keep your camcorder clean, and how to clean it if it gets dirty.

We will then shift to the topic of computer hardware. I will address how fast a computer you will need to edit your video, and whether you can upgrade your present computer. I will answer these questions:

- Should you buy an HP or Dell or Gateway?
- Should you build your own computer?

You will learn how to upgrade your computer to make it video-editing ready. For the brave, I've added a short tutorial on building your own computer. For all computer owners, I will show you the optimal settings for your hardware.

After guiding you through the computer and camcorder hardware stage, in Part III, I will give you easy to follow guidelines on the best way to operate your camcorder and capture the best quality video and sound:

- How do I shoot good video in low light?
- Do I need an external microphone?
- What are the best manual settings for shooting sports events?

Once your camcorder expertise is in place, in Part IV you will be guided through the computer editing process. We will go over the best software for each type of user. Using two of the top video editing applications (Ulead Video Studio 5 and Adobe Premiere 6) you will be shown how to import your video into a computer and edit it into a movie with transitions, title sequences, and special effects. Finally, we will go over all of your output options (Web video, VHS, DV, VCD, SVCD, miniDVD, and DVD). You will learn how to create your own DVD, complete with menus like a professional DVD.

The last chapter addresses the subject of filmmaking with a DV camcorder. I'll discuss the differences between video and film, write about how to make your video appear more like film, and recommend the best type of camcorder for shooting an amateur film project. I will also cover film festivals both online and off, and the future of DV in them.

You will find 11 projects throughout the book to help you test out what you have learned. By the end of this book, you should have a good understanding of the world of digital video, as well as the resources to keep you up-to-date on any new digital video technology, via the many Web sites listed throughout (at least until the next edition of this book comes out).

PART **I**

DIGITAL VIDEO: THE BEAUTY OF ZEROS AND ONES

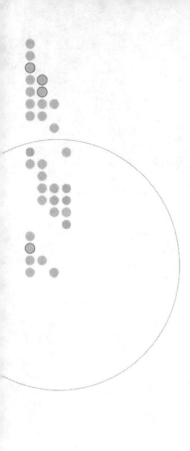

CHAPTER 1

THE HISTORY OF VIDEO: FROM ANALOG TO DIGITAL

Analog home video became a reality in the early '80s, offering the ability to record home movies with sound that could be played back in any VCR. As the home camcorder market grew, new formats offered more functionality, quality, and portability. 8mm, VHS-C, and later Hi-8 offered home users better video quality in increasingly smaller camcorder sizes.

Consumer Hi-8 offered semi-professional quality and was even used in some feature documentaries such as the movie *Hoop Dreams*. However, the analog video format had inherent limitations that left it vulnerable to the emergence of digital technology.

Digital video (DV) introduced even-smaller-sized camcorders, better quality, and improved editing options. Over the past few years, DV technology has further improved and prices have continued to fall, allowing DV to take over all but the lowest end of the home video market.

THE HISTORY OF VIDEO IN FAST FORWARD

When you go to the electronics store today, an increasingly large amount of the camcorders on display are based on the digital video format. Panasonic and Sony introduced the first consumer digital video format in 1997. This is now known generally as DV (also called MiniDV). In the short time since the introduction of DV, we have also seen the average home computer become fast enough to perform powerful video editing, increasing creative options. But before we delve further into the possibilities of current digital video technology, let us take a look back at how we arrived here.

JARGON

The term *DV* has several meanings. It is the acronym for the general term *digital video*. But DV is more commonly associated as the name for the most popular consumer digital video format, MiniDV. For the purposes of this book I will use DV in that context. When referring to digital video in general I will just use the term *digital video*. DV has one more meaning that will be explained in Chapter 2.

The idea of video display and camera as we know it was born in the late 1800s. In 1923, Vladimir Kosma Zworykin invented the first video capture device called the Iconoscope (measuring a meager one square inch) (see Figure 1.1). Four years later Philo Taylor Farnsworth transmitted an image of 60 horizontal lines (based on an idea he'd conceived of when he was only 16). Using Farnsworth's equipment, the 1936 Berlin Olympics became the first televised sporting event in world history.

Figure 1.1

At one square inch the Iconoscope was not exactly the most functional capture device.

Most consumer televisions in use today still make use of the same principles as originally used in the '30s—an electron beam scanning horizontal lines across a cathode ray tube creating a picture (see Figure 1.2).

Figure 1.2

This is a photo of Farnsworth possibly channel surfing on his early picture tube.

Early Analog Recording Technology

Early television, when not broadcast live, actually used film cameras pointed at video monitors to record footage; a process called kinescoping. The television industry relied on this complex cost-intensive method of recording for more than ten years until the invention of the video recorder.

The first competent video recording device was invented in the '50s by the AMPEX Corporation, building on magnetic recording principles conceived of as early as 1899. The demonstration of the Ampex Mark IV VTR at the 1956 NAB (National Association of Broadcasters) conference is considered the birth of video recording (see Figure 1.3). A color version of the Ampex VTR was released in 1958.

Figure 1.3

The Ampex Mark IV, the first video cassette recorder, was as roomy as a Cadillac.

Betamax and VHS Hit the Consumer Market

In May of 1975, Sony launched the first consumer video recorder, called the Betamax (see Figure 1.4). A year later, JVC released a competing video recording format called VHS. While Sony's Beta had better video quality, it was eventually overtaken by VHS. The demise of Sony's Beta was due to hardware limitations and market politics.

Figure 1.4

Behold, the first consumer model Betamax.

Technologically, Beta hardware was harder on the tapes so they had a shorter life. Beta recorders also had shorter recording time capacity. As a result, VHS was a better fit for the video rental business, which was a significant force behind video tape player sales. It surely did not help that Sony was very possessive of its technology while JVC was liberal with VHS licensing. The result was more VHS players on the market and more VHS rental titles, and that all led to the eventual death of consumer Beta.

The moral of the Betamax failure is that there are many factors you must consider when assessing which products are worth investing in. Just because Sony makes a product or it has superior technology does not mean it will succeed, as Betamax proved. The key factors appear to be performance, reliability, and market acceptance. Not just one, but all of these factors are needed for a product to make it.

Beta and VHS formats are based on analog recording technology (just like an audio cassette player). The word *analog* roughly means similar, but not the same. Therefore an analog recording is a representation similar to the original.

Analog technology attempts to duplicate the source (whatever you are recording) with voltage waveforms. An analog recording device writes these waveforms magnetically to tape. The quality of the recording depends on many things (that will be covered later in this book), but the ultimate weakness of analog technology is format instability. Every time you record a copy from the original tape, the waveform does not reproduce exactly, resulting in more and more deterioration of the original source. In an editing environment where video can go through several generational transfers, analog video begins to show its weaknesses.

THE EVOLUTION FROM ANALOG TO DIGITAL

The foundation of computers and digital technology is the *bit*. A bit is represented by two states—*off* and *on* (in computer code, *zero* and *one* represent these states, respectively). With eight bits, any number or letter in our alphabet can be represented (consequently eight bits are called a byte). Just as zeroes and ones can be used to represent letters, they can be used to represent images, sounds, and moving video. When you are surfing the Web, watching a DVD, or listening to a CD, you are experiencing a flood of data composed of zeroes and ones.

The advantage of digital data is that it is composed of a sequence of zeroes and ones that can be exactly reproduced, unlike analog data which is based on analog waveforms that can only be approximately reproduced. If you keep recording a copy of a copy of analog media you will eventually get data gibberish; however digital data will forever remain the same.

So no matter how often I make personal copies of the latest Weezer CD, I get the same audio quality as the master CD the record label delivered to the CD factory.

Besides offering superior format integrity, the newest digital video formats offer smaller-sized camcorders than even 8mm and Hi-8mm camcorders. The small MiniDV tape used in consumer DV camcorders allows incredibly small pocket-sized camcorders (see Figure 1.5). The FireWire interface (also called IEEE 1394 and i.Link) built into all recent DV camcorders enables you to connect your camcorder to any FireWire-equipped computer or another camcorder. This enables you to transfer video to your computer for editing.

JARGON

FireWire is a special interface developed by Apple (used on both PCs and Macs) that enables speedy data transfer, as well as the ability to hook up multiple devices. FireWire interfaces are included on all current DV camcorders (as well as most older models) allowing for easy transfer of footage from camcorder to computer (and back).

Figure 1.5

The Sony DCR-PC9 MiniDV camcorder is one of the smallest DV camcorders on the market.

DIGITAL VIDEO LONG-TERM PERSPECTIVE

As mentioned previously, *digital video* is a generic term meaning that the video is stored as zeroes and ones. When you buy a video camera, you need to decide not just whether you want a digital camcorder but what format digital camcorder you want. Just as there are several analog formats (VHS, 8mm, Hi-8mm, VHS-C, Super VHS, and so on), there are a number of digital video formats (DV, Digital8, DVD-RAM) and more on the way. Format differences in the case of the aforementioned analog formats are size of tape and recording quality. The differences between digital formats are comparable, with an additional difference, media type. Most current digital video formats use tape, but a few use optical disc–based media such as DVD-RAM discs.

Clearly, digital video camcorders are replacing analog video cameras. Eventually, within a few more years, you will not be able to even buy a new analog camcorder. So the question is no longer analog or digital, but which digital format?

There are a couple digital video formats to choose from right now, with more on the way. With this variety it is important to assess the performance, reliability, and market saturation when you decide on your digital camcorder format. Currently, there are two established consumer digital formats: *DV* (also called *MiniDV*), and *Digital8*. DV and Digital8 offer the same video quality; the only difference between the formats is the size of the tape they use. Released in the summer of 2001 was the DVD-RAM format. Currently, there are two camcorders that enable you to record up to two hours of footage on an optical DVD-RAM disc. Sony has also just released a new miniature tape-based format called *MicroMV*.

COMPATIBILITY WITH FUTURE FORMATS

Since we are very slowly approaching a new television format called HDTV, future compatibility might be a concern for some consumers. HDTV is slated to become the broadcast standard in 2006. HDTV differs from current analog TV in three ways:

- HDTV broadcasts digitally (the whole zero and one thing)
- HDTV has a wider aspect ratio than current TV (16:9 versus 4:3, or widescreen versus square) (see Figure 1.6)
- Up to four times higher video resolution

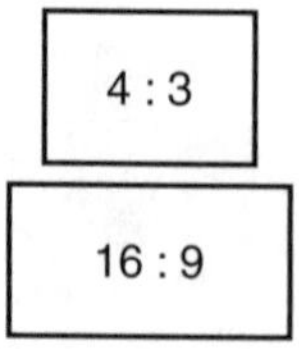

4 : 3

16 : 9

Figure 1.6

Observe the difference in aspect ratio (height×width) between a regular TV and HDTV.

HDTV sets will, for the foreseeable future, accept input from any camcorder with an analog out connection (which is all of them). The TV will just display the video in 4:3 format with black or gray bars flanking the picture (see Figure 1.7).

Figure 1.7

4:3 footage playing back on an HDTV widescreen monitor.

You should be wary only of investing in a new digital video format which lacks market acceptance. Without a large consumer base, costs will be higher on the camcorder, media, and accessories. Also, if the device uses non-standard media you will be out of luck if the manufacturer discontinues the product line. You should be even warier of formats that lack a FireWire port (which at least allows you a generic digital output option). An example of this is Sony's MiniDisc-based camcorder, which cost $2,000 and lacked FireWire or any other digital output jack (see Figure 1.8). Hitachi recently released a DVD-RAM camcorder which includes FireWire, however it is still too early to appraise its market acceptance.

Figure 1.8

The unsuccessful Sony DCM-M1 MiniDisc Camcorder was the first camcorder to use optical disc–based media.

CHAPTER 2

DIGITAL VIDEO BASICS

Digital video is more than just MiniDV and Digital8 camcorders. DSS (digital satellite system) set top TV boxes and hard disk–based video recorders (a sort of evolved VCR) like TiVo are also digital video devices. Many of these use totally different recording and playback schemes called *codecs*. Codecs are like foreign languages. Each has a different structure for conveying information even though on a basic level they are all a bunch of zeros and ones.

Set top is a generic term referring to electronic components that hook up to your television set.

Besides codecs, the other digital video dividing line is format. *Format* relates to the hardware implementation of a specific technology. MiniDV, DVCPRO, and DVCAM all use the same codec (the same core technology), but the formats are different. They differ in tape build, size, reliability, and length.

Some of these codecs and formats are ideal for the editing environment because they do not degrade like a VHS tape does after a copy of a copy is made. Some codecs are best suited for displaying video on the Web, storing video on CD, or sending video e-mail attachments.

New codecs and formats are a reality of technological evolution, and while newer ones may not be exactly compatible with older codecs or each other, the digital domain makes it much easier to transcode into the newer formats if necessary. As long as your camcorder can output video digitally via FireWire (or less ideally if you have analog to digital capture hardware) you will be in a good position to adapt.

If you are going to always output your movies back to your camcorder tape, you don't need to know about codecs (and you can skip much of this chapter). However, if you plan on creating DVDs, video e-mail, or Web video, you need to familiarize yourself with this technology. Furthermore, if you are interested in learning about all the digital video hardware options you have then you need to read about the various digital video formats covered in this chapter.

DIGITAL VIDEO CODECS

When you record video with your DV camcorder, inside your camcorder the video data is being written to tape magnetically as a sequence of zeros and ones. Those zeros and ones have a specific structure or order determined by a codec. The codec used in almost all consumer digital camcorders, both DV and Digital8, is called DV. (DVDs, however, use an entirely different codec called MPEG-2.)

Codecs are the foundation of digital multimedia data. *Codec* is short for compression/decompression. A codec is any technology used to compress or decompress data. JPEG images, MP3 files, and animated GIFs all are created and interpreted with a codec. Your computer, by means of codecs, is able to make sense of a particular video, graphic, or audio file.

There are two main types of codecs: *lossy* and *lossless*. Lossy codecs eliminate redundant image data to achieve the smallest file size possible, while lossless codecs substitute redundant image data with smaller code to maintain the integrity of the original video file through multiple generations.

Lossy Codecs

Lossy codecs are a great display/playback-only format. They are ideal for the Web where bandwidth is limited. Lossy codecs are also great for video e-mail, or interactive CDs where space is precious. While lossy codecs can look as good as a lossless codec in the first generation (as the picture quality of DVD movies proves), if you were to try to edit them, introducing recompression, they would start to degrade. JPEG (image codec) and MP3 (audio codec) are examples of popular lossy formats. The most prevalent video lossy codecs are MPEG-1, MPEG-2, and MPEG-4.

The weakness of lossy codecs, as the name suggests, is that the codec is not written to maintain quality as would be desired in the video production environment. This allows lossy codecs to be more efficient than lossless codecs that devote extra data to maintaining media integrity.

High bit-rate MPEG-2, as seen in DVD movies, will attempt to lose only video information that the human eye cannot perceive. Usually lossy codecs target detail and color to reduce file sizes. The result is that the more you compress, the more blocky and dull the picture gets (see Figure 2.1). If you have Digital Satellite TV then you might have occasionally seen picture artifacts (such as blocking) in fast-moving scenes.

Figure 2.1

MPEG compression can cause artifacts such as blocking in your picture; usually the more you compress the more blocking you get.

JARGON

Bit rate refers to how many bits (or how much data) a codec uses per second. The more bits the better quality is usually going to be, but more bits also results in larger file sizes.

Lossy codecs also have fewer keyframes than lossless codecs. Keyframes are central in the vocabulary of all codecs. A *keyframe* is a complete and distinct full frame of video. If you are editing your video you need every frame to be a keyframe. Obviously this requires more data. Lossless codecs limit the number of keyframes utilizing a technique called *frame differencing*.

Frame differencing takes advantage of the similarity between frames to save data. If a person is walking across a static background, a codec utilizing frame differencing will only encode the information of the person walking and any other changed pixels. Any pixel that remains the same from frame to frame will not be redrawn. Lossy codecs still have keyframes; they just have fewer of them.

Video as well as digital pictures are composed of pixels. A pixel is basically a digital mosaic tile. Image resolution is usually defined by the total number of pixels used or by the number of horizontal and vertical pixels. Every frame of NTSC DV video is composed of 345,600 pixels, and is 720 pixels in width and 480 pixels in length (for PAL video: total pixels = 414,720; dimensions = 720×576).

MPEG-1

MPEG-1 is an older, but still very useful lossy codec. The advantage of MPEG-1 is that almost all computers, whether Mac or PC, will be able to read it. Even more important, slower computers can handle MPEG-1 because it requires less CPU speed than newer codecs. Without a fast computer you can't play back MPEG-2 or 4 smoothly.

MPEG-1 has a bad name because people associate it with poor video quality. However this is more due to shoddy MPEG-1 encoders and not an inferior format. Software encoders like TMPGEnc, Panasonic, and Cinemacraft can produce impressive quality MPEG-1 video that, as mentioned before, will work on just about any computer. MPEG-1 is not perfect by any means, but it is far more useful than many people think.

The weakness of MPEG-1 is reproduction of fast action video. MPEG-1 can look as good as MPEG-2 at similar bit rates when people are standing around or walking slowly, but fast action appears choppy compared to newer codecs like MPEG-2 (see Figure 2.2). Also MPEG-1 is not capable of encoding interlaced video, so it will not look as smooth on TV as MPEG-2 which has interlace capability.

MPEG-1 is the codec used for all video CDs (VCDs). However, the VCD spec has a pretty low video bit rate (1Mbps), which results in VHS quality at best. If you are authoring MPEG-1 video files for distribution on CDs that will play back in computers, you can use higher bit rates that can deliver much better video quality.

What Exactly Is MPEG?

MPEG stands for *Moving Picture Experts Group*. You might be wondering who these people are. MPEG was created by the IEC/ISO (International Electrotechnical Commission/International Organization for Standardization). These organizations are to technology and consumer issues what the World Bank is to international economics, or the United Nations is to international diplomacy. It would probably take a whole book to explain their origin, how they operate, and what their strengths and weaknesses are. As the ISO states on its Web site (www.iso.ch), it is all about creating standards so the world works better. For example, all credit cards and phone cards are a product of an ISO standard, which stipulates that the optimal thickness of a credit card is .76mm (sounds reasonable to me).

MPEG continues to work on new audio and video standards (MPEG-7 and MPEG-21 are currently in development) which should improve all of our lives right up to when world peace is declared. The only way to join MPEG is to become a member of the National Standards Body in the country you live in. On the MPEG Web site (www.cselt.it/mpeg/) there is a link to more info on this.

MPEG-2

MPEG-2 is the codec for DVD movies. MPEG-2 was developed for digital television. It improves on MPEG-1 by adding higher bit rate capability and the ability to encode inter-laced video.

MPEG-2 is not really more efficient than MPEG-1, and since high bit rates are required for DVD quality video, file sizes can be quite large. A two-hour DVD movie requires 4+GB (that is 4000MB or about seven CD-Rs) of space; nonetheless it is still much more efficient than the DV codec, which would require 24GB. New DVD discs have two data layers allowing up to 9GB of data on a side.

As with MPEG-1, the quality of the encoder can really impact the resulting video quality. Cinemacraft and TMPGEnc currently are the best consumer MPEG-2 encoders (see Figure 2.2).

Some of the newer MPEG-2 encoders utilize *variable bit rate (VBR)* encoding. VBR encoding allows the encoder to vary the data rate in response to the complexity of the scene being encoded. Basically, the more movement and complexity a scene has, the more data will be required to properly encode it. The highest quality MPEG-2 encoders allow two-pass VBR encoding. This means that the encoder goes through the footage once to calculate how much complexity each scene has, and then in the second pass it uses that information to create the encoded VBR stream. Two-pass encoding usually takes twice as long as one-pass encoding, and the results, while better, may not justify the added encoding times for many users.

Figure 2.2

Originally a freeware application, TMPGEnc is one of the best MPEG Encoders on the market.

MPEG-4/DivX

Development of MPEG-4 started in 1993. MPEG-4 was intended to address the problem of large file sizes, which are not very useful on the Web or in other space-restrictive applications.

MPEG-4 has recently come into prominence due to a little hacking. Basically, a few programmers took Microsoft's MPEG-4 version 3 (Mpeg4v3) codec and changed a few things, most notably allowing Mp3 audio (instead of the lower-quality audio sound codec that Microsoft had built in to Mpeg4v3). This allowed even smaller file sizes than the original Microsoft codec and better sound quality. Recently, the creators of Divx have created an entirely new and original video codec, Divx 4.0, which is not based on the Microsoft codec.

Pretty soon people started copying DVD movies and encoding them into DivX, as the format allowed a two-hour DVD to fit onto one forty-cent CD-R. But keep in mind the whole ripping/encoding process takes between 3-20 hours depending on the speed of your computer and the encoding settings you choose. The resulting video quality is something between VCD and DVD, so it is not entirely cost effective if your time is worth more than one dollar an hour.

SVCD

The Chinese developed SVCD as a more affordable middle ground between DVD and what had already been a popular format in Asia, VCD. SVCD, like DVD, is based on the MPEG-2 codec, but it has a max video data rate of 2.6Mbps whereas DVD data rates can reach

10Mbps (see Figure 2.3). Including audio, the max total data rate is just under 2.8Mbps. SVCD resolution is 480 × 480 for NTSC, 480 × 576 for PAL. However many players that can play SVCD (such as the Pioneer 343) can play out of spec SVCDs, called XSVCDs, which can be sized at 720 × 480 for NTSC or 720 × 576 for PAL.

Figure 2.3

This is my Pioneer 333 playing back an SVCD I created on my computer.

SVCD, assuming you have a good encoder, is about S-VHS quality, so it might actually be an okay archiving distribution format for home movies. At the highest SVCD quality (just under 2.8Mbps) you can fit about 30 minutes of video on one CDR.

 While MPEG-2 and 4 are usually considered lossy codecs because that is how most applications use them, they can be calibrated to be more lossless by increasing the number of keyframes to 30 per second and eliminating frame differencing. While this will result in larger files sizes it will enable lossless editing.

Lossless Codecs

Lossless codecs are written to preserve video quality through the compression/decompression process. This makes them ideal for any high-quality editing application, but limits their usefulness in situations where space or bandwidth is at a minimum.

DV

DV is currently the most common lossless digital codec. It has a data rate of 3.6MB/s (or 25Mbit/s, hence the original name of DV25). The DV codec is used in many of the most popular digital formats (miniDV, Digital8, DVCAM, DVCPRO).

Some argument exists about whether DV is really a lossless codec. The most clinical answer to this debate is that it depends. DV has a compression ratio of 5 to 1, meaning that for every five parts of original data observed, it encodes just one part. So you are losing data from the start.

However the technical definition of lossless has to do with whether data is lost from the original encode. In this regard, well-written DV codecs such as the SoftDV, Main Actor DV, and Cannopus DV codecs have been shown to be lossless to the human eye over 10 generations of re-rendering (more than most users will ever re-render).

> *Rendering* refers to the processing that takes place when video files are altered in any way. Rendering is the most time-consuming element of the video editing process. Fortunately, as computer performance increases, rendering times will improve.

Keep in mind that quality loss can only occur if you re-render your video. This happens when you apply an effect, or add a title. But only the portion of your video where you have an effect or title is re-rendered. So if you just cut, paste, and move clips around, there is never any re-rendering taking place.

The Microsoft DV codec (used with most OHCI FireWire cards like the ADS Pyro) has not proven as lossless as the previously mentioned codecs. However as of DirectX 8 it has been greatly improved and comes closer to lossless performance.

MJPEG

MJPEG was the first well-known lossless codec. MJPEG is used primarily as an analog capture codec. MJPEG can achieve comparable quality to the DV codec but it requires more data to do so, so it is less efficient, requiring a faster hard drive and more storage space. Prior to the emergence of DV, MJPEG was the preeminent lossless codec. While it is still used with analog capture boards, DV has largely replaced it both in the consumer and prosumer markets (as many people now have DV camcorders).

DIGITAL VIDEO FORMATS

Whereas a video codec is a compression/decompression engine, format is the structure that houses that engine. Each digital video format has its own proprietary structure. In the case of tape-based digital video formats, tape size and recording length all vary depending on the format. Most current formats use the DV codec, but a few newer formats coming on the market use MPEG codecs.

The consumer digital camcorder market has two main formats: MiniDV and Digital8. Both use the same DV codec but record on different size tapes. The professional market also has two main DV codec-based formats—DVCAM, DVCPRO—which are engineered for maximum reliability. Newer MPEG codec formats, such as MicroMV, are still immature and do not yet offer the quality and reliability of current DV codec formats.

MiniDV

MiniDV (often just called DV) is the most popular digital video format currently on the market. MiniDV utilizes the DV codec. Tape size is very small (less then 2.5 inches in length), allowing for very small camcorder sizes.

The average MiniDV tape can record 60 minutes in standard play (SP) mode and 90 minutes in long play (LP) mode. Quality is the same in both modes, but recording in LP mode raises the chance of dropouts (when you lose picture and/or sound) because you are jamming more data on less space.

The rule is that your own camcorder can usually play back tapes it records in LP mode video, but other camcorders will not be able to play those same tapes back very well. My own experience with this problem was LP tape playback resulting in intermittent audio and video dropouts when using a different playback camcorder.

Newer tapes were released in 2001 that can record 80 minutes in SP mode. Generally, I prefer 60-minute tapes. The more footage on a tape, the more time consuming navigating through it will be. This of course reflects the limitations of linear tape media, limitations that make it vulnerable to an optically based video format which allows you to skip around with little or no delay.

Digital8

Digital8 also utilizes the same DV codec as MiniDV and DVCAM; the only difference is tape size. Digital8 camcorders can record on regular 8mm or Hi-8mm tapes (quality will be the same on either one) (see Figure 2.4). Sony markets a Digital8 tape, but it is just a remarked Hi-8mm tape.

front view · side view · back view

Figure 2.4

The Sony DCR-TRV730 Digital8 camcorder records digitally on 8mm and Hi8mm tapes.

MicroMV

MicroMV is the newest consumer digital format and was developed by Sony. MicroMV is rumored to be a Digital8 replacement, but this is just speculation for now.

MicroMV is a tape-based format that utilizes the MPEG-2 codec. Tape size is 50% smaller than MiniDV, allowing for even smaller camcorders (see Figure 2.5). Sony's first two models are the DCR-IP5 and DCR-IP7.

Figure 2.5

The small MicroMV tape size will allow for even smaller camcorder designs. Pictured here is the ultra compact DCR-IP7 MicroMV camcorder.

Sony claims its MPEG-2 codec provides quality on par with the DV codec (up to 500 lines of resolution). Since MPEG-2 is a more efficient codec, file sizes are much smaller, by 50% or more, so less hard drive space will be required.

DVCAM

MiniDV tapes use 10 micron tracks in SP recording mode and 6.7 in LP recording mode. DVCAM, which uses the same DV codec (so the image quality potential is identical) and the same tape size, uses 15 micron tracks in SP recording mode (see Figure 2.6). This makes DVCAM a more durable format (less prone to drop outs) with less recording capacity. DVCAM was developed by Sony as a more professional alternative to MiniDV.

Figure 2.6

The Sony DSRPD150 (which is the professional version of the DCR-VX2000) can record on DVCAM tapes (as well as regular DV tapes).

DVCPRO

DVCPRO (developed by Panasonic) is the highest caliber hardware that uses the DV codec. DVCPRO tapes are larger than DV and even Digital8. DVCPRO tapes utilize 18 micron record tracks as well as two separate tracks devoted to audio cue and tape control; this makes it the most robust of the DV codec formats. DVCPRO is used mainly for professional applications. For instance, one of the TV stations where I live uses all DVC Pro camcorders in the field (see Figure 2.7). Sony's DVCAM format is DVCPRO's chief market competitor.

Figure 2.7

The Panasonic AJ-D700 is a professional shoulder cam which uses the DVCPRO format.

Digital Betacam

Sony introduced this format in 1993 to replace the ubiquitous Betacam SP format, which was the dominant professional video format. Digital Betacam features a 2:1 compression scheme and records onto 1/2-inch tapes. Digital Betacam is currently the standard format used for most of the network television industry (see Figure 2.8).

Figure 2.8

The Sony DVW-700 Digital Betacam camcorder is currently one of the most popular camcorders in professional video production.

Future Professional Formats

Digital-S and DVCPRO 50 are the latest professional digital formats. They are based on new technology and coding algorithms. They are aimed to compete with Digital Betacam for the high-end professional video production market.

CHAPTER 3

THE FUTURE OF DIGITAL VIDEO

One of the big questions in the digital video industry these days is "When will digital video overtake film?" With George Lucas shooting the new Star Wars film, Episode 2, with a high definition digital video camera (Sony HDW-F900), it would seem that we are on the threshold. However, digital video technology still faces a lot of evolution ahead. Video resolution capability needs to get much better, and then computer processing power will need to get far faster to handle the higher data rates that go along with higher resolution video. Finally, digital projection quality needs to reach the level of film projection.

Once the technology is there, it will then take a considerable amount of time before all of this can be rolled out into your local theater. We will eventually watch movies at the theater via digital video projectors but it will not happen in the next few years.

In the meantime, digital video still is a remarkably capable technology for amateurs and professionals to both hone their filmmaking style and even make feature-length films. Consider this: The cost of a one-hour DV tape is ten dollars. The cost of one hour of 16mm film plus processing is more than $2,000; for 35mm film the cost is even higher. At these prices, DV is a better option for most amateur filmmakers.

You always have the option, if your film is good enough, to do a DV to film transfer. Spike Lee's recent film *Bamboozled* was shot mostly with three consumer Sony VX-1000 DV camcorders. He also shot the documentary *The Original Kings of Comedy* using DV camcorders.

ABOUT DVD

The most tangible high quality video distribution format appears to be recordable DVD, which is beginning to hit the market, and will eventually be as commonplace as the VHS VCR. While this won't equal 35mm projected film, it will provide a very high quality and convenient distribution format for independent filmmakers as well as families sharing their home videos.

DVD offers superior sound and video compared to the VHS format. DVD can resolve up to 525 lines of horizontal resolution while VHS resolves around 240. On the sound front, DVD allows for simple stereo sound, as well as 5.1 Digital Dolby or DTS sound (the latter two require a compatible sound system). With the right speakers DVD sound quality can rival or exceed anything you hear at your local movie theater (see Figure 3.1).

Figure 3.1

Consumer home theater packages are starting to become more common in your local electronics store. The Pioneer HTD-510DV is one example.

In addition to regular stereo sound, which will play back on anything, 5.1 Digital Dolby and 5.1 DTS sound are some of the more common DVD sound formats. To properly play back this format you need a receiver that decodes Digital Dolby or DTS signals. Also some DVD players come with onboard Digital Dolby decoders. On the hardware end you then need five regular speakers—two rear speakers, two front speakers, one center speaker (that sits in the middle between the two front speakers)—and finally a subwoofer, which can go anywhere (as low frequency sound waves are nondirectional). For a diagram of this, check out Figure 3.2.

However, you can record video with your VHS VCR, and current DVD players lack that ability. In the last few years, the only way you could create your own video that would be playable back on your DVD player was to author your own video CD (VCD).

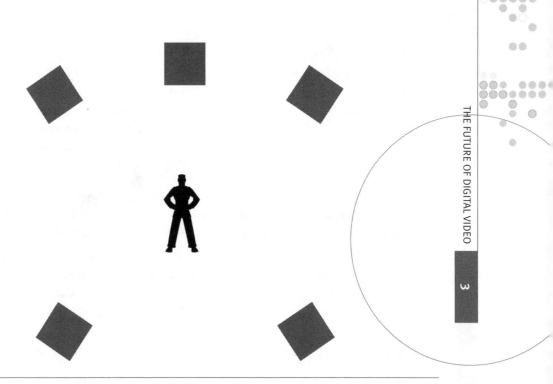

Figure 3.2

Dolby and DTS 5.1 surround sound speaker systems include five satellite speakers and a subwoofer for more immersive sound.

VCDs have much lower image quality than DVDs and some DVD players will not even play them back. Creating VCDs requires a computer, a CD burner, special software, and a lot of time and patience. Considering the sub-VHS quality you end up with, VCD creation has understandably never become very popular. With the recent introduction of recordable DVD drives, you now have the ability to author your own high-quality DVDs. This technology should prove explosive for both the computer industry and the creative possibilities of the home user.

Eventually, set top DVD recorders will take the place of VCRs, but right now the prices are high, the models are few, and the reliability is untested (see Figure 3.3). So the first few waves of DVD recording products will mostly be for the computer.

Figure 3.3

Tomorrow's VCR, the Pioneer DVR2000 standalone DVD recorder is an example of what we might be recording our favorite TV shows on in the next few years.

HOMEMADE DVDS

Computer-based DVD recorders are now available that will write DVDs playable in some set top DVD players. These recorders operate much like CD recorders (often called burners), though instead of writing data onto 650MB CD-Rs you can write data onto 4.7GB DVD-R/RWs or DVD+R/RWs (two competing formats). While you will be able to write regular data on these discs as you can with a CD writer, you will also be able to write video files that will play back in your set top DVD player. Now, you can write video files to CD as well, but you are limited to less than 15 minutes at DVD quality (and most DVD players won't play them back). Recordable DVD allows you to record up to two hours of high quality video. Software packages are already available that allow you to create your own DVDs complete with menu interfaces and multiple video and audio tracks.

The proliferation of consumer DVD recording will make it much easier for people to distribute their family videos to friends and family as well as archive their own library of home movies (especially as the media costs go down). Independent and hobby filmmakers will also benefit from having such a high performance delivery format for their creations.

Right now only a few recordable DVD drives are on the market, but far more models are expected to hit the market in the spring of 2002 if current timelines are maintained.

The holdup at least on the surface is due to competing formats. DVD-R/RW and DVD+R/RW are two different DVD formats, each supported by their own stable of manufacturers. While they both will play back on many DVD players, they are based on different underlying technology. It is still too early to predict which format will prevail (maybe both will).

Common sense also dictates that piracy concerns might have also been a factor in the delay of this technology's rollout. Nonetheless, due to built-in piracy protection called Macrovision (built in to the DVD format) you are unlikely to see any set top DVD recorders that would be capable of recording commercial DVD movies.

DVD+R/DVD+RW (DVD+R/RW)

DVD+R/RW, at least initially, had the most industry firepower behind it (HP, Sony, Mitsubishi, Yamaha, Philips, Ricoh, and others). As the name suggests, DVD+R/RW supports both writing and rewriting. DVD+R/RW currently sports up to 4.7GB disc capacity. Keep in mind DVD+R/RW disks are not compatible with all DVD players, so check the drive manufacturer to be sure your DVD player is compatible.   Also, VCDhelp (www.vcdhelp.com) maintains a very useful database of set top DVD players, which lists recordable DVD format compatibility.

DVD-R/DVD-RW (DVD-R/RW)

Developed by Pioneer, DVD-R/RW beat DVD+R/RW to the consumer market by six months. While DVD-R/RW had far less industry support initially, its speed to the marketplace may prove decisive in the long run.

DVD-R/RW drives allow write once (DVD-R) and rewritable (DVD-RW) DVD burning. 4.7GB DVD-R media cost $10 ($25 for the DVD-RW rewritable media) when it was introduced, but that price has already fallen to $5 and should continue to drop. Since the engineering behind DVD media is pretty much the same as CD media, you can expect to see sub one-dollar media prices eventually.

The first consumer DVD-R writer, the Pioneer DVR-A03 (rebadged as the SuperDrive in Macs), can write to DVD-R disks at 2x speed or 2.76MBps and rewrite to DVD-RW disks at 1x or 1.38MBps (see Figure 3.4). This is slightly faster than a 16x CD burner, which can write data at 2.4MBps; writing a full DVD takes around 30 minutes.

Figure 3.4

The Pioneer DVR-A03 is the first recordable DVD drive that can write consumer playable DVD discs.

Early reports suggest that DVD-R/RW is slightly more compatible with set top DVD players than DVD+R/RW. As with DVD+RW, check compatibility with your DVD player before buying.

DVD-RAM

DVD-RAM is another DVD format, one that has been on the market for close to two years but is not compatible with current DVD players. As a result DVD-RAM is really just a large rewritable storage format. With the plummeting cost of fast hard drives and cheap CD-RW, DVD-RAM has little appeal as a storage medium.

Recently a few disc-based camcorders have been released which record onto small DVD-RAM disks, and a few under-$100 DVD-ROM drives that will read (but not write) DVD-RAM have also been released (see Figure 3.5). However it is hard to see how DVD-RAM has a chance against DVD+RW and DVD-R, which offer consumer DVD player compatibility, allowing consumers to just pop their recorded DVDs right into their set top DVD players. Furthermore, future computers are infinitely more likely to have DVD+RW or DVD-R drives, which will further isolate the DVD-RAM format.

Figure 3.5

The Panasonic VDR-M10 camcorder records up to two hours of video onto 2.5-inch DVD-RAM discs.

FASTER EDITING PROCESS

Advances in video editing software on home computers continue to make for an easier user experience. Editing your videos is painfully easy in the newest crop of video editors. The only remaining inconvenience for some of these programs is rendering delays.

Most consumer video editing software requires re-rendering your entire video upon output, which can make the editing process up to twice as long. This is tolerable for short Web videos, but if you are editing hours of home movies this is a waste of your time.

Fortunately, some of the newest video editing programs such as Adobe's Premiere 6 and Apple's iMovie 2 (Mac only) don't have this problem. They enable you to edit your video and output directly to tape without any rendering delay (of course, special effects still need to be rendered). This feature is generally referred to as *instant timeline playback* (Apple calls it Play Through). Eventually, all programs will have this feature, but right now mostly just prosumer video editors have it. iMovie 2 is the only consumer-level sub-$100 video editor with this feature.

Top Consumer Video Editors

- Ulead Video Studio 5
- MGI Videowave 4
- Sonic Foundry VideoFactory
- iMovie 2 (Mac only)

Top Prosumer Video Editors

- Adobe Premiere 6
- Final Cut Pro 2 (Mac only)
- Ulead Media Studio Pro 6.5

Special Effects

With the latest video editing software, you can easily add special effects to your video. You can create your own black and white film that looks like it was shot in the 50s, or you can add more modern special effects. The only downside is that effects need to be rendered, which can be time consuming if you add a lot of effects. A number of prosumer video cards that feature real-time special effects are available. One such card is the Matrox RT2500 (see Figure 3.6).

The RT2500 delivers real-time effects and transition previews in Premiere; non-standard effects still need to be rendered. The real-time effects are only real-time on your computer monitor or output to an analog monitor. If you want to output to DV you still need to render. So most of these cards are real-time only in the sense that you can instantly preview effects and transitions at full quality on screen.

Figure 3.6

The Matrox RT2500 captures and outputs both analog and digital video, and includes a number of real-time special effects and transitions.

Even on today's fastest computers, rendering effects can still be a time-consuming affair. While a simple clip to clip two-second dissolve (where one image fades into the next) might only take 10 seconds, adding an effect filter to 10 minutes of footage can take hours to render. That is why studios have whole rooms of computers called *render farms* that are devoted to processing complex digital video special effects. So while simple cut, trim, and paste editing has started to reach the point of real-time editing, the advanced effects world is not there yet.

DV CONQUERS THE BIG SCREEN

With all the improvements of video technology, motion picture film still maintains a large visual quality edge over all current digital video formats. The best digital video cameras like the Canon XL1 or Sony VX2000 still deliver lower image quality than well-shot 16mm film, and there is no comparison when looking at 35mm film. The quality gap is shrinking, however.

New Star Wars Film Shot on Digital Video Camera

George Lucas is shooting the new Star Wars movie, *Episode 2: Attack of the Clones*, with a specially made Sony HD (high definition) digital video camera. The Sony HDW-F900 shoots at 24 progressive frames a second (24p) at 1,920×1,080 resolution. Keep in mind that the DV format by comparison captures video at 720×480 resolution.

Figure 3.7

The Sony HDW-F900 HD camcorder is being used exclusively to shoot the latest Star Wars prequel.

Progressive video is a display format that shows complete frames of video. So each frame of progressive video looks like a normal complete picture (a "full field" would be the technical definition). Interlaced video, which current NTSC televisions use, operates with interlaced frames of video. In interlaced video fields half of the display lines have picture information, and the other half are empty. Every 1/60 of a second the empty field gets replaced with a new half field of video, and the old half field of video goes empty, and so on. If you were able to freeze your video picture and look very closely you would see an effect similar to when you look out a window through vertical blinds. Interlaced video became a technology standard because at the time there was a limited amount of broadcast bandwidth, and interlaced video allowed a picture to have twice the field rate (60 fields) compared to the same sized progressive format (allowing for a smoother picture). With sports particularly, smoothness is more important then picture clarity.

Most technology professionals prefer the look of progressive video because it has more clarity than interlaced video. In any case, because film is a progressive-based format, composed of 24 frames per second of 35mm pictures, progressive video at 24 frames per second (24p) makes sense as an appropriate film substitute.

Lucas claims that the quality differences between 35mm film and the footage he shot with his digital camera are indistinguishable on a large screen. While some might disagree, such an effects-heavy film is a good match for this bold experiment. Film audiences can decide for themselves whether they agree with Lucas when the movie is released. In any case, digital video is only going to get better in the future, so even if Lucas is misjudging, video quality will eventually surpass film.

Digital Video Projection Technology

While the new Star Wars film is being shot via digital video, it will eventually be transferred to film allowing for compatibility with your local movie theater's film projector. However, some day your local movie theater will display movies with a digital video projector. Predicting when this will happen would be unwise, but it will eventually happen as film technology only has image quality going for it now, and once that edge is lost film will become ancient history.

CRT Projection

CRT projectors are an analog technology. They utilize the same cathode tube hardware as boxy projection televisions (as well as standard TVs). They weigh 60 pounds and up, not exactly ideal for mounting to a ceiling. If set up properly, they can still deliver the best video picture currently available, but newer technology that is cheaper and lighter is about to pass them by (see Figure 3.8).

Figure 3.8

If you can handle the size and price tag, the Runco DTV-873 CRT projector provides very good picture quality.

What is the current advantage of CRTs? Actual CRT tubes create the entire displayed picture (as opposed to a bright bulb projecting a smaller display—as is the case with LCD and DLP projectors), so the colors are less likely to be washed out. The most significant advantage of CRT is its ability to display dark tones correctly. On current non-CRT projectors, black often appears as dark gray. CRTs do have limited brightness capability; they max out around 260 lumens.

LCD Projection

LCD (liquid crystal display) projectors utilize the same technology used in flat screen monitors, commonly used in notebook computers. However, the LCD is quite a bit smaller, displaying a full resolution image that is projected with the use of a very bright light bulb and magnifying optics (see Figure 3.9).

Figure 3.9

The Toshiba B2 LCD projector is excellent for business applications but not so good for movie playback.

LCD projectors are much cheaper than comparable CRT projectors and only weigh between five and ten pounds. LCD projectors can produce very sharp image quality if you sit far enough away, and are generally preferred for business presentations, as the sharpness is ideal for graphs, pie charts, and text. For movies they are less ideal, as they can suffer from pixelation, also known as the "screen door" effect. This means you can see the empty spaces between all the projected LCD pixels, so it can appear like you are looking through a screen door (see Figure 3.10).

Figure 3.10

The screen door effect gets worse the closer to the LCD screen you are.

Anyone who has had enough notebooks or devices with LCDs knows that another problem that can arise is dead pixels, which can look kind of odd when projected on a large screen. Basically, this will cause black dots to appear on the displayed picture wherever there is a dead pixel (see Figure 3.11). Another problem with LCD projectors is that the bulbs only last between 1,000 and 2,000 hours and cost up to $500 to replace. These bulbs probably will get cheaper in the future.

Figure 3.11

Dead pixels result in dead spots on your projected display that can be rather distracting.

The main advantage of LCDs is that many affordable models come with three LCD chips. Each one handles a single color (like a three-chip camcorder): red, green, and blue. Three-chip systems usually offer better color fidelity and resolution than one-chip systems. Due to reflectivity advantages, the brightest projectors are also LCDs.

DLP Projection

Developed by Texas Instruments, DLP projection is the newest and most promising display technology. DLP stands for digital light processing. DLP projectors use a small wafer chip called a DMD (Digital Micromirror Device) loaded with hundreds of thousands of tiny mirrors that can be controlled by electrical impulses. Each mirror, when positioned correctly, displays the appropriate color (see Figure 3.12).

DLP projectors are even smaller than LCD projectors. Several models weigh less than three pounds. DLP projectors are also as inexpensive as LCD models. The main advantage of DLP besides size is image quality; they are far less prone to the screen door effect. As a result, the picture quality is usually much smoother, ideal for playback of DVD movies and home video. Currently, DLPs are the preferred projector for most new home theaters.

DLP projectors create images by reflecting light. This works well for producing colors but not as well for reproducing black. Consequently, this affects contrast performance (the difference between white and black) and black often appears as dark gray. However this problem has waned with each new generation of DLP. DLPs do produce dark colors better than LCD projectors. DLP projectors also have the same bulb life issues as LCD models.

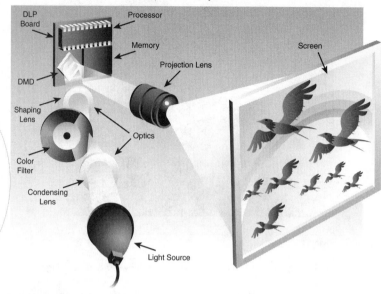

1 Chip DLP™ Projection

Figure 3.12

This diagram illustrates how DLP works; the area marked DMD (Digital Micromirror Device) is where all the image-creating mirrors are.

HDTV: WHERE DOES IT FIT?

HDTV is the newest television display technology. HDTV features a 16:9 widescreen aspect similar to the dimensions of a movie theatre screen and up to four times higher resolution than current TVs. Most of the new HDTV sets can display both interlaced and progressive video. Unfortunately, a lot of uncertainty still exists on HDTV broadcast standardization.

Currently, HDTV is broadcast at 1080i (1080 horizontal lines, interlaced video) but many technology experts are pushing for some kind of progressive-based format such as 720p (720 horizontal lines, progressive video). Current HDTV displays come without a HDTV tuner; you have to buy that separately. (And they wonder why HDTV sales are low.)

Furthermore, very little HDTV content is currently being broadcast and it is hard to say when this will change. The most compelling reason to own a HDTV is to play back widescreen/letterbox DVDs. Playing back your DV camcorder's footage on an HDTV display will offer little benefit over a conventional television. So until HDTV consumer camcorders are rolled out or HDTV broadcasts pick up, an HDTV purchase will be hard for even me to justify.

OVERVIEW OF NEW DIGITAL VIDEO TECHNOLOGY

We are still in a technological transition stage between older analog technology and newer digital technology. The DVD player and DV camcorder are prime examples of digital technologies that are now mainstream. As each of them took at least a few years to catch on and mature, you can only expect similar time frames for newly rolled out technologies.

Recordable DVD drives are the most promising of the new crop of technologies. However, recordable DVD drives are still very new, and the first batch of drives of both the DVD-R/RW and DVD+R/RW drives reflect that, as some set top DVD players won't play back the discs properly. If you are planning on buying one of these drives, check the compatibility with your current set top DVD player. As with all new technologies the prices are still high for the drives and media, but prices will drop over the next year.

PART II

HARDWARE: CAMCORDERS AND COMPUTERS

CHAPTER 4

DIGITAL CAMCORDER BASICS

Digital Camcorders are smaller, lighter, provide better sound and video quality, and interface vastly better into the computer editing environment than current analog camcorders. Furthermore, with the falling prices of DV camcorders, only a narrow price gap remains between the cheapest analog camcorders and DV camcorders.

But DV camcorders are not perfect. The two biggest problems that affect DV camcorders are low light performance and motor noise being picked up from the camera's microphone. As I will discuss in this chapter, these problems are intrinsically tied to limitations of current DV hardware. When buying a camcorder, look out for these flaws in particular. As the format is refined, these issues will hopefully become less common. Despite these problems, the advantages outweigh them and most of us really have no reason to buy anything but DV in the current market.

ABOUT GENERAL CAMCORDER COMPONENTS

Before investing in such a pricey toy/tool, familiarize yourself as much as possible with the basic elements of a DV camcorder. Most camcorders share the same basic hardware and features. What separates them is hardware quality, ergonomics (how well the camera is designed), and accessory availability (this is more important for some users than others). While a higher price usually suggests a better product, one or more camcorders usually stand out in terms of the price/performance ratio (that is, how much you get for your money).

All camcorders are composed of a few basic elements:

- Lens
- Imaging device (which collects the image)
- Recording hardware such as a tape drive
- Viewfinder
- Microphone

The quality of these basic hardware elements determines camcorder performance and reliability.

All camcorders also have a stock group of features: zoom lens, image stabilization system, various picture effects, and other bells and whistles. Many of these features you will never use. Prioritize what you need in a camcorder so that you can make the most of your purchase dollars.

The imaging chip is the heart of a camcorder. Imaging chips record the optical information that makes up your recorded picture. Along with the lens, the quality of your imaging chip determines the quality of your recorded picture. Obviously, when buying a camcorder, the most important consideration on your checklist should be the imaging chip.

CCD

Currently, all camcorders use charge-coupled devices (CCDs) for their imaging chips. CCDs are small wafer chips composed mainly of a photo-sensitive coating (see Figure 4.1). This photo-sensitive coating is filled with small electronic capacitors, which are charged by the electrons in light.

The capacitors are separated in a grid-like structure. Each cube in the grid is known as a pixel. The more pixels, the better the resolution. The larger the pixels, the better the low-light performance. Consequently, higher-end camcorders tend to have larger CCDs and some also have more pixels.

Recently, CCD size has been getting smaller and pixel counts have been increasing in many newer camcorders. The obvious result of the smaller chips has been poor low-light performance, but the increased pixel counts have also improved video resolution in good lighting.

Figure 4.1

The CCD (charge-coupled device) is the imaging device used in all recent camcorders, as well as most digital cameras.

CCDs come in two flavors: progressive and interlaced. Interlaced video is that standard television display format used all over the world, whether NTSC (North America), Secam (France), or PAL (Europe and Asia).

Interlaced CCD

Interlaced video is kind of an odd display format that was developed within certain technological limitations (such as limited data bandwidth). With good luck, interlaced video will become a part of video history, but it still is a major player in present video technology, even in HDTV (high definition television).

The term *bandwidth* originated in the radio broadcast era. Technically it means the numerical difference between upper and lower frequencies on an assigned radio spectrum. The wider the bandwidth, the more information could be transmitted over that radio spectrum. But we are now entering the age of fiber-optic data transmission (with other transmission technologies likely to follow), and the word bandwidth has evolved to also mean how much data can be moved across a communications channel in a set amount of time.

Interlaced video is composed of 60 half fields for NTSC or 50 half fields for PAL every second. Each interlaced field only contains video information on every other scan line (see Figure 4.2). The advantage of interlaced video is that motion is smoother because more than 60 moments get captured. The disadvantage is that this comes at the expense of picture resolution. Interlaced video is basically capturing twice as much of the action, but it is delivering half the image information on each field.

Figure 4.2

Interlaced video is composed of two half fields of interlaced video information every 1/30 of a second.

Progressive CCD

Progressive video, on the other hand, is composed of full frames. As a result, progressive video looks sharper than interlaced. Computer screens are all progressive displays and many of the newer HDTV televisions and DVD players are capable of progressive video mode. Motion picture film is also a progressive format, displaying 24fps (frames per second).

All camcorders that feature progressive video mode also can record in interlaced mode (see Figure 4.3). The advantage of getting a camcorder with progressive video mode is that every frame of your video is also a 720×480 video still. With a good quality progressive video camera, you can get some very nice looking video stills that are ideal for the Web, e-mail, or picture CDs straight from your video footage.

Figure 4.3

Progressive video is composed of one complete field of video every 1/30 of a second compared to interlaced video's two half fields of video every 1/30 of a second.

Progressive video mode is not without drawbacks. It does not work very well recording fast action such as sports, because 30p (progressive) captures half the number of frames of 30i (interlaced) video. But for slow stuff (where people move at a walking pace or slower), it performs well.

Sixty fields of progressive video a second would of course capture sports as well as 30i and be visually superior, but current televisions do not support that. In fact, when you output 30fps progressive video from your camcorder to your television, it does not look as good as it would on progressive display like a computer monitor. Progressive-capable camcorders display each progressive frame twice on interlaced televisions to fill the sixty fields. As a result the playback can have a stuttered look.

Sony's high-end camcorders produce some of the best interlaced video; unfortunately none of them have 30fps progressive video mode. A few high-end models offer 15fps progressive mode, but this is unusable for anything but extracting stills. This makes choosing between interlaced and progressive capability even more difficult.

Interlaced video is not incapable of producing good video stills, but requires a more involved process. Each captured still from interlaced video contains two half fields. If the still is taken from a fast action video, the presence of two different fields will be obvious. The still will have a window blind effect (see Figure 4.4).

You have to export the still from your video-editing program and then import it into an image-editing program like Adobe Photoshop (www.adobe.com). Photoshop has a deinterlacing filter, which gets rid of one of the fields of video. You can then either use line duplication or interpolation to fill the empty lines of the removed video frame. Interpolation (where the program guesses appropriate image fill data) usually looks better than duplication mode. So while you technically lose half the resolution information, the result is not as dramatic. Still, the quality is always going to be below that of a progressive still.

Figure 4.4

This split screen shows the same frame of video in both interlaced and deinterlaced form. The interlaced side displays the characteristic stuttered window blind effect, whereas the deinterlaced side looks very smooth.

If little or no movement occurs between the capture of the interlaced frames, you often won't have to deinterlace at all. The advantage of this is that you do not lose image resolution, as you retain both fields of video information. I should also note that Paint Shop Pro has an easy to use deinterlace filter, which lets you discard one of the fields and utilize interpolation.

Whether interlaced or progressive, most CCDs used in DV camcorders suffer from a noticeable problem when compared to analog camcorders: poor low-light performance. CCDs need light to generate a picture, but the increasingly higher pixel resolution (to meet DV picture quality) on the same size or even smaller chips results often in dismal low-light performance (see Figure 4.5).

Figure 4.5

Unfortunately many DV camcorders don't perform well in low light, which defines most home shooting environments.

Hardly any of the sub-$1500 consumer camcorders I have used can equal the low-light performance of my old Sony CCD-TRV101 Hi-8 camcorder, bought in 1994. DV camcorders clearly produce superior picture quality outdoors or in brightly lit rooms, but in average room light and below many DV camcorders perform disappointingly.

Unless you want the headache of having to worry about lighting, demo the low-light performance of any camcorder you are considering buying. Never believe the low-light specs given by camcorder companies—they are written by people with marketing degrees. The low-light issue hopefully will be improved in the future, but it is still a major issue with consumer DV camcorders right now.

Many new camcorders feature low-light, and even zero-light modes. Low-light modes usually reduce the frame rate and work with various degrees of success (often very little) to lighten your picture quality. Zero-light modes project an invisible infrared beam up to ten feet in front of your camcorder, and pick up an image from that. Sony includes this feature, which they call Nightshot, on the greatest number of camcorder models. However, video taken in these modes has a pronounced green cast to it, or appears black and white.

Three-Chip CCD Camcorders

The highest-end camcorders usually have three CCD chips (also called *three-chippers*). Each CCD is responsible for collecting one of the basic colors red, blue, and green (see Figure 4.6). The resulting picture quality has warmer, more accurate colors than any one-chip camcorder can provide. In addition, three-chip camcorders usually have better low-light performance and resolution because they capture more picture information. Currently, the Sony VX2000, which has three 1/3-inch CCDs, is by far the best low-light performing consumer camcorder.

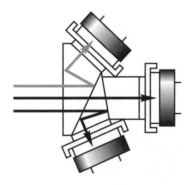

Figure 4.6

In three CCD camcorders a prism separates the red, blue, and green colors, which are then recorded by three separate CCDs.

Three-chip camcorders tend to be fairly large, since they have to fit three CCDs. Thus far, the smallest three-chip camcorders from Sony and Panasonic have been much larger than the smallest one-chip camcorders. If you can handle the size, the video quality on a three-CCD camera like the Sony TRV900 is well worth it (see Figure 4.7).

Figure 4.7

The Sony TRV900, one of the smaller three-chip camcorders, is still much bigger than one of the smaller one-chip camcorders like the Sony PC-9.

CMOS

CMOS (complementary metal-oxide semiconductor) is a new imaging chip technology that is capable of smaller form factors, lower power consumption, and cheaper production costs than CCDs (see Figure 4.8). So far CMOS chips have mostly been used in low-cost webcams. However, the Canon D30, one of the best professional-style digital cameras on the market, uses a three-megapixel CMOS chip and delivers outstanding picture quality.

Figure 4.8

The CMOS imaging chip with its better low-light capability could someday find its way into camcorders.

CMOS offers the potential of better low-light performance and lower video noise levels than current CCD technology (though future CCD technology may also offer that).

JARGON

> *Video noise* is a result of pixels not getting enough picture information (usually a result of inadequate light) as a result the CCD displays a random color. The resulting effect is a disperse white or color laden snow throughout your video image (see Figure 4.9).

Figure 4.9

Video noise looks like snow throughout your video picture.

Time will tell whether CMOS makes it into camcorders. When it does, treat it as untested technology.

LENS

Lenses are the second most important components of a camcorder. A poor lens can be prone to image distortion and color aberration.

Image distortion can occur when you have the zoom at maximum or minimum settings. At minimum settings you can get slight *barrel distortion* where straight lines not in the center of the picture bow away from the image center (see Figure 4.10). At max zoom setting you can get slight *pincushion distortion* where straight lines not in the center of the picture bow towards the image center (see Figure 4.11).

Figure 4.10

Barrel distortion causes vertical lines that are not in the middle of your picture to bow away from the image center.

Color aberration is technically called *chromatic aberration*, which means colors display incorrectly. For example, sometimes blacks can appear purplish. However, a camcorder's automatic White Balance usually compensates for color aberration.

Lens size also affects how much light can get to the CCD. The smaller the lens, the more likely the camera is to have poor low-light performance.

Sony has added Carl Zeiss lenses on some of its higher-end camcorders. Carl Zeiss has a venerable reputation for manufacturing quality professional camera lenses. However, in the last few years many companies have started to use their quality brand names to sell more mass consumer items. Keep in mind Mercedes Benz is now selling a $30,000 model, which is probably below their historical standards. So don't be taken too much by the branding. In general, while it is safe to assume higher-priced camcorders tend to have nicer lenses and components, this is not *always* the case.

Because image quality depends on both the lens and CCD chip, the best way to assess a camcorder is to judge quality of the recorded video.

Figure 4.11

Pincushion distortion is the opposite of barrel distortion and happens most commonly when you reach the max settings of your optical zoom.

BATTERY OPTIONS

Battery technology has improved like everything else. Most new camcorders feature Lithium Ion batteries, which have a much smaller physical size, compared to older Nicad batteries. Lithium Ion batteries also can be recharged without regard to making sure the battery is fully drained. With Nicad batteries you allegedly had to fully drain your batteries before recharging them if you wanted to ensure optimal battery life (many tech experts think this is a myth).

You have fairly good battery options for most digital camcorders (see Figure 4.12). The smallest DV cams tend to be less suited for long play batteries, but most models have them (they just tend to stick out clumsily from your little cam).

Large battery
clumsily sticking out

Figure 4.12

A large extended life battery can make your compact camcorder quite a bit less compact.

Sony DCR-TRV camcorders historically have the best battery options. This is a result of one part good engineering and one part having the largest consumer base to sell accessories to. Most of the other manufacturers have between two and three battery options that will work on each particular model (a one-hour, a two-hour, and a four-hour battery). The one thing you need to know about camcorder batteries is that they are very un-standardized. Each company has its own proprietary designs, which often vary between models. So when buying extra batteries, pay special attention to which batteries are compatible with your camera.

The word *proprietary*, when used alongside batteries, memory cards, or attachments (external lights, microphones), is code for "this device will only work with our stuff." For example, a proprietary external microphone from Canon will only work on specified Canon camcorders.

VIEWFINDER

The viewfinder is as old as the invention of the camera (see Figure 4.13). Camcorders have video viewfinders, which are either color or black and white. Almost all new digital camcorders have color viewfinders.

Figure 4.13

Using the viewfinder will allow your camcorder battery to last longer.

Interestingly enough, a few of the highest-model prosumer digital camcorders (Canon XL1, Sony PD150) have black and white viewfinders because professional video camera operators find it easier to focus images in black and white.

When comparing viewfinders, check the pixel resolution count. The more pixels the better the resolution of the viewfinder.

LCD MONITOR

LCD (liquid crystal display) is the monitor technology used in notebook computer displays and most flat-panel monitors. Small LCD flip-out monitors have been included on many digital camcorders since they hit the market in 1997. Almost every new DV camcorder on the market right now features an LCD monitor.

LCD monitors are a great feature on a camcorder because they free you from having to stick your eye in the viewfinder. Their ability to swivel into various positions allows you more shooting options. They do have two main weaknesses, though. First, using your LCD will drain your battery faster than using the viewfinder. Second, most LCDs do not work very well in the bright sun because the picture generally becomes hard to see.

In my experience, a 700mA battery (which is the average size of included batteries) will last as long as an hour using the viewfinder and between 30 and 45 minutes using the LCD (depending on the size and power consumption of your LCD). LCD power consumption varies more than viewfinders, so it is harder to give exact specs on how much using your LCD will impact the battery.

Common sense dictates that larger LCDs will use more battery power, but the number of pixels has an effect too. While a large LCD with the most pixels might look the best, it will also drain the most power. Large LCDs often have low pixel counts relative to their size, which helps power efficiency (see Figure 4.14). Small LCDs often have high pixel counts to compensate for their small size. Personally, I like the 2.5-inch LCDs on the pocket DV camcorders, especially in situations where the camera needs to be as transparent as possible. A 3.5-inch swing out LCD has a significantly larger appearing foot print, even though it does not make a camera much larger physically. If transparency is not a factor, the larger LCDs screens are preferable to most people.

LCD screens usually allow you to adjust screen brightness. The downside of altering LCD brightness is that you can lose proper reference to the light levels of your recorded video. I usually keep brightness at the default middle position.

Figure 4.14

Large LCDs usually have fewer pixels per square inch than small LCDs. This enables them to have a large viewing size without excessive power consumption.

MICROPHONE

Sound quality is one of the most important-yet-overlooked features on a camcorder. Good sound is as important as video for anything but silent pictures. Unfortunately, sound quality on DV camcorders is a mixed story. DV camcorders record sound at 16-bit 48kHz stereo (CD quality is 16-bit/44.1kHz). You can also record four tracks of 12-bit 32kHz sound, but you are better off adding extra tracks if needed in the computer video editing process, where you are not limited to 32kHz.

DV Audio Explained

Digital audio has two defining parameters: sample rate and bit resolution. *Sample rate* translates to how often a sample of the source audio (that is, whatever audio you are recording) is recorded. *Bit resolution* translates to how many bits (binary digits of information: 0 or 1) are used to describe that sample. If you were to open a sound file in a music audio program and magnify it extensively you would eventually be looking at the bit resolution. 24-bit resolution allows for more faithful recording of the source than 16- or 8-bit (see Figure 4.15).

Sample rate is measured in kHz (kilohertz). Music CDs are 44.1kHz. DV audio is 48kHz. DVD audio is 96kHz. That means that DVD audio has twice as much sample data compared to CD and DV. However, the human ear (and more importantly most consumer sound hardware) is often not capable of discerning much difference between 44kHz and 96kHz sound.

Bit resolution differences seem to be more detectable to the human ear than sample rate differences. CD and DV audio is 16-bit. DVD audio is 24-bit.

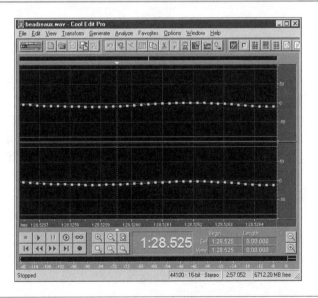

Figure 4.15

The higher the audio bit rate, the smoother and more accurate your recordings will be.

As far as the specs go, DV camcorders should have much better sound than their analog counterparts. However, many camcorder microphones are pretty average. Mic quality is going to show up more when you are recording subjects with a wide frequency response like a concert, and then playing things back on a high-fidelity home theater system. Many people are not doing this, so the average camcorder microphones are adequate in most home video applications. However, for filmmaking or professional applications, where any motor noise is unacceptable and more versatility is required, the built-in mic is usually not acceptable.

DV camcorders have somewhat unique sound issues. The tape drive on DV camcorders operates at twice the speed of analog camcorders because DV writes more data to tape. The result of the increased speed is more friction, which results in more audible noise of the tape mechanism. Onboard camcorder mics tend to pick up some of this motor drive noise. The result varies from a hiss to a low mild drone. Some users don't notice it; some are driven crazy by it. The unfortunate reality is that the quietest camcorder I have owned is again my trusty Sony TRV101 Hi-8 analog camcorder.

The best solution to the problem is to avoid DV camcorders that have this problem (but since most do this can be difficult). The only ones that seem to avoid this problem almost entirely have DSPs (digital signal processors) which digitally screen out the motor noise. The Sony TRV900 is an example of this (see Figure 4.16).

Figure 4.16

The Sony TRV900 features an audio DSP (digital signal processor), which filters out any noise from the camcorder's tape drive.

Some camcorder companies have responded to this problem. JVC in particular used to have some of the louder models, but now they make some of the quieter ones. I would just recommend demo-ing the camcorder's ability to record audio in a quiet room and then playing back the footage and listening to the sound.

The problem of tape drive noise is exacerbated by what is called *audio gain control*, not to be confused with auto gain control, which your camcorder uses to make your video brighter (I will discuss this later in Chapter 12).

Audio gain control alters the gain on your microphone. Gain determines how sensitive the mic is to external noise. If you are videotaping a child talking who has a weak voice, audio gain control is good because the camcorder will adjust the gain to make the voice more audible. On the other hand, if you are videotaping in a quiet museum, the audio gain control might jack up the gain (searching for sound), honing in on undesirable things like the air conditioner system, or buzzing fluorescent lights.

Only a few of the highest-model DV camcorders enable you to turn audio gain control off and set your own audio levels. Therefore most people are just going to have to live with the limitations of audio gain control. Using an external mic will not eliminate audio gain control (unless you have a camcorder that allows manual audio). However, an external mic should minimize motor drive noise.

OPTICAL AND DIGITAL ZOOM

All camcorders have zoom lenses of some kind. Because of size constraints, DV camcorders actually tend to have smaller optical zooms (around 10x) than analog camcorders. This is because altering the distance between two lenses inside your camcorder creates the optical zoom. Most DV camcorders are too small to accommodate enough distance for a powerful optical zoom. By reducing lens size, a small DV camera can accommodate a longer optical zoom, but this usually hurts image quality. Digital8 camcorders, since they are larger due to bigger tape media, can accommodate longer optical zooms (see Figure 4.17). Most Digital8 models average a 20x optical zoom.

front view   side view   back view

Figure 4.17

Digital8 camcorders usually have more powerful optical zooms than DV camcorders because their larger size allows for them.

All camcorders have digital zooms, which activate once you zoom past the limits of your optical zoom. At that point all you are doing is digitally enlarging your video, which results in diminished resolution (see Figure 4.18). Bottom line: Digital zooms are not worth using because you compromise the quality of your video. Go into your camcorder menu and disable it permanently. So, ignore the fact that a camera has 500x digital zoom. It creates pixilated images and cannot be used effectively without a tripod. It's only good for surveillance.

If you want that pixilated effect you get with the hyper digital zoom, you are better off applying that effect in your computer with video editing software, after the fact.

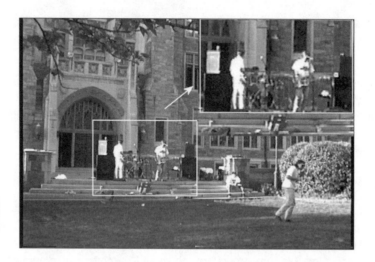

Figure 4.18

The digital zoom digitally enlarges your picture, which results in unacceptable picture quality. Do not use it.

OPTICAL AND DIGITAL IMAGE STABILIZATION

If you have seen *The Blair Witch Project*, you probably were a little ill because of the prolific camera shaking that riddled the film. Since the days of 8mm home movie cams, home videos tend to have an annoying shakiness to them.

This is not just because we are spoiled by television and movies, where camera movement is always smooth and professional. The human optical system has sophisticated built-in stabilization. Throughout your day, your body is rarely as perfectly still as a camera tripod, yet the world never appears to be as shaky as old home movies. This is because your eyes constantly adjust to accommodate for little head and body movements.

If you have ever consumed too much alcohol, you have probably witnessed the failure of that optical image stabilization system and the world probably started to look like an old home movie.

Camcorder image stabilization systems attempt to achieve the same thing by constantly altering the picture to compensate for camera movement. While the human body's optical stabilization system can compensate for pretty large movements, camcorders will only cover small movements and shakiness.

There are two prominent image stabilization technologies: digitally based systems and optically based systems.

Digital image stabilization (DIS) constantly moves your picture digitally to compensate for shakiness. Older DIS implementation compromised video quality because it would crop the outside of the picture image by a certain amount to allow the camera picture to be shifted a little to the left when the camera shook to the right. New DIS technology dedicates the outside portion of the CCD to image stabilization so that turning on DIS does not reduce picture quality in any way. The general advice used to be to disable your DIS, but now there is no reason not to use it unless you are looking for a jumpy picture effect.

JVC Wide Mode

Thanks to the extra CCD space devoted to image stabilization, some new JVC camcorders offer a wide mode video option. The wide mode feature basically gives you sort of a built-in .7x wide-angle lens. When in this mode, the camcorder utilizes that extra video data on the outskirts of the CCD to give you a wider picture (this can save you the trouble of buying an external wide angle lens). However, you are unable to use DIS mode when utilizing this feature. You also, for whatever reason, can only utilize this wide mode feature when you are in progressive video mode. Since I shoot most of my footage in this mode, this is not a downside for me. JVC has this feature on the JVC 8ou, 9ou, 98oou, and DV2000 camcorders.

Optical image stabilization (OIS) is considered to be a superior stabilization approach, but fewer camcorders use it because it costs more to implement (see Figure 4.19). The clearest advantage OIS has is low-light performance. DIS can hurt low-light performance, while OIS has no effect.

Figure 4.19

This is a diagram of the optical image stabilization system used in some Canon camcorders.

OIS was developed by Canon but it is also used in some higher end Sony and Panasonic camcorders. OIS operates by attaching small motors to the lenses inside your camera. When shakes occur, the motors move the lenses in order to keep the picture projected onto the CCD completely stable (resulting in a stable video picture).

The downside of OIS is that it requires more battery power than DIS, though I don't think the difference is significant or large enough to take away from the advantages of OIS.

SPECIAL EFFECTS

Virtually every new camcorder includes an array of special effects that you can apply to the video you capture (see Figure 4.20). Each manufacturer offers a different package of effects. The standard effects include goodies like black and white, sepia (a yellow-tinged black and white), strobe, video echo, film like mode, and low light modes.

Figure 4.20

Most camcorders come with the ability to apply special effects to your video while shooting, or during playback.

Once you set the desired effect in your camcorder, your LCD or viewfinder will immediately alter your video with that effect. So you can go through all the different effects to see which one fits what you are shooting best. Sony is particularly good with effects implementation, as you can jog dial through effects on-the-fly. My JVC camcorder forces me to select the effect in the menu and then exit before I can see what it looks like, which is more tedious.

JARGON

The *jog dial* is a wheel control mechanism implemented on most camcorders to navigate and control internal settings (see Figure 4.21).

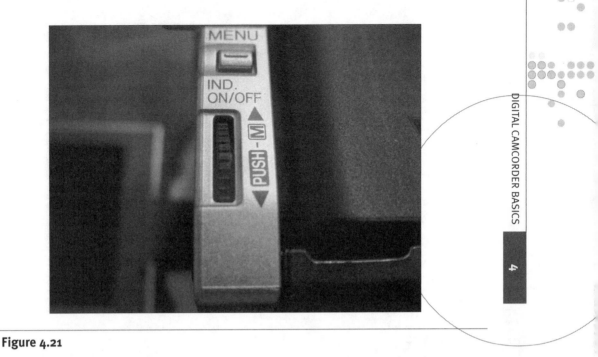

Figure 4.21

The ubiquitous jog dial is the main interface on most camcorders for controlling most camera settings.

AUTOMATIC AND MANUAL SETTINGS

Manual settings allow you to compensate for the limitations of your camcorder's automatic settings (see Figure 4.22). Automatic settings try to accommodate for as many shooting conditions as possible. But it is impossible for automatic settings to cover every shooting situation. Even as automatic settings improve, they will never be perfect. So if you have exacting standards or requirements, manual settings are an absolute requirement.

All DV camcorders have some manual controls. Prosumer camcorders provide a larger set of manual controls, giving you more shooting control. If you tend to enjoy tweaking, you want a camcorder with manual settings. If you are shooting for professional applications, you really have no choice.

Keep in mind that if you don't want to have to worry about manual settings, most of the time automatic mode can provide great video results. It is mainly in extreme lighting conditions (bright sun, low light) that having the option of manual controls can help you get noticeably better video quality.

Figure 4.22

All camcorders have internal menus, which allow you to control various camera settings.

Auto and Manual Focus

Manual focus is the most common manual control (though in truth many camcorder users don't ever use any manual controls). This lets you override the auto focus, which is often necessary in low light when auto focus mechanisms tend to fail. Auto focus systems use the middle of the frame to determine focus, so if you want to have something off center in focus you will also need to go manual.

Manual focus controls vary greatly as well. The most sensible, the *focus ring* around the camera lens (as you would find on a professional film camera), is featured on every Sony DV and Digital8 camcorder (see Figure 4.23). Some Panasonic and Canons have this, but just one JVC model (the new DV2000) does; the rest of the JVC camcorder models force you to use the menu jog dial to focus (which is not exactly ideal).

Figure 4.23

Many camcorders feature a focus ring that allows you to manually control the focus of your video. This is an important feature in low-light situations where the auto focus system tends to fail.

Auto and Manual White Balance

Automatic white balance, like a good laundry detergent, makes sure your whites stay white. When your white balance is off (which can happen under difficult lighting conditions) the color white can appear greenish, yellowish, or bluish. Manual white balance controls featured on many DV camcorders allow you to point the camcorder at something white and lock in the white balance setting. However, if the light changes in the room or you move to another room, you will have to recalibrate the white balance setting.

Unless your camcorder has a bad auto white balance, for most home video work sticking with auto is the best approach.

Auto and Manual Exposure

Camcorders, like cameras, emulate the design of the human eye. The black dot in the middle of the human eye is called the pupil. The pupil is part of a structure called the iris. The iris controls the pupil to allow more or less light into the eye. When encountering bright sunlight, the iris constricts the pupil, so less light gets in and you don't get blinded. In a candle-lit room, the iris dilates (enlarges) the pupil allowing more light to enter the eyes so you can see better.

Exposure works the same way. High exposure is like the dilated pupil, low exposure is like the pin hole pupil. Automatic exposure in most camcorders works pretty well except in very bright or really dark lit situations (see Figure 4.24). In bright sunlight, camcorders tend to overexpose things, causing your picture to be too bright. Colors will get a washed out look; any light colors will often appear white (see Figure 4.25). These white areas are called hot spots.

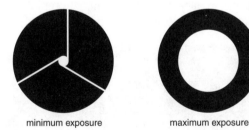

minimum exposure   maximum exposure

Figure 4.24

Controlling exposure also allows you to achieve various video effects. Full exposure brings more light into the camera and makes everything in focus. Minimal exposure allows you to minimize incoming light and allows for selective focus control.

In low-light situations, the auto exposure is not high enough, resulting in a picture that is too dim. In regards to the latter, a lot of camcorders that perform poorly in auto mode in low light conditions can't be helped much by manual exposure because the problem is the light sensitivity of the CCD, not the exposure levels.

Figure 4.25

Exposure to excessive light can result in blinding whites that take over your video picture.

Exposure is measured in F-stops in the film camera world and the highest end DV camcorders utilize this format as well. Higher F-stops represent lower exposure levels (less light); low F-stop settings represent higher exposure levels (more light).

The Canon XL1 features an F-stop ring on the lens of the camera delivering the ideal professional level of control. Lower-end DV camcorders (analog as well) have a certain number of AE (auto exposure) modes for generic shooting situations: one for sunlight, one for snow, one for desert, and so on. Midrange DV camcorders usually have various plus or minus numbered systems to allow you to go from between -6 (minimum exposure) to +6 (maximum exposure) (see Figure 4.26).

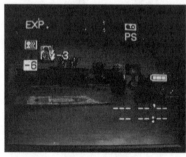

Lowest exposure setting   Highest exposure setting

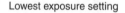

Figure 4.26

Camcorders all vary in their exposure control interfaces. JVC allows you to vary exposure between +6 and -6 settings.

A few of the best DV camcorders (Canon XL1 and GL1, Sony TRV900/1000 and VX2000) include a feature beyond simple manual exposure which paints zebra lines in the viewfinder/LCD on any part of your picture that is overexposed—also called *hot spots* (see Figure 4.27).

Figure 4.27

Some higher end camcorders include a feature which marks out overexposed areas with zebra lines.

Altering exposure also determines the depth of field. *Depth of field* is camera jargon for how much of your camcorder's field of view is in focus. If you are interested in having something in the foreground of your picture in focus and everything beyond that out of focus, you want very little depth of field, so you need to set the exposure low (see Figure 4.28). This technique is useful if you want the audience to focus in on a certain thing. If you want the foreground and the midground to be in focus (medium depth of field), a medium exposure is ideal. Finally, if you want the largest depth of field (everything in focus), set the exposure as high as possible.

Auto and Manual Shutter Speeds

Shutter speed is as old as the film camera. Shutter speed determines how long the shutter is open for each frame. The longer it is open, the more information it records. So if you were able to keep the shutter open for 10 seconds and you filmed a busy intersection, the resulting image would be an unintelligible smear of all the image data during that time.

The slowest shutter speed you will find on a camcorder is 1/4 of a second; most do not go lower than 1/60sec. At this speed, fast moving objects such as cars will look smeary (at least if you extract individual stills). The benefit of slow shutter speed is low-light performance because the more picture information the camcorder can record, the more light it will absorb as well.

Figure 4.28

By setting my exposure extremely low I was able to put the foreground in focus and the background out of focus.

If you lower the shutter rate below 1/60 in interlaced video mode or 1/30 in progressive video mode (which only some camcorders feature), you will lose some image resolution. However, the improved low-light performance may be worth the trade off for you.

Slow shutter speeds don't work very well though for fast sports, as quick moving things will suffer from motion blur (see Figure 4.29).

This is where fast shutter speeds come in (see Figure 4.30). If you want to analyze a golf swing, you need to be able to increase the shutter speed as high as possible. The higher it is, the more likely you are to get clean stills of the entire club motion. Because the smaller the duration of time you see an image, the cleaner the still. The effect of the high shutter is similar to the effect of a strobe light. If you have ever seen people dance near a strobe light you can recall that with each flash everyone appears frozen in time (even though they are moving fast). In the movie *Traffic*, there were a number of scenes where the filmmaker utilized a really high frame rate to achieve this interesting stroboscopic effect.

Sony and Canon DV camcorders have by far the most shutter speed options, with some models ranging between 1/4 and 1/15,000. JVC comes up short in this department, only delivering 4 shutter speeds: 1/60, 1/100, 1/250, and 1/500. Bottom line: If you are into videotaping NASCAR racing, don't get a JVC (unless you can afford the JVC GY-DV500, a professional DV shoulder cam).

Figure 4.29

As shown in this figure, slow shutter speeds are unacceptable for fast moving subjects. This effect is known as motion blur.

Figure 4.30

A fast shutter speed is necessary to record fast action scenes smoothly.

STILL PICTURE CAPABILITY

The ability to take digital stills with your camcorder is all the rage in recent camcorder design. The problem is that digital still cameras perform far better at taking stills than the best DV camcorder with this capability built-in. Furthermore, digital cameras are much smaller and cheaper. At issue is technology cramming. Just as you cannot put the amenities of an RV in a Suburu Justy (or whatever your micro car of choice is), you can't merge a digital camera with a digital camcorder (if it is possible, it has not been done well yet).

NTSC digital camcorders take video at a resolution of 720×480, which is dictated by the DV codec. Some digital cameras, however, have resolutions of 1,600×1,200 and above. As a result, the CCD imaging chips for each format are going to have totally different design priorities. Nice digital cameras have 1/2 inch 2–3+ megapixel CCDs. Most DV camcorders don't even have a megapixel CCD, but within the limited resolution range of the DV codec, a two-megapixel chip would produce too much information anyway.

Many new DV camcorders are starting to feature the ability to take digital stills, but this requires a separate storage medium and transfer method. Most use Smart Media cards, which are common in digital still cameras. Sony models use a proprietary format called Memory Sticks that resembles a stick of gum (if they made gum really thick, blue, and hard to chew).

NOTE

Digital Camera Storage Media

Smart Media, Compact Flash, SD cards, and Memory Stick are all storage formats used in digital cameras, PDAs (such as Palm Pilots), and other electronic devices. These storage formats have no moving parts and can retain data without external power (see Figure 4.31).

Figure 4.31

Smart Media, Compact Flash, and Memory Sticks are the most common storage formats for digital devices.

For still image transfer, older camcorders used serial connection, which is really slow and unreliable. The newest camcorders use USB, which is much faster. Extra cables, storage on a separate media card, and so on can eventually become more of a hassle than having a separate digital camera.

I personally prefer the progressive video mode option when I want a still from my camcorder. Progressive video frame grabs are great for pictures headed for the Web. If you need a high-quality printable photo, a digital camera with a large 1/2-inch megapixel CCD is really the only good solution.

I am also a fan of the flash capability camcorder makers are starting to include, because it is useful for progressive still quality, and also the flash adds a cool effect when shooting video. Unfortunately, most camcorders won't let you just activate the flash in video mode without freezing the video frame for a six-second still, which I find rather limiting.

There is an advantage in having everything you want in one device, and if you can find a model that meets that, fine; but compromises will have to be made. Right now the digital still feature is more gimmicky than useful. The only good thing about this still camera integration is that camcorders have a big advantage over many still cameras in the battery department.

ANALOG PASS THRU

Analog pass thru or *on-the-fly analog encoding* is a relatively new feature on many DV camcorders. This highly useful feature allows you to connect any source with an analog output such as a VCR, DVD player, or an old camcorder and transcode that video into the DV format over the FireWire and into your computer (or to record onto your DV camcorder's tape) (see Figure 4.32).

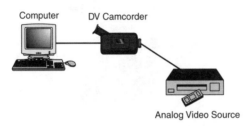

Computer   DV Camcorder

Analog Video Source

Figure 4.32

Many of the latest DV camcorders allow you to input analog video from your old camcorder or your VCR and digitize it.

This is obviously very useful for digitizing old home movies shot on analog camcorders, among other things. Sony, JVC, and Canon all have models that feature it.

ACCESSORY SHOE

The camera shoe allows you to mount an external microphone or light to your camcorder (see Figure 4.33). It can really be useful for achieving higher quality sound or better lighting. Keep in mind that external attachments can be a hassle and can make your life more complicated than necessary. Ideally, home users should look for a camcorder with onboard hardware that suits all their needs, but this is not always possible.

hot shoe

Figure 4.33

Many camcorders come with accessory shoes. *Hot shoes*, which are a type of accessory shoe, allow you to power and control various optional accessories.

The Hot Shoe Explained

A *hot shoe* resembles an ordinary accessory shoe and can work as an ordinary shoe. But what makes a hot shoe unique (or "hot") is that it will power and control compatible attachments from the camcorder electronics. Each manufacturer makes their own proprietary attachments that will only work with their camcorders.

The advantage of a hot shoe is simplicity. With a hot shoe and a compatible attachment you don't need a separate power supply in the case of light attachments, or a mic cable in the case of microphones (see Figure 4.34).

Figure 4.34

The advantage of a hot shoe is that you can hook up a proprietary microphone and the sound data is transferred via the shoe (no mic cable required).

If you need an accessory shoe but your camcorder does not have one, you can buy a $15 shoe adapter that attaches to the bottom of your camcorder.

FIREWIRE (IEEE 1394, I.LINK)

FireWire is a data transfer technology developed by Apple Computer. It is similar to USB except that it is capable of carrying far more data, up to 400Mbps. Early model DV camcorders had questionable FireWire implementation, with compatibility varying from model to model. However, pretty much every DV camcorder released after 2000 has fully operable FireWire in and out (except European models, which often have DV-in disabled for tariff reasons). Exceptions exist, and some camcorders don't work with some computer operating systems, so you should always make sure a camcorder you are considering is compatible with whatever hardware or software you plan on using it with.

FireWire cables have two types of connectors: a small four-pin connector (commonly included on camcorders) and a larger six-pin connector (commonly included on computer FireWire cards) (see Figure 4.35). FireWire cards come with a cable with a six-pin connector on one end for the card and a four-pin on the other for your camera. If you need to transfer footage between two DV camcorders, you will need to buy a cable with a four-pin connector on each end.

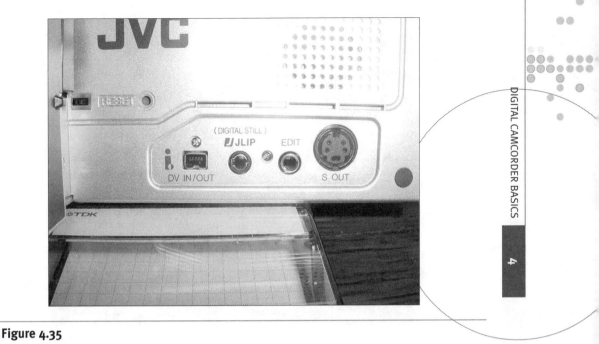

Figure 4.35

All new camcorders come with FireWire connectivity. On this camcorder it is labeled DV IN/OUT.

MEDIA OPTIONS

There are two main format media options for DV camcorders: Digital8 and MiniDV (note that the terms MiniDV and DV are used interchangeably in the industry). There are also optical-storage–based camcorders hitting the market. So far there are only three models that use optical media, and none have made much of an impact.

MiniDV (DV)

MiniDV is the most widely implemented digital video tape format. Most consumer digital video camcorders on the market today use MiniDV tapes (see Figure 4.36). Their physical size is halfway in between an 8mm tape and an audio microcassette tape. They hold 60 minutes of video in SP mode and 90 minutes in LP mode. Recently an 80-minute tape has been introduced. You can also get 30-minute MiniDV tapes.

They cost about $10 a piece, but that price continues to drop. The small tape size allows for some remarkable tiny camcorders. MiniDV will probably continue to be the dominant digital acquisition format until a similarly compact optical or hard-drive–based format can replace it (which could happen at some point in the future).

Figure 4.36

MiniDV tapes used in DV camcorders are about half the size of 8mm tapes (used in Digital8 camcorders).

Digital8

Developed by Sony utilizing the same compression scheme as DV camcorders, the only difference is that Digital8 camcorders record onto 8mm video tapes.

The advantage of 8mm tapes right now is cost (around $5). You can use 8mm or Hi-8mm tapes in your Digital8 camcorder with equal results. The larger form factor of 8mm tapes also allows for more durable camcorder construction. As a result, I think Digital8 cameras make great edit and archiving decks even if you already own a DV Camcorder.

However, the biggest advantage of Digital8 (at least with models introduced before 2001) is that it will play back your old 8mm and Hi-8mm tapes and convert them into DV on-the-fly into your computer via FireWire. While many new DV camcorders have what is called *analog pass thru* (this means you can feed analog video into the camera and it will digitally output it over FireWire or record it to tape), this requires that you have a working 8mm or Hi-8mm deck or camcorder to feed the signal. A Digital8 camcorder allows you to dump your old 8mm camcorder if you still have one, yet still have access to all your old footage (as well as the option to digitize it).

OPTICAL MEDIA

The newest potential DV data format is optical media. This technology will at least make its way onto your computer via recordable DVD drives that should eventually replace CD burners. But it could become a dominant storage technology in camcorders as well.

The advantage of optical media is that you can quickly get from one part of your footage to another much quicker than with tape media, which requires comparably clumsy tape rewinds and fast forwards. The complexity and touchiness of tape drives will certainly not be missed if optical media becomes dominant. So far, there have been three camcorders utilizing this concept, but none of them have caught on due to use of non-standard optical media formats and sub-par video quality (see Figure 4.37).

Figure 4.37

The Hitachi DZ-MZ100A was the first DVD-RAM camcorder on the market.

The most ideal optical media format looks to be DVD+RW, which started rolling out *en masse* in the spring of 2002. Camcorders based on small DVD+RW discs could give tape-based DV cameras serious competition. As of the publication of this book, there are no DVD+RW camcorders on the market. And even when there are, I would dissuade any format-jumping until this technology can prove itself in the market.

CHAPTER 5

CHOOSING THE RIGHT CAMCORDER

DV camcorders are expensive devices that can well make up the cost in memories for a family, in creativity for a hobby filmmaker, as a method of making money for a videographer, or all of the above. DV camcorders start as low as $400, with most of them around the $1,000 range and a handful of models over two grand. While they all record footage using the same DV codec, the image quality varies considerably depending on the hardware of each camcorder.

You need to determine whether you are a budget buyer, specific needs buyer, price/performance buyer, or a high-end buyer. The budget buyer can only afford to spend so much and wants the best camcorder they can get within their price range. The specific needs buyer requires certain features that only a few camcorders are going to have. The price/performance buyer wants to buy the best performing camcorder for the money. The high-end buyer wants the best camcorder regardless of cost.

THE DIFFERENT CAMCORDER TYPES

In choosing a camcorder, I advise accepting the fact that you will probably not find the perfect DV camcorder. I am not speaking philosophically, either, but rather to the reality of currently available models. The DV format—in respect to its potential—is really only at the fair to good stage on the technology evolution time line. The models with the best video and sound are bigger than most prefer, or don't have a progressive video mode like the Sony DCR-VX2000. Most smaller models have average to dismal low-light performance, and many have bad audio with respect to motor drive pickup. Nevertheless, even the worst DV camcorders produce very good-looking video given adequate lighting.

Subcompact Camcorders (Pocket Cams, Wrist Cams)

The latest miniature camcorders (or *cams*) are remarkably cool looking devices weighing as little as a pound and small enough to slip in a jacket pocket. They have viewfinders and 2.5-inch flip-out LCDs. I call them *wrist cams* because you hold them on the side, which taxes the wrist far more than the common palmcorder design, held as the name suggests by the palm. Subcompact cams are much more transparent (they blend into their surroundings) when compared to palmcorders, which look deceptively larger with a 3.5″ LCD screen swung out (see Figure 5.1).

Figure 5.1

The JVC DVP3u is currently the smallest DV camcorder.

Subcompact camcorders would be great for documentary use or general home video work if they worked well enough. Unfortunately these cams have severe technical and ergonomic limitations. They usually have bad low-light performance and/or bad sound quality. The only one that performs really well is the Sony PC120 (and its predecessor the PC110), but it's not all that compact. The PC120 is also really awkward to handle, as are most subcompact camcorders. The Sony TRV30 palmcorder, which is only slightly bigger, performs better and is much easier to handle, as are most palmcorders. Subcompact camcorders, due to their small size, are awkward to handle and are hard to keep steady, resulting in a shakier picture. Given all these limitations, if you really want a subcompact, I would recommend the Sony DCR-PC9, which delivers pretty good video quality, has an external mic jack, and will easily fit in a jacket pocket.

Compact Camcorders (Palmcorders)

Compact camcorders are often not much bigger than the average subcompact wrist cams. The two main differences are the LCD size and the palmcorder design. The LCD size has its obvious advantages, though it makes these camcorders look bulkier.

The palmcorder design allows better placement of components (see Figure 5.2). For example, the microphone is usually more removed from the tape drive, reducing the chance of motor noise pickup. The palmcorder design also usually accommodates larger lenses than the subcompact cams, allowing for better low-light performance. Finally, these camcorders are easier to keep stable as they rest naturally on your palm, affording smoother, less shaky footage.

front view   side view   back view

Figure 5.2

The palmcorder design is the most common camcorder design on the market.

Midsize Camcorders

The latest midsize camcorders offer incredible image quality for the price. They are the camcorder of choice for many professionals as well as consumers who want the best quality possible.

The Sony VX2000 and Canon GL1, two of the most popular midsize camcorders, weigh between 2 and 3 pounds. More awkward than heavy, these cams are not big enough to rest on a shoulder, so they have to be held as you would a compact palmcorder, which can be fatiguing. (For more information on these two models, see the section "Best Prosumer Camcorders," later in this chapter.)

The larger form factor allows for better mic placement and higher-quality sound. Midsize cams can also house multiple larger CCDs. The VX2000 has three 1/3" CCDs, which deliver higher resolution and better low-light performance. It is physically impossible to fit three CCDs that big into compact camcorder dimensions. These cameras are also less prone to shake due to the size and weight.

The popular Sony TRV900 is one of the smallest midsize cams, weighing in at 2 lbs (look ahead to Figure 5.14). The TRV900 has a smaller form factor than the GL1 or VX2000 and looks like many other consumer camcorders (making it more transparent). Despite the unassuming design, the performance is top-notch.

Large Camcorders

Large camcorders have similar or slightly better-quality video than midsize cams. Their main advantage is that they are shoulder mounted so they are going to deliver the steadiest picture. They also feature removable lenses, which gives you more shooting options. All smaller camcorders have fixed lenses. Professional videographers who are used to shoulder-mounted cameras are going to be more comfortable with one of these models. The Canon XL1 is the most popular large DV cam (see Figure 5.3).

Figure 5.3

The Canon XL1 features three 1/3" CCDs, a removable lens, and progressive video mode.

Large cams also look more professional. While a smaller cam like the TRV900 shoots great video, you look more like a tourist than a professional videographer using it.

Budget Camcorders

If you are on a tight budget, there are still a fair number of good DV options for you. Budget DV cams will have lower video quality (still better than analog) and fewer bells and whistles. However, they still possess the advantages of DV—a lossless video codec and the ability to easily input video into a computer.

Digital8

Digital8 camcorders are positioned in the budget price zone with models between $500 and $1,000. One advantage of Digital8 is tape costs: Five dollar 8mm tapes are half the price of MiniDV tapes (though MiniDV tape costs are falling). Sony recommends Hi-8mm tapes but there does not seem to be any performance difference between 8mm (which are cheaper) and Hi-8mm tapes in Digital8 camcorders. Sony now labels its Hi-8 tapes for Digital8 or Hi-8 use.

Most current Digital8 cameras have average quality CCDs that deliver resolution of between 375 and 400 horizontal lines. Their low-light performance is average. The two highest model Digital8 camcorders have a better CCD, which appears identical to that used in the acclaimed Sony TRV20 (predecessor to the TRV30), delivering closer to 500 lines of resolution.

While the large size of Digital8 camcorders does not appeal to a lot of consumers, there are benefits. Digital8 camcorders can have a higher optical zoom capability. Most models have at least 20x. Since they are bigger, they tend to be easier to keep steady without shaking. Also they match the form factor of Hi-8mm and 8mm camcorders that many of you are already familiar with. I also think Digital8 camcorders are more durable because all the parts are bigger and thicker.

Since most of the lower-end models have similar video quality (in fact, the newest models actually have smaller CCDs than the previous Digital8 models), I don't see a point to recommend any one of them. The cheapest Sony Digital8 camcorder should give you the most value since it has the same CCD and internal mechanics as the others.

However, the Sony DCR-TRV730 stands out because it has a really nice megapixel CCD, so the image quality is great (see Figure 5.4). The DCR-TRV830 has the same CCD (and a larger 3.5" LCD) but comes with a wacky external printer mounted on the top for printing still pictures (see Figure 5.5). (Both the TRV730 and TRV830 feature the ability to take digital stills.) The printer is clunky, has really high media replacement costs, and prints really small unimpressive pictures.

Figure 5.4

The Sony DCR-TRV730, which features a 1.1 megapixel CCD, is one of the best performing Digital8 camcorders.

Figure 5.5

The Sony DCR-TRV830 is identical to the 730 except that it adds a larger 3.5-inch LCD, and a funky detachable external printer.

Recommended Model: Sony Digital8 DCR-TRV730

The Sony DCR-TRV730 has a much better CCD than lower model Digital8 camcorders, but is still priced very low (well under $1,000). The picture quality is identical to the MiniDV model TRV20. The only con to the 730 is the small 2.5" LCD.

Entry Level DV (MiniDV)

There are many DV camcorders priced in the budget range ($500–$1,000). They have quality limitations similar to those that affect Digital8 camcorders, but have a much smaller form factor (that is camcorder size) since the MiniDV tape is smaller.

Since they are smaller they tend to have lower-powered optical zooms (they average 10×). A few models feature up to 20× optical zooms (a few of the Panasonic models). However this can require a smaller lens size, which affects image quality. Fortunately, in the case of the Panasonic models, image quality is not compromised.

DV camcorders, due to their small size, can be hard to keep steady. The small DV cams that fit the palmcorder design are the easiest to steady as they have a nice balance between compactness and handling. The pocket cams conversely are more prone to unsteadiness.

The smaller size of DV cams also affects sound quality. Since everything is so close together these cams are more prone to picking up motor noise on your recordings than older and larger analog camcorders. Also, as stated before, the DV tape drive operates two times faster than older analog tape drives. So larger DV camcorders are not automatically immune to motor noise pickup.

Recommended Models: Panasonic PV-DV101/201/401/601

All of these models share the same hardware (good CCD, impressive 20x optical zoom, camera housing, and tape mechanism). They only differ in size of flip-out LCD and memory card/still picture options (see Figure 5.6). Price range for all models is $500 to $750.

Figure 5.6

The Panasonic PV-DV601 is one of the best budget DV camcorders on the market.

BEST PRICE/PERFORMANCE CAMCORDERS

Purchasing a mid-range camcorder is a good way to obtain the most for your dollar. The way the retail world works is that the highest quality and newest products are usually overpriced. Early adopters are forced to carry a disproportionate amount of the product development cost.

Take one small, usually imperceptible step down in quality and usually you get a much better deal. Considering that technological purchases fall under the *in danger of obsolescence* category, and will probably be replaced every 2–5 years, there is no sense in spending twice as much for maybe a ten percent improvement in quality. The ideal purchase zone is right where quality advantage mirrors the extra cost you have to pay. When the price begins to exceed the quality advantage, you are getting into the area where you are burning money for very small gains in performance. Consider the example of electronic pets. The Sony AIBO dog costs $1,500, while the similar Tiger Electronics I-Cybie costs just $199. Bottom line: Sometimes you can get a similar product for much cheaper.

Recommended Model: Sony DCR-TRV30

This camcorder follows the palmcorder design. It is very similar to the Sony PC120 internally (same CCD), but it has a far superior form factor and has a bigger lens (see Figure 5.7). It also has better sound than the PC120, as palmcorders allow for better mic placement. If digital stills are important to you, the TRV30 takes the highest quality stills of any DV camcorder currently on the market. It also has a USB port for fast transfer of digital stills.

front view   side view   back view

Figure 5.7

The Sony TRV30 has a 1.5 megapixel CCD and delivers the highest image quality of any current one-chip camcorder.

Video quality is very good in most lighting conditions. In low light it is acceptable, but not nearly as good as the Sony TRV900/1000 or VX2000. This camera, like most Sonys, has solid battery options (as far as purchasing an additional battery).

Since this is a one chipper, the color quality is not going to match a three-chip camcorder, but in terms of resolution the TRV30 approaches 500 lines. As far as reputation for reliability, Sony is one of the best.

The only significant down side to this camera is that it lacks 30fps progressive video mode, which allows you to grab individual frames of video as full-frame still pictures. This camcorder has an accessory shoe, 3.5-inch LCD, analog pass thru, and external microphone jack. The average price is $1,300.

Recommended Model: Canon Optura 100MC

The Canon Optura 100MC is replacing the popular Optura Pi, but it is a totally different camcorder. Actually, the new Optura 100MC closely resembles the Sony PC110 and PC120 both in appearance and in features.

The Optura 100MC has an interlaced 1.3 megapixel CCD, which means no more progressive video on the Optura series. (Unfortunately, progressive video mode seems to be becoming less common on the latest model camcorders.) The CCD is larger, at 5/16", than most new DV models, especially compact models. This should mean good low-light performance, which most compact camcorders lack (see Figure 5.8). The average price is $1,350.

Figure 5.8

The Canon Optura 100MC is a high performing compact DV camcorder with competent low-light performance.

Recommended Model: JVC GR-DV2000U

The JVC DV2000 is a pretty good camcorder though not as good as the 9800u model that it replaced. For whatever reason, the JVC replaced the 1/3-inch CCD with the 1/4-inch one. This camera has better digital still capability than its predecessor, though not as good as the Sony TRV30. The DV2000 also has USB for transferring digital stills.

The coolest thing about this camcorder, as well as the 9800u and 9500u models before it, is the automatic lens cover. When you turn the camcorder on and off, the lens cover slides open or closed automatically (similar to many digital cameras). This can really reduce lens maintenance, as well as those 'lens cover left on' recording fiascoes. However, if you use lens attachments, this won't be as useful for you.

The DV2000 has 30fps progressive video mode, an accessory shoe (the first JVC model in years to include it), 3.5-inch LCD, analog pass thru, and external microphone jack (see Figure 5.9).

Figure 5.9

The JVC GR-DV2000U offers a progressive CCD, which allows you to take 30 full frames of video per second.

Discontinued Models Worth Considering

The Canon Optura Pi is a camcorder that has an earned reputation as the best low-light performing one-chip camcorder (see Figure 5.10). You would have to get a three-chipper to do better.

The Optura Pi is also one of the lowest priced and smallest camcorders with optical image stabilization (the original Elura has OIS but it is no longer on the market). It is slightly smaller than the Sony TRV30. The Optura Pi has 30fps progressive video mode, which allows you to grab 720×480 stills anywhere from your video footage.

Figure 5.10

The Canon Optura Pi offers the best low-light performance of any one-chip camcorder, and also features a progressive CCD.

The only con on the Optura Pi compared to the other camcorders mentioned in this section is that it delivers lower resolution, around 430 lines. Nevertheless, with the superior low-light performance and low price tag, I highly recommend the Optura Pi, especially to users that never want to mess around with manual settings.

This camcorder also has an accessory shoe, 3.5" LCD, analog pass thru, and external microphone jack. Average Price is $900.

As for Sony's discontinued models, the TRV20 is the predecessor to the TRV30 and is identical to the TRV30 with the exception of a smaller 1.1 megapixel CCD. However, the TRV20 still performs better than most new model camcorders and should be priced very competitively. Its average price is $1,100.

Also note that the JVC GR-DVL9800u and GR-DVL9500 are the best small progressive video camcorders produced yet. They are fairly compact with a large 3.5" LCD. They both have a big 1/3 CCD that produces great quality video, and performs comparatively well in low light. The 9800u has improved sound quality over the 9500, with less motor drive pickup (see Figure 5.11). Neither camcorder has an accessory shoe (but you can get an adapter for $20). The 9800u can capture megapixel stills to memory card; the 9500 cannot. The average price is $700 to $950.

Figure 5.11

The JVC GR-DVL9800u is my favorite DV camcorder in the JVC line. The 9800u offers high picture quality, a progressive CCD, and an automatic lens cover.

BEST PROSUMER CAMCORDERS

Some prosumer camcorders can definitely fall in the price-performance zone (with the increasingly competitive market, the number seems to be growing) but for many prosumer models you often have to pay a premium for the best technology. There are two reasons for this:

- Prosumer models sell less so they need to generate a higher profit on each camcorder.
- Product development costs are front loaded so that if you buy a camcorder right when it is released, you are paying a premium.

Indeed paying for innovation is often an unforgiving experience. Besides overpaying, you are more likely to experience problems with products that are not entirely perfected yet. The early Sony VX2000s had sound problems (audible hum) that were fixed in later models. Sony replaced the early models that had problems. But ideally, you want a one-way camcorder purchase (from the store to your home, not back and forth).

What makes a camcorder "prosumer" is debatable. Generally speaking, three CCDs and extensive manual controls are the current qualifiers for this class. Manual controls are a must for any serious videographer, but most home users are unlikely to use them. While prosumer camcorders have lots of additional manual controls, they still feature all the automatic controls found on consumer camcorders. So if you can handle the weight of some of these camcorders and don't feel the larger size is a problem, they are worth buying just for the superior image quality alone.

Recommended Model: Sony DCR-VX2000

As far as image quality and sound quality, the Sony DCR-VX2000 is the best camcorder under $5,000 on the market right now. This camcorder is used on many news shows for field work; you have probably seen it used on FoodTV and MTV as well. It delivers great color fidelity, high resolution, and has the best low-light performance of any current sub-$5,000 DV camcorder.

The only important feature missing from this camcorder is 30fps progressive video mode. The DCR-VX2000 has 15fps progressive video mode, which is only useful for extracting stills. At 15fps video is just too jumpy. If they had included 30fps progressive video mode this camcorder would be absolute perfection (realizing of course that such quality could not readily fit in a form factor any smaller).

The VX2000 has an accessory shoe, 2.5″ LCD, analog pass thru, and external microphone jack (see Figure 5.12). Its average price is $2,300.

Figure 5.12

The Sony VX2000 offers exceptional video quality and low-light performance for around $2,000. This camcorder is the best there is right now in the consumer market.

Recommended Model: Canon GL1

This camcorder borrows from the looks of the Sony VX1000/VX2000. While the quality is not up to the VX2000 standards, the price is lower.

The biggest selling point of the Canon is the high-quality Fluorite lens which features a long 20x zoom. However the three-CCD imaging system is a notch below the lens quality. As a result the lens quality accentuates the failings of the imaging system. Many buyers are not going to want to spend that kind of money on a camcorder that delivers resolution just slightly above 450 lines. Sound quality is also not as good as the VX2000 or TRV900, as it tends to pick up a little motor noise and there are no manual audio controls. Low-light quality is solid, noticeably cleaner than the TRV900 but not as good as the VX2000.

Probably due to the lens, the GL1 does have really great color quality. The GL1 also has an accessory shoe, 2.5″ LCD, analog pass thru, and external microphone jack (see Figure 5.13). The average price for the GL1 is $2,000.

Figure 5.13

The Canon GL1 delivers prosumer image quality with three CCDs and a high-quality Fluorite lens.

Recommended Model: Sony DCR-TRV900

Resembling the classic Sony Handycam design, which has been a fixture on the camcorder scene since the release of the first compact 8mm video camcorders, the TRV900 delivers a formidable professional level of performance not too far off from the VX2000. Because it uses smaller CCDs, the biggest difference is low-light performance. Nonetheless the TRV900 is still one of the best low-light performers.

The TRV900 may be the perfect middle ground between professional performance and portability, although it is still noticeably larger than the average DV palmcorder. Early generation TRV900s had a problem with eating tapes, but that has since been fixed.

The camera utilizes an audio DSP chip, which eliminates motor drive noise so sound quality is very clean. The TRV900 also has an accessory shoe, 3.5″ LCD, analog pass thru, and external microphone jack (see Figure 5.14). The average price is $1,600.

Figure 5.14

The Sony TRV900, still one of the better prosumer models, was the first camcorder to provide professional image quality at a price within consumer reach.

CHAPTER 6

CAMCORDER ACCESSORIES

The accessory phase of the camcorder purchase would be a useful arena for psychologists to screen for compulsive buyers. There are so many things you can get for your camcorder that you can waste extraordinary amounts of money on things you don't need. So figure out what you do need, make a list, and don't waver from it.

If you are interested solely in a simple point and shoot camcorder for home video applications, there are a handful of well-made camcorders in the budget to prosumer range (listed in the previous chapter) that will satisfy all your needs (except for maybe a tripod and extra battery).

If you are shooting for professional applications or making a film, or are just obsessed with that extra ten percent of quality, then there are accessories you will need. The maxim to remember is *never overbuy* (the acronym of which is appropriately N.O.). DV camcorders and their accessories—due to their high cost, smaller consumer base, and threat of obsolescence— tend to have lower resale values on eBay than large market tech items like a CD burner. As a result, when you overbuy, you always lose money. We are not dealing with extinct animals or rare artifacts. Your camcorder accessories will always be at the camera store waiting for you if you need to buy them.

I have provided a handy chart at the end of each accessory description with my recommendation on whether you should consider a particular accessory. It is all based on what type of camera user you are—consumer, prosumer, filmmaker, or professional. Look to these charts for guidance before purchase.

LENS FILTERS AND ATTACHMENTS

Outside of the basics (tripod, camera case, and extra battery) the world of camcorder accessories can involve significant costs and a formidable learning curve. The latter point is lost on too many over-shopped consumers. Regardless of your budget, unless you are willing and able to handle the learning curve of advanced accessories you should hold on to your money and stick with a nice automatic camcorder.

On the other end of the spectrum, if you are willing to tackle the accessory learning curve, you should focus on the accessories you need.

Common to the still camera world, lens filters and attachments are just as useful on a DV camcorder. Lens filters can be used to reduce haze, brighten colors, eliminate sun glare, reduce brightness, and even add effects. Lens attachments can extend your zoom range and widen your picture. DV camcorders (even prosumer models) all have environment and hardware limitations that lens filters and attachments can ameliorate.

It is important to consider the advantages and disadvantages of filters and attachments. If you want your camcorder to provide the most pain-free operation, filters and attachments can present more complications than benefits. The simpler your camcorder operation is, the more likely you are to want to use it. If you get a good camcorder, the difference between auto mode–based footage by an amateur and expert tweaking by a honed videographer under most lighting conditions is not going to be all that significant. It is only under certain conditions such as low light and bright light that a manual proficiency will produce better results.

However, if you are shooting for professional applications you are going to need to be well versed in lens filters and attachments. As a professional you need to be able to produce good video 100% of the time. Appropriately using manual mode and appropriate filters might only mean a 10% relative improvement in overall footage. Nonetheless, obtaining a professional skill level means that you are smarter than your camcorder and are therefore worth hiring.

A downside of any filter or lens adapter is that they all affect your image resolution to a small varying degree depending on the quality of the adapter. The resolution loss varies from incalculably small to as much as 3%–5% reduction, depending on the quality of the lens. Since video has much lower resolution than film, lens quality can be significantly lower before resolution is affected. The slight loss is usually outweighed by the advantages of the filter or adapter, but you should be aware of the downside of using filters and adapters.

Filters and adapters also increase the possibility of lens flare (see Figure 6.1). Lens flare is a reflection of the sun or light on the lens causing circular bands of light in your picture. (Some people actually use this effect for artistic reasons—Photoshop and Paint Shot Pro actually let you add a lens flare effect to images). Lens flare is often seen in outer space pictures or in wide landscape shots in older films.

Figure 6.1

Lens flare is caused by external light reflecting off the internal optics of a camera.

A significant problem introduced by most filters and adapters is that they can disrupt your camcorder's automatic settings, forcing you to go manual. This problem is going to vary from camcorder to camcorder, so there is no blanket way to avoid it (except to avoid filters).

Wide-Angle Lens Adapters

Wide-angle lens adapters enable a wider field of vision for your camcorder. The one thing you might notice when you first start using your camcorder is that it has a narrower field of vision than you do (see Figure 6.2). This is most evident when filming subjects at close distances. You might be 3 feet away from the subject, but when you look in the viewfinder you appear to be even closer, often too close to properly frame the subject. In these situations a wide-angle adapter enables you to get a wider picture without having to take one or two steps back.

JARGON

Framing (or to *frame a shot*) refers to the composition of your video; basically, how you position what you are filming within the video frame.

Figure 6.2

Your camcorder, which just has one lens, has a narrower field of vision (as represented by the smaller rectangle) than a human, which has a two-lens optical system (as represented by the larger rectangle).

Wide-angle adapters come in various strength levels from .7x (less strong) to .4x and higher. The lower the decimal of strength, the more you are going to start getting the fish eye effect, which is similar to the effect observed when looking through a hotel room peep hole (see Figure 6.3). Depending on what you want, that effect can be desirable or undesirable. This effect starts to show at anything stronger than .5x. So if you want a general use wide-angle adapter, go for .5x and up.

JVC makes a few camcorder models that enable you to get a wider picture when shooting in progressive mode. The Progressive Wide Mode achieves the same effect as a .7x wide-angle lens would. The camcorder makes use of the outside pixels of the CCD, normally used for DIS (Digital Image Stabilization); consequently you won't be able to use DIS and Progressive Wide Mode simultaneously.

Wide-angle adapters often disrupt the camcorder's auto-focus ability. If you have this problem, your only recourse is to focus manually when using the wide-angle adapter.

Figure 6.3

The more powerful your wide angle lens, the more curvature your picture will display. This is an exaggerated example of the fish eye effect.

TABLE 6.1 SHOULD YOU CONSIDER A WIDE-ANGLE ADAPTER?

Accessory	Consumer	Prosumer	Filmmaker	Professional
Wide Angle Lens	✓	✓	✓	✓

Telephoto Lens Adapters

Telephoto adapters (also called converters) increase the power of your zoom (see Figure 6.4). So if you are displeased with the strength of your zoom, a telephoto adapter can give you more range for closer shots.

Figure 6.4

A telephoto adapter will lengthen the power of your zoom and bring you closer to your subject.

Keep in mind that the more you zoom, the narrower your camcorder's field of vision. With a narrower field of vision, camera shakes are much more pronounced, to levels that your camcorder's image stabilization is not going to compensate for. In these situations it is advisable to use a tripod.

TABLE 6.2 SHOULD YOU CONSIDER A TELEPHOTO ADAPTER?

Accessory	Consumer	Prosumer	Filmmaker	Professional
Telephoto Adapter			✓	✓

Lens Filters

Lens filters encompass a large group of attachable problem solvers and visual effects tools. They allow you an enhanced degree of control over your camera in many shooting conditions that can arise.

UV Filters

A UV filter is the most common camcorder and camera filter on the market. UV filters are also called haze filters because haze is caused by naturally occurring ultraviolet light. Video and film cameras are more sensitive to UV light than the human eye. Excessive UV shows up as a bluish cast. This is most likely to occur at high altitudes (because the higher you are the more UV there is) or with wide landscape shots, especially those over large bodies of water.

In all other shooting conditions, UV filters have close to zero effect on your video picture. Since UV filters are the cheapest filters, they are commonly recommended to camcorder owners for lens protection alone (not at all because salesman like to sell).

It is much easier to clean or replace a UV filter if it gets dirty, scratched, or broken than to replace your camcorder's lens. However, most camcorders have recessed lenses, so damage to the lens is pretty unlikely. If you use your camcorder in situations that will cause the lens to get dirty, a UV filter might be a good thing to have.

TABLE 6.3 SHOULD YOU CONSIDER A UV FILTER?

Accessory	Consumer	Prosumer	Filmmaker	Professional
UV Filter	✓	✓	✓	✓

Polarizing Filters (Polarizer)

Polarizing filters are really handy in certain situations. A polarizer is most useful for outdoor photography, where it helps to eliminate glare and bring out colors, especially the blue in the sky. If you are shooting through glass such as a car window, a polarizer will eliminate reflections that would otherwise obstruct the shot (see Figure 6.5).

Figure 6.5

A polarizing filter can eliminate reflections and window glare.

A polarizing filter has an outer ring that you rotate to get your desired effect.

TABLE 6.4 SHOULD YOU CONSIDER A POLARIZING FILTER?				
Accessory	**Consumer**	**Prosumer**	**Filmmaker**	**Professional**
Polarizing Filter			✓	✓

Neutral Density Filters

Neutral Density (ND) Filters enable you to lower the amount of light coming into your camcorder without having to adjust exposure. This is important when you want to maintain a smaller depth of field (an effect which causes the foreground to be in focus and the rest of the shot to be out of focus), but also need to lower the light levels. If you had to use exposure controls to lower the light level, you would also be increasing the depth of field, which would undermine the shot. Without ND filters, videographers, filmmakers, and photographers would have far fewer shooting options.

ND filters come in various strengths, which coincide with how much light they eliminate. The Sony TRV900 and Canon GL1 have built-in ND filters. The Sony is a 2.5 ND filter, and the Canon is a stronger 4.5 ND filter. Each .3 equals one F stop, so a 2.5 filter brings down exposure by seven stops.

TABLE 6.5 SHOULD YOU CONSIDER AN ND FILTER?				
Accessory	**Consumer**	**Prosumer**	**Filmmaker**	**Professional**
ND Filter			✓	✓

Color and Special Effects Filters

Color filters, often called *gels*, can add artistic casts to your video. There are also a number of special effects filters. The starburst filter adds a bunch of fake-looking starbursts to your video (exciting). These special effects filters were not even that great before computer editing rolled along, and now I don't see any reason to use them.

> **JARGON**
>
> A *cast* is a transparent tint that alters the color of your image. A cast can occur unintentionally because of a faulty automatic white balance or intentionally by using a color filter or by altering the white balance.

Within your computer editing environment, you can alter your video color or add any number of special effects with more creative control and versatility than any filter can offer. Furthermore, with a filter the results are permanent; in contrast, with your computer there is always the Undo command. The only downside is rendering times (which are ever decreasing), but how many feature films do you plan on shooting every week?

TABLE 6.6 SHOULD YOU CONSIDER COLOR FILTERS?

Accessory	Consumer	Prosumer	Filmmaker	Professional
Color Filters			✓	✓

TRIPODS AND MONOPODS

A tripod is a three-legged camcorder (or camera) stand that enables you to raise or lower the camcorder, pivot up and down, right and left (also called panning), and tilt (see Figure 6.6).

Figure 6.6

A tripod enables you to take steady footage, and frees you from having to hold the camcorder for extended periods.

The tripod is one of the most important accessories. Even a cheap $20 tripod can be a very useful asset in your video shooting. Investing in a nicer tripod will simply give you smoother panning options (and possibly a heavier, more durable build).

More expensive tripods use a fluid-filled head, allowing for smoother motion. Cheap tripods don't move as easily, but if you have a steady hand they are definitely workable and the much lower price makes them very tempting (also, a little oil in the joints will make them work more smoothly). Your best bet is to go to a camera store that has both varieties and try them out.

If you think you can manage with the non-fluid model, you are better off buying one cheaply at Wal-Mart (or a similar discount store). I bought a non-fluid head tripod at Wal-Mart for $20 and it works great and is super light (the pricier fluid-filled head models tend to be heavier, which can be good and bad).

Tripods come with certain problems: They require a lot of floor space and are unwieldy to retract and set up. For shooting situations where either of these two failings cannot be accommodated, there is the monopod. The monopod is a one-legged camcorder (or camera) stabilizer/stand. Monopods can be set up very quickly and require no more floor space than a quarter (see Figure 6.7). They are also rather inexpensive and can be found for around $30. They are obviously not as stable as a tripod, but some of them have a swing-down foot, making an "L" at ground level, which adds stability.

Figure 6.7

A monopod is far more compact than a tripod, and offers quicker setup.

If you have a camcorder with a bottom-loading tape mechanism, you will have to disconnect your camcorder from the tripod before you can change tapes.

TABLE 6.7 SHOULD YOU CONSIDER A TRIPOD?				
Accessory	**Consumer**	**Prosumer**	**Filmmaker**	**Professional**
Tripod	✓	✓	✓	✓

STEADICAMS

The Steadicam was invented in 1973 and it revolutionized the film and television industry, enabling a single cameraman to get shots that had previously been impossible. Many television shows like *E.R.* use Steadicams extensively. Steadicams work by isolating the movement of the camera operator's body from the camera. Stability plus freedom of motion give the Steadicam an advantage over the conventional Dolly (a method of stabilization where the camera rides along a track) in many shooting situations.

Tiffen Company (www.steadicam.com) makes a Steadicam model for small camcorders called the Steadicam Jr. (see Figure 6.8). It sells for around $600 and includes an LCD monitor. There are also free plans on the Internet showing you how to build your own faux-Steadicam for $30 (not including the cost of the LCD if you need one).

Figure 6.8

The Steadicam Jr. is a Steadicam built for small to medium sized camcorders (under 4 pounds).

TABLE 6.8 SHOULD YOU CONSIDER A STEADICAM?				
Accessory	**Consumer**	**Prosumer**	**Filmmaker**	**Professional**
Steadicam			✓	✓

MICROPHONES

As discussed earlier, one of the weaknesses of most DV camcorders is the sound quality. DV tapes run twice as fast as their analog counterparts. The higher speed results in more friction and a louder tape mechanism. Newer camcorders are starting to improve in this area, but because of the higher write speed DV tapes require and small camcorder sizes this is likely to be a lingering problem from model to model.

An external microphone can often lessen the problem of tape motor drive noise (but not always). Aside from the motor drive noise issue, a camcorder microphone, like the automatic settings on your camcorder, is not going to be ideal for every shooting situation. If you are shooting home videos then an external microphone can often introduce more hassle, adding to the camcorder size (and possibly adding a dangling cable). But for professional applications or independent film work, you are going to need to use various external microphones.

Many newer camcorders feature a hot accessory shoe, which enables you to use proprietary microphones. The advantage is that the proprietary mics transfer the audio signal through the hot shoe, so you don't need to worry about hooking up an extra cable. The disadvantage of these proprietary mics is that you usually only have one model choice and the quality is often mediocre.

Microphone quality is only one of the reasons to use an external microphone. Location of your sound source is an equally important reason. You could have the nicest camcorder in the whole world, but if you are trying to capture the sound of a speech among a large crowd, you will often pick up more noise from the audience than you would like. An average microphone near a sound source will always sound better than the best microphone more than ten feet away. This is why the camcorder microphone (which is usually removed from the sound source) is never going to be the master of all things. At best, the built-in camcorder microphone will merely be adequate in most situations.

Different external microphones, like different lens filters, have varying specializations and will be appropriate for varying things. If you decide you need to use an external microphone, you then need to decide which microphone is most appropriate for the application.

Dynamic and Condenser Microphones

Technically speaking, there are two types of microphones: dynamic and condenser. Dynamic microphones (or *mics*) do not require any electricity to operate. They are less sensitive and usually lack the frequency response of condenser microphones. However, their insensitivity makes them more useful in applications where a condenser would pick up too much unwanted noise. Stage mics tend to be dynamic because they are less sensitive to handling and don't pick up unwanted peripheral noise.

Condenser microphones require power and are more sensitive. They are capable (depending on the quality of the microphone) of delivering wider frequency response. Except for situations where you can get the mic basically within inches of the sound source, you will want to use some kind of a condenser microphone.

All microphones—both dynamic and condenser—are engineered with a certain pick up pattern. This determines what the microphone hears. An omnidirectional pattern means sound is picked up in all directions, whereas a unidirectional pattern means sound is only picked up in one direction (see Figure 6.9).

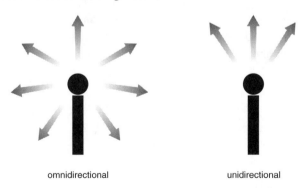

omnidirectional   unidirectional

Figure 6.9

An omnidirectional mic picks up sounds from all directions, while a directional mic only picks up sound from certain directions.

Omnidirectional and Directional Microphones

Omnidirectional microphones are the most common general use microphones. As the name suggests, their pick up pattern is everywhere. They are good for picking up room tone, which is useful when making a film. This gives you background noise that you can use later in the sound editing process. They also work well if you can get them really close to your desired sound source. In all other situations, omnidirectional microphones pick up too much peripheral noise.

Directional microphones have directional pickup patterns, allowing you a greater ability to capture and control your sound. Most camcorder-mounted microphones will be some form of a directional mic.

Handheld, Shotgun, and Lavalier Microphones

A final microphone designation has to do with the physical design of the microphone. Handheld microphones feature the basic cylinder design you see used in television interviews or at your favorite karaoke bar (see Figure 6.10). Handhelds come in dynamic and condenser versions, though dynamics tend to tolerate hand holding better. Handhelds are the most affordable microphones, but they are often the least useful for video work.

Figure 6.10

The standard handheld mic; every karaoke user knows it all too well.

Shotgun microphones are long, slender, directional microphones that resemble a gun barrel (see Figure 6.11). These mics are usually mounted on the camcorder's accessory shoe or a microphone boom (which is a retractable pole used to get close to a sound source). Most shotguns are condenser microphones and they can be very expensive, ranging from $100 to several thousand dollars. Shotguns are the most widely used microphones in professional video and film applications.

Figure 6.11

Shotgun microphones have a narrow pick up pattern that rejects unwanted peripheral noise.

Finally, lavaliers (or *lavs*) are the small microphones you see attached to clothing on television talk shows (see Figure 6.12). Lavs can be wired, but more often are attached to wireless systems, which can be very expensive. The advantage of lavs is that they are positioned on the actual sound source and can be easily concealed in the clothing. The disadvantage (besides price) is that wireless systems can be troublesome as far as interference, cable jostling, and battery consumption. Sound quality is inferior to a well-boomed shotgun microphone. Also, the more sound sources you have, the more complicated a lav system becomes.

Figure 6.12

Lavalier microphones are used on most talk shows and in other applications where you need to get close to the sound source but remain transparent.

Built-In Camcorder Microphones

The microphones included with DV camcorders vary in quality. An average camcorder will perform well enough in home video environments, but it is not the best tool for recording wider frequency sources such as an orchestra. If you want the best sound possible without the use of an external microphone, you will need to get a higher-end camcorder like the VX2000. But even then there are many situations where an external microphone will work better.

Bottom line? The built-in camcorder microphone is good enough for most home video work but insufficient for professional applications or filmmaking.

External Microphones

External microphones come in many different varieties, each appropriate for different applications. They are probably the most expensive of all camcorder accessories, with prices ranging from below $100 to well over $500.

TABLE 6.9 SHOULD YOU CONSIDER AN EXTERNAL MIC?				
Accessory	**Consumer**	**Prosumer**	**Filmmaker**	**Professional**
External Microphone		✓	✓	✓

Cardioid and Supercardioid Microphones

Cardioid microphones are directional mics. *Cardioid* derives from the Latin word for *heart*, as their pick up pattern is heart-shaped. Cardioid microphones have the widest pick up pattern in the directional mic class (see Figure 6.13). They basically pick up everything in front and on the sides of the mic and reject anything behind.

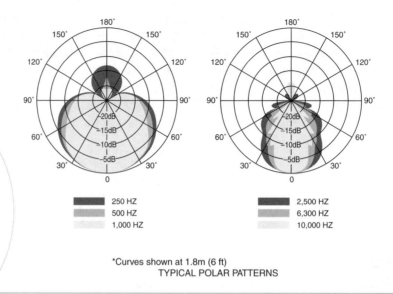

*Curves shown at 1.8m (6 ft)
TYPICAL POLAR PATTERNS

Figure 6.13

Most microphones you buy come with a diagram illustrating their pick up pattern.

Supercardioid microphones have a narrower and longer pickup pattern. This narrower pattern allows them to pick up a sound source from farther away than a cardioid microphone can, while also screening out unwanted peripheral sounds. Most shotgun mics are supercardioids. There are also hypercardioids, which have an even narrower pick up pattern than supercardioids. Both super- and hypercardioid microphones pick up a little behind the microphone (this is called a figure 8 pick up pattern). This makes them potentially a good choice for a documentary filmmaker who wants to have his voice picked up from behind the camera while interviewing subjects.

All directional microphones suffer from a peculiar audio quirk called the *proximity effect*. Basically if your sound source is too close to the microphone, the mic will pick up excessive bass (and you will sound more manly). If excessively close to the mic, the sound will become highly distorted. The only way to reduce this effect is to increase the distance between the mic and sound source.

Stereo Microphones

The microphone included with your camcorder is stereo, which means that it records separate left and right audio channels. Stereo recording operates much like the human auditory system. The separate left and right audio channels give the listener an audio image of the source. For instance, with a stereo mic in front of an acoustic rock band, the listener might be able to tell you that the guitar player was on the left and the banjo player was on the right. This is called *stereo imaging*, or seeing with sound. Without the stereo image you could not discriminate the location of the sound.

Many high-quality external shotgun mics are actually mono (one channel of audio only). Due to the narrow pickup pattern of the shotgun mics, there is not as much benefit in a stereo image as with a cardioid or omnidirectional mic. If you are interviewing people in a documentary, stereo imaging is not necessary. In fact, a high-quality mono recording will often pick up the voice of the interviewee better.

Wireless Microphone Systems

Wireless microphones allow many options that wired microphones do not (see Figure 6.14). They also introduce a lot of cost and hassle that make them not ideal for home video applications.

Figure 6.14

This is a UHF wireless microphone system made by Samson, composed of a receiver, which mounts to the camcorder's accessory shoe, and a wireless microphone/transmitter.

With a wireless system, you need a transmitter and a receiver and lots of batteries. UHF seems to be the more stable wireless format, though no wireless system is totally immune to interference problems. Most television talk shows and news programs use wireless lav systems. Wireless mics are also used in many rock and roll shows, so barring the rare interference problems they can deliver professional sound. Expect to pay at least $500 for an intro-level UHF transmitter and receiver.

Microphone Guide

The following guide recommends different external mics for different shooting situations:

TABLE 6.10 RECOMMENDED MICS FOR DIFFERENT PURPOSES

Event	Stereo	Cardioid (Directional)	Shotgun (Supercardioid)	Wireless
Birthday party	✓	✓		
Sporting event			✓	
Wedding	✓		✓	✓
Musical concert	✓	✓		
Public speaker			✓	
Filmmaking	✓	✓	✓	✓

If you plan on a wide range of shooting applications and can only buy one external mic, a stereo or hybrid mic is recommended. A hybrid mic includes multiple pickup modes, usually stereo and directional. Specific model microphones are covered in Chapter 14, "Camcorder Sound."

LIGHTS

Due to the low light limitations of many camcorders, especially DV camcorders, a video light attachment can be a semi-useful accessory (see Figure 6.15). However, they are to some degree an imperfect solution because of size and power restrictions.

Figure 6.15

External lights allow you to capture video in otherwise unshootable locations (moonless nights, dungeons, and so on).

Aside from a few JVC models, most DV camcorders don't come with a built-in light. The light you see on most new camcorders is a flash and will only work for still picture taking.

However, many camcorders come with hot shoes, which will accept proprietary or non-proprietary video light attachments. The advantage of the proprietary light is that it will often be powered by the camcorder so you won't have to worry about a second power supply. Of course, this will adversely affect the battery life of your camcorder (solution: buy a bigger battery).

Most video lights are small and project a flashlight-like beam that is really only useful for shooting at close range. The limited focal length (the illuminated area) of the most light attachments makes them somewhat useless for wider shots (see Figure 6.16). A more professional lighting solution, the light kit, will be discussed later in this book.

Most external lights range in power from 3 watts to 20 watts. The most powerful external lights from Canon and Sony require external power, specifically the same type of batteries used on most of their standard camcorder lines.

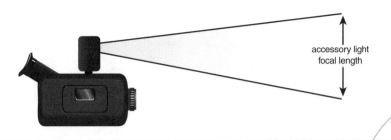

accessory light
focal length

Figure 6.16

External lights are limited by their size as far as how much light they can throw on your scene.

TABLE 6.11 SHOULD YOU CONSIDER A CAMCORDER LIGHT?

Accessory	Consumer	Prosumer	Filmmaker	Professional
Camcorder Light		✓	✓	✓

RECOMMEND ACCESSORIES CHART*

TABLE 6.12 RECOMMENDED ACCESSORIES

Consumer	Prosumer	Filmmaker/Professional
Extra battery and tripod	Extra battery, tripod, wide angle adapter, external microphone	Extra battery, tripod, wide-angle adapter, ND filter, external microphone, external light (or some kind of light kit)

*Please note that this is just a general guide.

CHAPTER 7

SHOPPING TIPS

The first part of a good camera purchase is thorough research. More time spent, for more data, will yield better purchasing decisions. If shopping causes you a neurochemical rush, focusing on the research will sober you up. Remember that there is no perfect camcorder; you just need to find the model that affords the fewest compromises.

Once you decide which camcorder you want, you then have to figure out where to buy it. Online retailers usually have the best prices and selection, but many consumers are more comfortable at local retailers where they can get more tactile assurance. Some combination of the preceding two, whether demoing locally and buying online or finding a price online and trying to get a retailer to match it, is probably the ideal. However, with some of the nicer camcorders your only purchasing option will be online. In general, the cheapest online electronics outfits use low prices as bait. They will never sell you anything for the low prices they advertise unless you buy a bunch of overpriced accessories. Always, pay a few extra dollars for a quality online retailer.

RESEARCHING YOUR PURCHASE

If you are interested in getting the most performance for the money, you need to be able to assess the various camcorders. This is easy with computer products, as there are many magazines and Web sites loaded with resources. However, DV camcorders are expensive items, so comprehensive reviews and comparisons are scarcer.

Camcorders also are a bit more complicated to assess than computer chips or video cards, because there are more variables involved. Despite all this, there are still adequate amounts of useful and free information via the Internet and newsgroups, as well as a few magazines and books that will enable you to make a better camcorder purchase.

A DV camcorder is a rather large investment that will hopefully serve your needs for many years. Unfortunately, not all camcorders are created equal and spending a lot of money will not ensure you get the best results. Look at buying a camcorder as an onerous chore, not as an exciting excursion. Once you are certain in your head of what is the best camcorder for your needs, only then are you ready to buy.

The most important thing you can do is research. The more you read and study about Harry S. Truman, the more likely you are to become an authority on Harry S. Truman. The same goes with anything else, including camcorders.

There are a few bad shopping instincts to avoid:

- **Buying the most expensive**—The most expensive camcorder is not always the best and it might not be the right camcorder for your needs.

- **Buying based on the published specs**—Specs should be given general consideration, but they often don't translate to performance. The Canon Optura Pi is one of the better mid-priced camcorders, but it has only a 410,000 pixel CCD—far lower than many other camcorders that actually have poorer image quality. Also, the often-published blurb that the DV format is capable of over 500 lines of resolution means nothing. Bottom line: Never believe a company's published specs when it relates to the camcorder's resolution or low-light performance.

- **Buying based on brand name reliability**—This is the least harmful of the bad instincts, but it is still blind shopping behavior. Bottom line: Performance from one manufacturer's model to the next can vary greatly, and newly introduced models, even by well regarded companies, tend to be buggier than models that have been out a while.

- **Buying based on the salesperson recommendation**—This is the most harmful habit of the shopper. Even if the salesperson is your husband or wife of fifty years, do not believe what they say. Bottom line: Those who wear the salesperson vest or nametag are sometimes the enemy.

To make the wisest purchase you just need to keep researching. Eventually the best camcorder for you will emerge from that data. This brings us to the next question—where are the best places to research a camcorder purchase?

Magazine and Books

A few magazine publications devote themselves solely to camcorders. The problem is that they are dependent on advertising dollars, so their reviews are often reserved when it comes to negative things. In fact, one of the prominent camcorder magazines this last year stopped publishing video resolution ratings in their reviews.

Sound and Vision, one of the best multimedia publications, still has uncompromising reviews with more ratings and technical measurements than even I know what to do with. Unfortunately, they only occasionally review camcorders. They also have an abbreviated but good free online site at `http://soundandvisionmag.com` (see Figure 7.1).

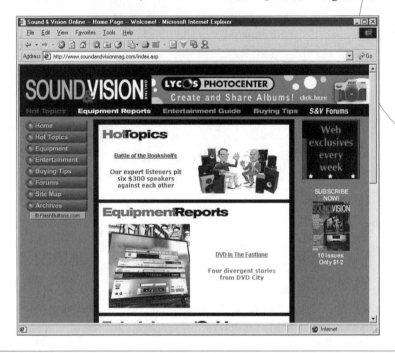

Figure 7.1

The Sound and Vision magazine and Web site provide informative and objective reviews of all kinds of multimedia products.

Consumer Reports (`www.consumerreports.org`) has a good overview every year or so and is probably the best magazine resource right now, but they are pretty general in their analysis. The site has a small number of free articles, with access to all articles if you subscribe (see Figure 7.2).

Overall, the magazine world is not a highly recommended research source. Books are more likely to be honest, as they have no advertisers to please. On the negative side, you are getting the expert opinion of only one or two people who can't possibly have tested every camcorder on the market. Moreover, books don't come out more than once annually, so there is a chance they are going to be dated. (Please note: This book is the lone exception.) And books cost $20 and up. Most of us want free resources.

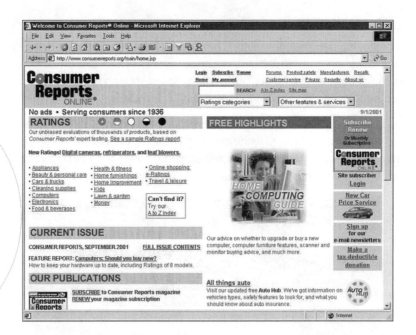

Figure 7.2

Consumer Reports is one of the most well regarded and unbiased sources of product reviews.

The Web

The Web or Internet is a free resource, assuming you have Internet access. If not, any local library usually has a number of computers available for Internet surfing.

The Web has a number of large and small review sites, personal home pages, and forums (also known as message boards) with information on camcorders as well as video editing. Each individual site varies, in content amount and quality, but all of these resources together offer a fairly robust and objective view of camcorders and many issues that relate to computers and video editing.

Epinions (http://epinions.com) is a large Web site that features reviews written by average consumers (you can submit your own as well) on all sorts of products including camcorders (see Figure 7.3). The quality of reviews varies, but you can get a pretty good idea of the pros and cons of the more popular camcorder models (as there are a large number of user reviews on each).

DV.com (http://dv.com) is one of the best professional DV-related sites on the Internet (see Figure 7.4). The Web site is more geared for professionals, but they have a great user forum and their reviews and articles are usually very informative and objective.

Figure 7.3

Epinions is an innovative Web site which allows the general public to post reviews on just about any product on the market.

Figure 7.4

DV.com is a Web site that covers DV technology from a professional viewpoint. The site has articles, reviews, and a busy forum.

The World Wide Users Group (WWUG—http://wwug.com) is a conglomeration of user forums on the Internet devoted mostly to video and multimedia-related products. You can read through users' posts or post your own questions (see Figure 7.5). Video professionals, most of whom are pretty knowledgeable, frequent the boards.

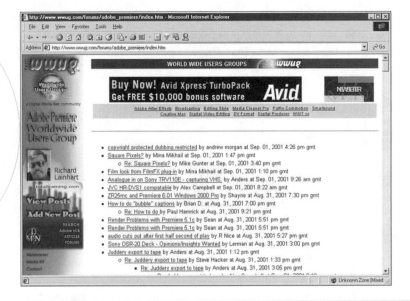

Figure 7.5

The World Wide Users Group features multiple forums devoted to multimedia hardware and software.

Small Niche Sites

The Internet enables anyone to start their own publication (even the fedora-clad Matt Drudge). I started PCvideomaker.com a few years ago in response to the lack of good resources on computer video editing. Eventually I merged PCvideomaker.com into Multimedian.com, which covers all forms of multimedia creation (see Figure 7.6).

Other niche sites worth checking out include

- 2-POP (http://www.2-pop.com/)
- DV & FireWire Central (http://www.dvcentral.org/)
- Consumer DV Reviews (http://www.consumerdvreviews.com/)

With the crash of Internet advertising you can't really make money with these types of sites, but it makes a great hobby. One of the foundations of the Internet is doing things for the fun of it, not the money.

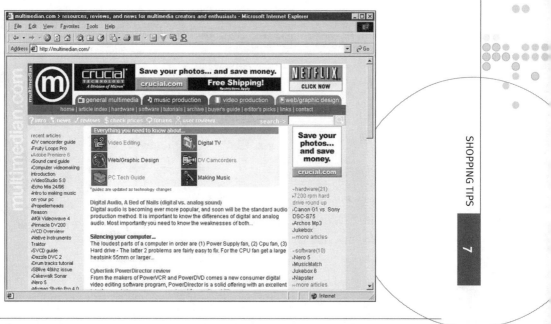

Figure 7.6

Multimedian.com is a small niche site that covers all facets of multimedia creation.

Personal Web Sites

John Beale's personal Web page (`http://www.bealecorner.com/trv900/`) started off as a site dedicated to the Sony TRV900 camcorder, but has become one of the better DV resources on the Internet (see Figure 7.7). The site has the look of an average home page with a very basic unassuming design, but it is loaded with serious content on all facets of DV technology (reviews, camcorder comparisons, tips, links). Another site similar in simplicity and also a quality DV resource is Adam Wilt's DV Web page (`http://www.adamwilt.com/dv`).

Hopefully these sites will serve as an example of the Internet of the future, where more individuals create their own resource-filled home pages. Unfortunately, right now most people prefer to consume rather than produce.

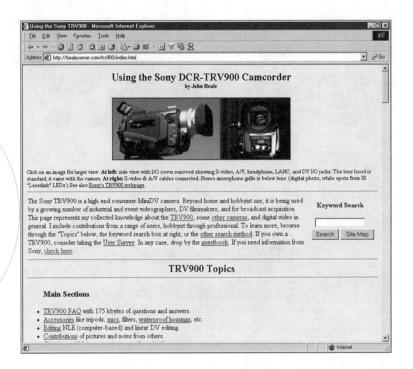

Figure 7.7

John Beale's Web site covers his extensive knowledge and experience with DV and includes links to many relevant external resources.

Newsgroups and Usenet

Newsgroups are the best resource of information currently on the Internet. Newsgroups are a cross between e-mail and the Web. The idea of technologically aided mass group discussion started with dial-up BBSes in the late 70s. BBSes were *bulletin board systems* where people could communicate, similar to how a Web forum or message board works except that the interface was all text-based (as opposed to HTML). Usenet developed around the same mass discussion principle but utilized the Internet as a foundation. As the Internet grew, Usenet replaced the popularity of the BBS system. Today, Usenet is composed of thousands of newsgroups based on every imaginable topic. For our purposes, the best newsgroups are `rec.video`, `rec.video.production`, and `rec.video.desktop`.

Usenet (and its many newsgroups) is technically not part of the World Wide Web. It has its own separate Internet protocol. You need to have access to a newsgroup server to read or post on newsgroups. Most major ISPs (*Internet service providers*) include newsgroup server access. Access to newsgroups is usually achieved through an e-mail client such as Microsoft Outlook Express (see Figure 7.8). America Online has its own built-in newsgroup reader interface.

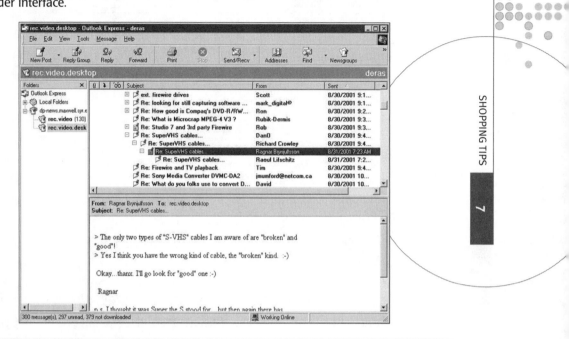

Figure 7.8

Outlook Express and similar e-mail programs are a popular way of accessing newsgroups.

However, even if you don't have access to a newsgroup server you are not out of luck. Google Groups (http://groups.google.com), formerly Deja.com, indexes most newsgroups for viewing with any Web browser (see Figure 7.9). At the Google Groups Web site you can read or post via a friendly HTML interface.

Thanks to services like this, newsgroups have gained an even wider appeal. Newsgroups are an ideal source for information because of their uniform text-based structure and mass of users, many of whom are professionals and experts in their respective fields.

Even if you have access to a newsgroup server, I recommend using Google Groups to search and read through the newsgroups as it works much better (at least for searches). Google Groups enables you to do complex searches through all or just specified newsgroups, even allowing you to limit returned data to posts submitted in the last month, year, and so on.

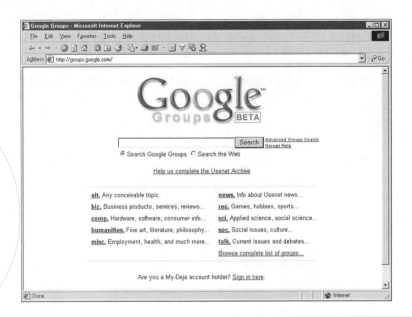

Figure 7.9

Google Groups (formerly Deja.com) enables you to read and post to newsgroups from any Web browser.

There is special newsgroup reading software available, too, but you are not going to be able to archive as many months and years of posts as they have on the Google Groups servers. As you read through the posts, a pattern should emerge of what camcorders would best suit your needs. The more you research the clearer this pattern will be.

ONLINE SHOPPING

Online shopping offers convenience and value over conventional retail shopping. Sometimes it is your only purchase alternative, as you can't buy some of the better camcorders in local retail stores. There are legitimate failings to online shopping, but balanced against the positive aspects they are pretty small.

The biggest advantage of online shopping is lower cost. Prices are cheaper because online retailers have lower overhead. Also, you usually don't have to pay sales tax for online purchases. Unless you live in New York, Los Angeles, or Chicago you simply can't buy a lot of things in physical stores, as selection tends to be limited (especially when it comes to electronics). There is a much better selection online, and everyone is a click away from it.

The Internet has a number of shady, borderline retailers which advertise the lowest prices but won't sell to you unless you are willing to buy several overpriced extras. On the other end of the spectrum, there are a number of very good online retailers which charge a bit more but have very good reputations, solid customer service, and prompt shipping. The rest are somewhere in between. If you don't care about customer service and just want a cheap price on a camcorder then the middle-priced retailers probably will offer the best deal. I usually buy from a reputable middle-priced retailer.

Retailer Ratings Web Sites

In the mail or phone order days, it was hard to find out whether a retailer was reputable. Thanks to the Internet, this is no longer a problem. Retailer rating sites help keep consumers informed, and retailers honest. Before you buy from anywhere you should always visit a retailer-rating site to check the retailer's reputation.

ResellerRatings.com (http://resellerratings.com) was the first Web site where shoppers could rank online retailers and leave comments on their experience (see Figure 7.10).

Figure 7.10

ResellerRatings.com is a highly recommended resource for checking the reputation of various online retailers.

There are other Web sites that rate retailers, such as Gomez (http://gomez.com) and Bizrate (http://bizrate.com). While they are both reputable, they don't cover as many companies as ResellerRatings.com and are geared more as a service to price search engines (covered next) than as standalone sites for consumers to read about retailers. So they are not as useful.

Price Search Engines

Price search engines are an essential tool for any Internet shopper. Price search engines are similar to Internet search engines, except that they catalog merchant prices, enabling you to search for the best price on almost any product. Some specialize in computer gear, others in books, and some cover just about every product category.

Some of the top price search engines include the following:

- Cnet's Shopper (http://shopper.com)
- Pricewatch (http://pricewatch.com)
- MySimon (http://mysimon.com)
- Pricegrabber (http://pricegrabber.com)

Pricegrabber, one of the bigger price search engines, has just added a well-implemented user review system that resembles the ResellerRatings model (see Figure 7.11). Because Pricegrabber gets extensive amounts of traffic, it should prove to be one of the better ratings resources.

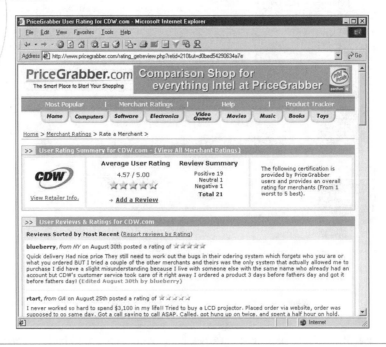

Figure 7.11

Pricegrabber.com now includes user reviews of online retailers.

Another great price search engine, Pricewatch.com, is one of the oldest and best price search engines for computer parts (see Figure 7.12). While Pricewatch predominantly covers computer retailers, you can find some camcorder (and other general electronics) prices there too.

The tricky thing about search engines is that the lowest prices are listed at the top. As a result, merchants often have really low prices, but then try to make up the difference by charging outlandish shipping prices. The increased competition in the price search engine industry has resulted in these search engines putting pressure on retailers to list their shipping prices to avoid this problem. Consequently, things have improved. Some search engines even add shipping cost to the prices, showing you who really is the cheapest.

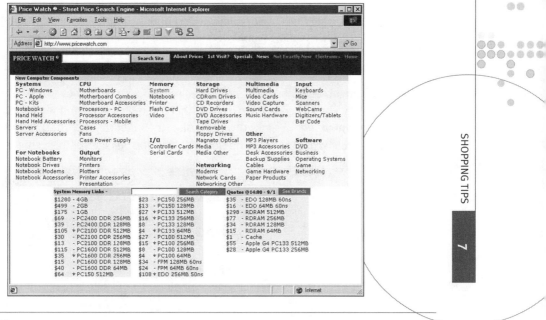

Figure 7.12

Pricewatch features a very basic interface which makes searching for prices easy.

Many of the search engines also have merchant ratings, which reflect previous buyers' experiences with a company. Gomez ratings (based on a three-star system) are the most frequently used and they are fairly reliable. It is almost always worth it to pay a few extra dollars for a two- or three-star rated merchant. Merchants with really low ratings that always have the lowest prices usually are not worth dealing with. The low price is simply the bait and they are never going to sell only the camcorder at that low price unless you buy a bunch of overpriced accessories.

Price search engines make money from the retailers they catalogue on their engine, which puts them in a compromising situation as far as wanting the most retailers possible on their service. The risk is that many of the retailers are lousy. Hopefully, in the future, price search engines will get better about not even listing bad retailers, but until then, utilizing a retailer rating resource will provide sufficient protection from falling into the hands of a degenerate merchant.

Bargain Sites

Over the last few years bargain/coupon sites have proliferated on the Web. These were really big before the Internet crash because countless Internet companies flush with money were providing great deals and coupons, often underselling products to increase their market share.

The Internet crash refers to the period of time during 2000–01 when the overinflated tech economy finally fell apart. During this period the Nasdaq went from over 4000 to under 2000 and many tech companies folded.

Post–Internet crash, these sites are not as packed with deals, but some of them are worth occasionally checking out. Keep in mind that these sites make money from referrals (if you buy something via a link on their site they get a kick back). Techbargains.com (`http://techbargains.com`) is one of the more popular sites of this genre (see Figure 7.13).

Figure 7.13

Techbargains is a Web site dedicated to online bargains and deals.

Online Auctions

Online auctions are great for selling your old gear or buying older merchandise. They are less impressive when it comes to buying new items, as you can often find a better price from an online retailer.

As it stands now, eBay is the only viable auction site on the Internet (see Figure 7.14). Yahoo auctions is the closest competitor, but it is a graveyard in comparison.

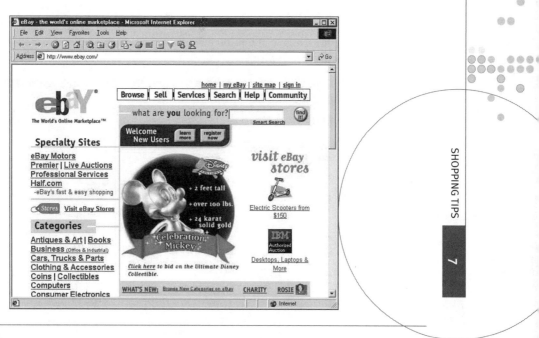

Figure 7.14

eBay is the only auction site on the Internet that matters.

When it comes to new products, the prices at eBay are not all that great. eBay, due to its size and pop culture popularity, tends to reflect the general public more than the net-savvy public. It only takes two non-savvy bidders (trying to outbid each other) to drive up the price of an auction. So even if a majority of bidders know a certain camcorder can be bought from an online retailer for about $900, if just two bidders have the weekly ad from Best Buy (which lists the price at $1100) as their point of reference, then the auction can go higher than it should. Of course, selling on eBay can be great, as you benefit from the above problem.

Older products (by which I mean products that are no longer available from retail channels) or lesser-known ones are ideal products to buy on eBay as they do not tend to suffer from price inflation.

eBay is also a great tool for dumping your old technology before it loses most of its value. If you really keep up-to-date on the latest technology, you can often upgrade to the latest gear for close to the price of selling your replaced gear. The downside of this is that constantly reconfiguring and upgrading your system can be excessively time consuming. Furthermore, the latest technology usually needs to be on the market for several months at the very least before a clear picture of performance and reliability can be ascertained.

eBay also makes it easy to determine what a fair price is for products. All you have to do is search through completed auctions and see what the average winning bid price was for recently concluded auctions.

If you are unfamiliar with eBay, one of the major features is the user feedback system. Next to everyone's user name on eBay is a number, in parenthesis, that represents their feedback rating (see Figure 7.15).

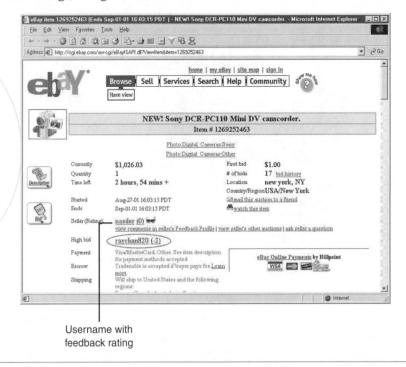

Username with
feedback rating

Figure 7.15

Be attentive to the user rating of eBay buyers and sellers; this rating can help you judge the reliability of a user.

Taking the amount of positive feedback comments a user has received and subtracting the number of negative feedback comments generates the feedback rating. If you click the number, you will get a screen where you can read through all the user comments to better assess the seller or buyer (see Figure 7.16).

If you are new to eBay, you will have a zero next to your name as well as a pair of dark sunglasses (refer to Figure 7.15). After 30 days you will no longer have the shades next to your name. If you ever change your username, you will have to wear the shades again for 30 days. Not having a lot of feedback is not a big deal if you are a buyer (though some sellers won't sell to users with a zero feedback rating). However, if you are a seller, having very little feedback will hurt your auction's sale price, especially if you are selling an expensive item such as a camcorder. Without a high enough feedback rating, buyers are unable to discern whether you are a legitimate seller.

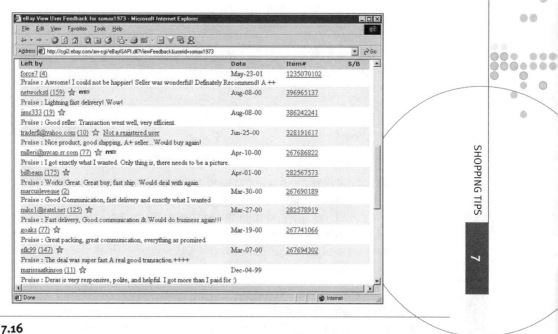

Figure 7.16

On the user comments screen you can click the feedback provider's name to find out information about them and what they bought from the seller.

As far as buyer protection, eBay has a free insurance program, which covers all auctions. But it only covers up to $200 minus a $25 deductible. For more expensive items, there are escrow services that, for a small fee, will hold all auction funds until you receive and are satisfied with the product. As it extends the timeframe and fees, some sellers are not fond of escrow services, so make sure your seller is willing.

Online Credit Card Fraud

Many people fear giving out their credit card numbers online. According to one study, consumers perceive credit card fraud to be twelve times more common than it is. In reality, credit card fraud is three to four times more common on the Internet than the physical world, so it is a legitimate concern.

You can minimize your fraud risk in several ways. Don't ever enter your credit card number into a Web site that is not secured with encryption. To find out if a site is secure, check the site's URL in the location bar at the top of your browser window. The address should start with *https* instead of *http* (see Figure 7.17).

Shopping at only the bigger sites or, even better, limiting how many different stores you shop at will also lower the chance statistically that you will be a fraud victim.

Figure 7.17

Always make sure you are on a secure site before entering credit card information.

Big Internet retailers are not immune to problems. Egghead.com, the largest online computer retailer, was hit last year by Russian hackers. I know this because my credit card company called me and informed me of the problem, but apparently my card never was affected. In this instance, Egghead did take proactive measures, informing all the credit card companies of past Egghead customers. However, a small site might not have the personnel to do that.

In general, you are just going to have to accept that there is a slightly higher risk shopping online, but even with that risk only a small percentage of people will have a problem. Since you are not responsible under federal law for unauthorized credit card purchases (what the thieves buy), getting your card number stolen is more of an inconvenience than a financial tragedy.

BUYING AT YOUR LOCAL RETAIL STORE

Local retail stores, also called *brick-and-mortar stores*, historically are more expensive compared to their online competitors. And though this gap is starting to close a little, online competition still has the advantage of no sales tax. On small items (books and CDs) the sales tax at retail stores usually corresponds to online shipping costs, making for a more competitive arena. But for high-priced items, sales tax can be significant, far exceeding the cost of shipping.

Retail stores allow you to actually see, handle, and possibly even demo the product you are interested in. This is obviously an advantage. On the other hand, the chain electronic stores don't carry many of the better camcorders (Canon GL1 and Optura Pi, Sony TRV900 and VX2000). You also have to deal with annoying sales people (and their warranty cult). Convenient returns is another factor, but most of the chains charge 15% restocking fees on camcorder purchases. The only exception I know of is Sears, which as of the publication of this book does not charge any restocking fee.

OTHER THINGS TO KNOW BEFORE BUYING

You should also be on guard against restocking fees and unnecessary extended warranties both when shopping online and your local retail stores. Some merchants apply restocking fees when you return a product. Furthermore, increasingly, merchants are pushing extended warranties on customers.

Restocking Fees

Restocking fees are one of the potential land mines of online and retail shopping. A restocking fee is a 10%–20% charge applied on all returns by some merchants. Even Best Buy and Circuit City charge restocking fees on some of their products. Any merchant who charges a restocking fee is required to post information to that effect on their site.

Restocking fees are not unreasonable in some instances, but some unscrupulous merchants use them illegitimately, applying a restocking fee even if they were in the wrong.

A few years ago when I was less tech-savvy, I bought a computer from an outfit that had the cheapest prices listed in *Computer Shopper* magazine. They sent me a broken computer with all the wrong components. It took well over a month to get my money back minus the 15% restocking fee. Other people were not so lucky with this operation and they lost all their money. Eventually the FBI shut the place down. Apparently they reopened under a different name a few months later.

This transpired before retailer ratings sites even existed. Thanks to the Internet, these types of merchants exist in far smaller numbers than they used to, but they will always be around as long as people shop solely by price.

Extended Warranties

In the long run, paying for warranties and insurance whenever it is offered is going to cost you far more money than you could possibly save. If it were a good deal, the insurer would be losing money. Camcorders though fall under an exception for some users.

Standard three-to-five year camcorder warranties start around one hundred dollars. Companies that charge $200 and up are ripping you off. In general, I don't think a warranty that costs more than $100 is worth investing in.

Camcorders have many moving parts and electronics packed into small quarters. They will likely go through a good amount of handling and possibly even weather exposure. For these reasons, a camcorder is far more fragile and prone to breaking than a television or a package you send in the mail, so insurance is not an entirely bad idea.

For people who know they are going to use their camcorder extensively or for those who might want to sell their camcorder at some point, an extended warranty makes sense, assuming it is not too expensive. For the light user, warranties are a waste of money. Camcorders suffer from defective units like anything else, but these problems are going to show up in the first few months of ownership when you are still under warranty.

Stores are increasingly trying to strong-arm consumers into buying extended warranties (also called performance plans) because they make a lot of money on them. Some stores give a kick back to the salesperson, which encourages them to press customers. Other stores like Best Buy just create an atmosphere where it is expected of every employee if they want to stay in good standing.

An interesting Web site called BestBuySux.org (`http://bestbuysux.org`) chronicles the system Best Buy uses to maximize performance plan sales. Basically, every morning and evening all the employees meet, and the person who has sold the most performance plans is supposed to tell everyone else how he or she was able to do it. This is all both amusing and disturbing, the minimum wage version of the film *Glengarry Glen Ross* (a dark film about a shady real estate sales firm).

You really have to be vigilant to get out of these stores without buying an extended warranty plan these days. So don't waste your time trying to reason with these people; just say no and if they keep pushing the hard sell, resort to the *zip it* mantra.

CHAPTER 8

CAMCORDER MAINTENANCE

Camcorders are complex electronic devices with numerous components that could potentially break. The increasingly small size of camcorders has in some cases made them more fragile as well. The weather, magnets, thieves, and your concrete patio can all prove fatal for your camcorder. Educating yourself about all the risks and learning a few tips can keep you from losing your electronic investment.

The biggest source of maintenance is related to the tape drive of the camcorder, which becomes dirty over the device's life. Your tape drive is also the component on your camcorder most likely to fail because of its inherent complexity. Keeping your tape drive in order requires occasional cleaning as well as extra care when loading and unloading tapes.

STORING YOUR CAMCORDER

Your camcorder is an expensive, fragile gadget. As long as you remember a few important things, you can forget about the expensive potentially fragile part and have fun with it like any other toy.

A camcorder bag is a wise investment and should be among the first three accessories you buy (see Figure 8.1). It does not have to be technically a camcorder bag. Any bag that has at least a quarter inch of padding and matches the size of the camcorder plus maybe an extra tape and battery is good (you can always go bigger). In fact, you are better off if it does not look like a camcorder bag, which might attract thieves.

Homeowner or renter's insurance will usually cover your camcorder if it is stolen from inside your house (or apartment), but not if it is stolen outside of your house. You may want to check with your insurance company to find out their policy specifics.

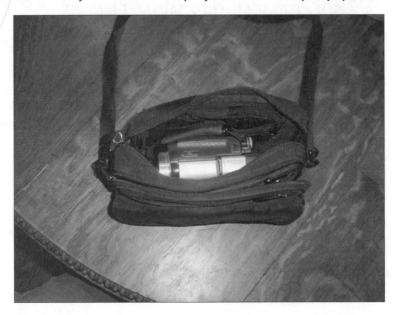

Figure 8.1

A camcorder bag helps protect your camcorder from dust, scrapes, and inclement weather.

The bag should have Velcro or zipper closures to keep out dust and water. A water resistant material is recommended too. Darker colors allow you to better see dust or dirt that might have found its way in your bag.

CAMCORDER ENEMIES

The following are just a few camcorder enemies, which can ruin your camcorder or cost you hundreds of dollars in repair bills:

- **Dust and particulate matter (which is a blanket term for all small particles)**—If they get into your camcorder to any significant degree (which can be defined as being able to see it in your camcorder), they can cause all sorts of problems. The most relevant would be contaminating the tape drive head, which, when rotating across your magnetic tape at fast speeds, can cause audio and video dropouts. If it gets bad, you can physically mess up both your tapes and your tape head. The tape head is basically the engine of you camcorder so if that goes, fixing it will be a few hundred dollars at least (of course, every camcorder repair probably will run that high).

> *Dropout* is a term used to describe when video or audio cuts out during your recording. This is the most common recording/playback error on digital camcorders.

Over time even the most responsible of you will find a little dust inside the camcorder. All you need to do is get a can of compressed air sold at most electronics stores (see Figure 8.2). (You can get it really cheap at Sam's Club—two cans for $8.) Then just thoroughly spray out any dust you see.

Figure 8.2

Compressed air is the best way to clean out the inside of your camcorder.

Solution—Make sure your hands are clean when loading and unloading tapes. Keeping your camcorder within a closed and clean bag whenever you are not shooting. Don't lend your camera to dirty people.

- **Sand**—Sand is obviously even worse than dust. Even one grain of sand is too much.

Solution—Make sure you are extra careful if you take the risk of bringing your camcorder to the beach. If any sand gets in your camcorder, break out the compressed air can and spray (while holding your camcorder upside down).

- **Moisture and condensation**—When it is really humid out, your camcorder could potentially have problems. Moisture + electronic components = potential problems (see Figure 8.3).

Figure 8.3

High humidity and excessive heat, as re-enacted by my dishwasher, can disable your camcorder.

Solution—Some of the newer camcorders are programmed to shut off if there is any internal moisture/condensation present, to protect the camcorder. This is helpful, although it can sometimes make your camcorder inoperable for up to an hour. If you are going from the cold outside to a warm house, make sure your camcorder is in an insulated bag, or has time to adjust to the temperature change before using it.

- **Extreme temperatures**—Excessive heat can do any number of things to internal components. Cold weather reduces battery life by up to half. Going from extreme cold to warm and back can cause fogging and condensation, and then that condensation can freeze (see Figure 8.4).

Figure 8.4

Extreme temperature changes can cause your camcorder lens to fog up.

Solution—Never store your camcorder in an environment that is colder than 65 degrees or warmer than 85 degrees. When operating the camcorder in extreme temperatures, allow transition time between hot and cold environments. If you are shooting exclusively outside in the cold, keep your camcorder outside even during shooting breaks (in an insulated bag). Keep your camcorder batteries insulated from the cold.

- **Pavement or other hard surfaces**—Your camcorder plus the force of gravity minus the stopping power of a hard surface can equal tragedy. The smaller the camcorder the more unfortunate drops will be.

Solution—Buy a tough camcorder. This is one of the advantages of the Digital 8 camcorders and the bigger DV models, because they handle drops far better than a pocket cam will. Of course, this does not mean they won't break too, but they are more likely to handle some bumps and bruises.

- **Water**—Obviously water is harmful to any electronic item. It can cause internal electrical shorts in the short run and corrosion over the life of your camera. Camcorders are not waterproof, or even water resistant.

Solution—They make underwater housings for camcorders, which provide obvious underwater protection (see Figure 8.5). They would work well shooting in heavy rain too. These housings can also be used as camcorder armor when shooting scenes that put the camera in harm's way.

Figure 8.5

Underwater housings allow you to take your camcorder into shark infested waters.

More on Cold and Warm Temperatures

Cold temperatures affect the performance of your camcorder battery. So it is important to keep your camcorder batteries at room temperature both in storage and prior to use.

The smaller the camcorder, the more potentially dangerous internal condensation can be because there is no empty buffer space. Personally, I have had numerous lens fogging instances in my early filming years when going from a cold shooting environment to a warm one without problems. However, if you can afford to wait the temperature transition time, you will be minimizing the risk of problems.

The Sun

The sun is potentially dangerous to your camcorder. Shooting the sun for too long without movement has the theoretical potential of damaging your CCD, your camcorder's imaging chip. However, I have yet to find a confirmed incident of this. The brighter the sun (midday), the more risk you have. Shooting a sunset therefore produces little risk.

Also if your viewfinder (not the lens) is pointed at the sun, it can definitely fail permanently. This is because the optics of the viewfinder basically act as a magnifying glass. So if the sun shines through the viewfinder for any extended period of time, it can melt the internal screen.

CLEANING YOUR CAMCORDER

Camcorders occasionally need to be cleaned because of residue build-up that comes from your videotapes. This residue can clog your video head, resulting in video and audio dropouts while recording or playing. Most video experts recommend cleaning the video head every 20 or so hours of use. The other alternative would be to wait until you see audio and video dropouts or you see residue on the tape head or drive.

There are two ways to clean your camcorder—cleaning tapes or a special swab and cleaning solution (see Figure 8.6).

Figure 8.6

Cleaning tapes offer a convenient way to renew your camcorder's tape head.

Cleaning tapes are recommended by most camcorder companies. DV camcorders use dry cleaning tapes (don't *ever* use wet). They look like ordinary MiniDV videotapes; however, they possess special cleaning powers. These tapes use abrasion to clean off residue. Because they are abrasive, you should only run your cleaning tape for five seconds at a time (any longer and you could damage your video head). To run your cleaning tape, you just pop it in the camcorder and press play for five seconds. If the first run does not do the job, you can rerun it up to three times, pausing one minute between runs. If this method fails to do the job, the next step is to use cleaning fluid.

Cleaning your camcorder with cleaning fluid requires the correct tools and precise (or at least careful) motor skills. If you can't pull this off, you are better off letting a professional clean your camcorder.

The best cleaning fluid for your camcorder is 99% Isopropyl alcohol. However this is hard to find. You can obtain it from Radio Shack over the phone (1-800-THE-SHACK) for about six dollars, but there is a hazardous chemicals tax of $20 you have to pay. 91% Isopropyl alcohol that most drug stores carry can be used if you can't get your hands on 99% Isopropyl alcohol. However the 91% leaves nominal residue, which could hurt your camcorder (but usually does not).

Some people suggest using denatured alcohol, but I strongly discourage this because denatured alcohol leaves an unacceptably high level of residue.

Aside from cleaning solution, the other important tool is the cleaning swab (see Figure 8.7). You cannot use cotton swabs to clean your camcorder because any shed lint that sticks to the video head will potentially damage your head when that piece of lint is sandwiched between your tape and the spinning video head.

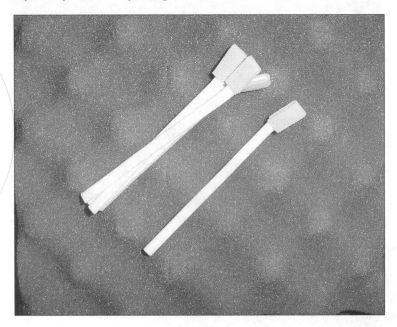

Figure 8.7

When cleaning your camcorder, use only lint free swabs.

You need lint free chamois or foam cleaning swabs. Both are carried in Radio Shack stores. I prefer the chamois swabs.

Depending on the ergonomics of your camcorder, you may want to remove the tape cover of your camcorder to get a better access to your video head and tape drive. Camcorders use lots of tiny screws, so if you are removing any make sure you are working on a large, clean, and well-lit table.

You need to thoroughly clean the video head and the tape drive. The video head (sometimes called a drum) is the shiny cylinder inside your camcorder which is responsible for reading and writing tapes.

Wet your swab to a medium level of saturation and then place it on the video head. With some other tool (such as a mechanical pencil without lead) spin the drum slowly around while maintaining light pressure on the swab against the video head. Continue until the head is clean. Make sure and reload on alcohol and change swabs if your swab becomes dirty.

Once the video head is done, proceed to the tape path. The tape path is any hardware that comes in contact with the tape (guides, pins, rollers). Clean the tape path thoroughly. Some experts advise against alcohol-based cleaners for the rubber rollers because eventually alcohol can cause rubber to dry out and crack. However, I tend to think that unless you over-clean your camcorder, by the time the rubber starts to crack (several years down the line if ever), you will probably be on to your next camcorder. If you want to be safe, Radio Shack sells rubber conditioner/cleaner that safely cleans rubber rollers. Also, if the rubber rollers don't appear dirty, you can just pass on cleaning them.

If you are wealthy or are not detail-orientated, professional cleaning is your only alternative. Cleaning is not hard, but if you are not willing to be careful and thorough, then you might as well pay someone else who will be. Retail electronic stores—like Best Buy and Circuit City—will clean your camcorder, although you might get a better deal at a local camera shop that you trust.

Your camcorder lens will probably be what you clean most often. Your lens can easily become dirty with soot or even oil from your fingers (produced from your pores). Keeping your lens clean is important both for taking clear video and for maintaining your lens. Camcorder lenses usually have a coating on them that can be deteriorated by things like finger oil over time.

Make sure that you keep the lens cap on when you are not shooting, as that will reduce the need to clean it. Also avoid touching the lens with your fingers. JVC makes a few camcorder models with automatic lens covers that eliminate this chore.

When cleaning, use 99% or 91% alcohol along with a chamois cloth. Often you will only need to use a cloth if the lens just has lint on it. A compressed air can is another good way to blow lint off your lens.

CHAPTER 9

COMPUTER HARDWARE BASICS

Computer power continues to increase exponentially every year. Computer video editing, which used to be a trying affair, is becoming ever more pain-free, thanks to faster hard drives and CPUs. With the latest version of Adobe Premiere 6 and any new computer with a FireWire card, you can finally experience the promised convenience of non-linear video editing. You can now edit your home video footage and output to tape without any render delays.

However, when it comes to adding special effects or encoding into a different video format (such as for the Web), prepare for long rendering and encoding times even on the fastest computers. Simple two-second dissolves between one scene and the next take only a few seconds to render, but if you need to add extensive special effects to your footage, the rendering times can add up.

THE MINIMUM AND RECOMMENDED SPECS

The slowest brand-new computer sold today is fast enough for video editing (see Figure 9.1). Increased computer performance will only benefit you in speed gains on effects rendering times, or rendering times when encoding in other video formats (such as VCD, video e-mail, and so on).

Figure 9.1

Even an affordable Emachines computer is fast enough for digital video editing.

If you are only interested in simple editing then you don't need to spend extra money on the fastest computer. If effects and rendering in other video formats is important to you, buy the fastest computer for the money.

While every camcorder outputs different quality video depending on its hardware, all computers basically output the same quality video—a quality that is equal to the source. A better computer can do things faster, but it will not improve on the quality. Because DV video output quality is basically identical on every computer, the price/performance ratio is theoretically easier to measure with computers than it is with camcorders. If a $1,000 computer can render video twice as fast as a $750 computer, the $1,000 computer is the better buy.

However, you won't find published performance specs on every computer. And the quality of the internal components has a lot to do with speed. One 1.5 gigahertz system can be much faster than another if it has better internal components. Component quality also affects stability, which most would agree is also very important. As a result, learn what components make up a computer before you buy, and know which component models perform the best for your needs.

CPU

CPU stands for central processing unit. CPUs are also commonly referred to as processors. CPU speeds used to be rated in MHz (megahertz), but now that we have reached 1000MHz and beyond, the GHz (gigahertz) speed measurement will soon become predominant (someday we will even have terahertz).

The CPU is the processing brain of your computer system. Historically, the faster the CPU, the faster your computer operated and completed tasks. This is not always the case anymore. CPUs made by different companies—Intel, Motorola, and AMD, for example—have somewhat different architectures that also affect performance. Software companies sometimes optimize their software for a certain chip architecture. Generally speaking, right now, a 2GHz Pentium 4, 1.4GHz AMD Athlon, and 867MHz Apple G4 perform about the same overall (see Figure 9.2).

Figure 9.2

The two top CPUs in the PC world are the Intel Pentium 4 and the AMD Athlon.

Intel and AMD make chips that conform to the X86 architecture, which all Windows operating system–based programs operate on. Apple has an entirely different architecture to their chips. Consequently, you can't normally run a Windows program on an Apple computer or vice versa. They do, however, make emulators, which enable you to run most Windows programs on an Apple, but this causes a substantial performance hit.

Minimum CPU

The minimum CPU speed for video editing within the OHCI DV FireWire protocol is 450MHz. Older models and even current non-OHCI FireWire cards–such as the Pinnacle DV200, Digital Origin MotoDV, Cannopus DvRaptor–allow for video editing down to 200MHz. Presently, I would recommend at least a 600MHz CPU for OHCI FireWire cards. The Apple CPU performs well at lower speeds, so I would recommend 400MHz and up CPUs if you are going with an Apple computer.

JARGON

> OHCI is a hardware specification for FireWire (IEEE 1394). In other words, it is a specified design and implementation of FireWire technology. Because Microsoft has chosen to primarily support OHCI FireWire cards in their operating systems, they are likely to be the dominant FireWire cards on the market for consumers.

Intel CPUs are the conservative choice, mostly because they often have more video-editing–compatible motherboards. This is most likely because Intel motherboards have less chipset variety than AMD systems.

AMD is a much better value recently, and while their chips are great, their track record is less stellar when it comes to motherboards. However, AMD system stability has improved greatly over the last year and their market share continues to grow. I use an AMD-based video editing system, and with all the most recent drivers I have no complaints. The more entrenched AMD becomes, the more its stability will likely rival Intel. Many Intel motherboard chipsets (even the famously stable BX chipset) historically suffered from compatibility problems when first introduced.

> *Motherboards* are the foundation of every computer. All computer components plug into your motherboard. Motherboards are ultimately responsible for making sure all your computer components work together. The quality of the motherboard is the most important factor in computer stability.

Recommended CPU

If you plan to add any effects, or encode into different video formats, then you might as well have all the horsepower you can reasonably get, so buy the fastest CPU for the money. This is usually the third or fourth fastest model CPU. If you buy the fastest CPU you will always pay a premium. Bottom line: You can usually pay about half as much for the CPU model that is only around 10% slower.

Hard Drive

Hard drives are the storage medium on a computer, your computer's file cabinet or long-term memory (see Figure 9.3). Hard drives are composed of several magnetic disks—one on top of another—on a spindle encased in a metal housing. A read/write head that resembles a record player arm glides across the disks, accessing and/or writing data.

Figure 9.3

While hard drives keep getting larger storage capacities, they continue to maintain the 3.5" bay size.

Hard drive performance depends highly on the rotation speed of the disks. If you buy a stock Dell or Compaq computer, you will likely end up with a 5400rpm speed drive. A 7200rpm is far more ideal (though not absolutely necessary) for video editing or other multimedia work. Prices on fast 7200rpm drives have never been cheaper, so if you are upgrading or building your own system, the small premium is worth it. As cheap as CPU prices have fallen, storage technology has maintained an even faster increase in performance per dollar.

IDE (Integrated Drive Electronics)

A few different types of hard drive interfaces are presently on the market. A hard drive interface determines how your hard drive speaks to your motherboard (see Figure 9.4). The most common hard drive interface is IDE, which is on most stock consumer computers. IDE has two channels generally, allowing you to connect two devices (hard drives, CD burners, and so on) on each channel, for a total of four.

Figure 9.4

The IDE channels are where the hard drives and CD/DVD drives interface with the motherboard.

IDE comes in various flavors: ATA 33, ATA 66, and ATA 100 (ATA stands for Advanced Technology Attachment). The ATA number relates to the max-sustained data transfer rate. That means that on an ATA 33 board, you can get faster data transfers than 33MB per second (33MBps). The fastest current IDE hard drive is the IBM 60GXP, which averages 38MB/s read speed. While this is quite fast, it hardly satisfies the potential of the ATA 100 interface. However, hard drives are capable of reading in bursts (small increments) up to twice their average speed. The IBM 60GXP can read up to 60MB/s burst speed, which at least necessitates having a motherboard that supports ATA 66.

You can use an ATA 66 or ATA 100 hard drive on an ATA 33 motherboard (or an ATA 33 drive on an ATA 100 motherboard); you will just never exceed 33MBps in average or burst speed. All new motherboards will be ATA 100, so it is not going to cost you anything extra to have.

SCSI (Small Computer System Interface)

SCSI (pronounced "scuzzy") is a higher performance hard drive/storage interface which allows for faster storage transfers and more devices, with less of a hit on your CPU compared to IDE. SCSI drives are also more expensive and require a SCSI card or SCSI-equipped motherboard. With the rise of low-cost, high-performance IDE drives (and the

oftentimes difficult SCSI setup), SCSI is less appealing for most multimedia computers. SCSI still offers better performance, but when you consider the cost, it is not worth it. If, however, you were building a Web server that was going to get incredible amounts of traffic (or maybe a professional music studio), then SCSI would be the best choice.

RAID (Redundant Array of Independent Disks)

RAID is the hotrod in the world of hard drive interfaces. Technically, RAID is a controller used within an IDE or SCSI interface. RAID allows you the ability to control multiple hard drives (collectively known as an array) in a number of ways. RAID Level 0 (also called striping) allows you to write data to two drives simultaneously, doubling your storage performance. RAID Level 1 allows you to mirror data to two disks simultaneously, so if one of your hard drives fails, you have a backup drive intact. With four drives you can run in RAID Level 0 + 1, which allows you to both stripe and mirror your drives, so you get twice the speed, along with the backup advantages of RAID.

A few years ago there was only SCSI-based RAID, which was too costly for the average consumer. In the last year, a number of IDE RAID solutions have come on the market. Many new motherboards include it onboard. The downside of IDE RAID is that it takes more system resources than SCSI. But on a personal computer, the price advantage makes it more attractive. If you are running a Web or office server, SCSI-based RAID is always better; otherwise IDE RAID is fine.

Other Interfaces (FireWire, USB)

USB is a standard interface on most modern computers (see Figure 9.5). USB is ideal for connecting keyboards, printers, and some portable music players. The limitation of USB is speed. USB is not fast enough for high-quality video capture. It will work for backing up your video files to external USB hard drives, but even then you have better options. USB 2.0 is a newer version of this hardware technology. USB 2.0 has transfer speeds that rival current FireWire, but the technology has an uncertain future because manufacturers have started to favor FireWire.

FireWire (also called IEEE 1394 and sometimes i.Link) is the latest, most interesting hard drive interface option (see Figure 9.6). It offers the portability of USB, but has much higher data transfer rates (as fast as 400Mbps) making it ideal for video capture. You can also hook up and use more than one external FireWire drive at a time, similar to SCSI.

1394b, the next generation of FireWire currently in development, will have between 800 and 1,600Mbps, or up to 3.2 Gbps transfer speeds, depending on the hardware implementation.

Figure 9.5

Almost every desktop computer made in the last few years has two USB ports on the back, usually right under the power supply.

Figure 9.6

FireWire is showing up on more computers, but often you have to add a PCI card in your computer. This figure shows the connectors on a typical PCI FireWire card.

RAM

RAM (random access memory) is your computer's short-term memory system (see Figure 9.7). The main advantage of the RAM is speed, since it has no moving parts. If there is a disadvantage, it is storage size (though after you reach a certain amount of RAM, more is not likely to improve performance). RAM used to be expensive, but now it has fallen to all-time price lows, so you have no excuse for having less than 128MB of RAM. 128MB is enough for most users, but if you want to be safe or need to have multiple power hungry applications open at the same time, go for 256MB.

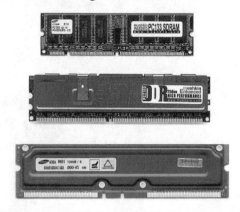

Figure 9.7

RAM is your computer's short-term memory. Currently there are three types of RAM: SDRAM, DDR RAM, and Rambus RAM (pictured from top to bottom).

On Win98/Me I have seen little performance difference between 128 and 256 (though the difference between 64 and 128 is significant). Windows 98/Me can't handle more than 512MB, and really does not manage RAM very well past 128MB. Windows 2000 or XP has much better RAM management, and can handle more than 512MB of RAM, but for most video editing projects you see little performance advantage beyond 256MB.

The RAM market is starting to get complicated with different RAM types. Pentium III systems use PC133 SDRAM, Athlon systems use PC133 or DDR-RAM (Double Data Rate RAM) depending on the motherboard, and Pentium 4 systems use SDRAM, DDR-RAM, or RDRAM (Rambus RAM) depending on the motherboard. DDR-RAM and RDRAM are faster than PC133 SDRAM, but most current hardware and software has not proven to take much advantage of that speed. DDR-RAM right now is the best price/performance option, but it only works in DDR-RAM compatible motherboards.

Don't be confused with all the RAM types when it comes to upgrading. There are only three types of RAM in newer computers, and your manufacturer's Web site will tell you which RAM your computer uses. Online memory retailers like Crucial Technology (http://crucial.com) will allow you to easily find the exact type of RAM for your computer if you want to upgrade.

Video Card

Every computer has a video card that enables the computer to display graphics on the monitor (see Figure 9.8). Video cards are generally evaluated by their 2D and 3D speed and image quality. Most gamers care about speed (frames per second), whereas CAD (Computer Aided Drafting) designers care more about 2D image quality.

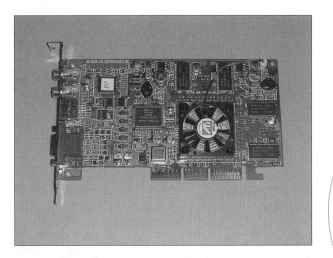

Figure 9.8

Video cards are responsible for generating your monitor display. For 2D work, which includes video editing, most cards, regardless of costs, perform similarly.

While 3D performance—mostly used in the latest, most innovative games—varies greatly depending on the price, 2D performance—used for everything else—is pretty comparable in most consumer video cards, even the cheapest. Image quality is kind of a wild card, as paying more won't necessarily mean better quality in consumer cards. The professional 2D cards used by CAD designers aren't worth the high cost for video editing work.

Video editing is generally a 2D endeavor, so you need not waste a lot of money on the latest greatest 3D gaming card. Any 2D card will fair pretty well. Some of the low-end ATI and Matrox cards have very good image quality and are also highly affordable.

Sound Card

Generally speaking, sound cards do not have much to do with the video editing process. Sound card quality is not going to have any effect on your audio because your audio never leaves the digital domain. You import sound through the FireWire card as zeroes and ones—the sound card is never in a position to alter your audio. A better sound card, if you have really good speakers, is just going to make your audio sound a little more faithful to the source (see Figure 9.9).

We are on the threshold of do-it-yourself (DIY) DVD authoring, which uses 16-bit and/or 24-bit audio. Most consumer sound cards are 16-bit. Since your camcorder records in 16-bit, you gain no audio quality advantage upsampling to 24-bit. Even when a camcorder format is released that does support 24-bit audio, a 16-bit sound card will still be fine because, again, your video and audio enters your computer through the FireWire port, not your sound card.

Figure 9.9

Your sound card will rarely, if ever, be involved in the video editing process.

Upsampling is when you raise the sample rate of a sound file—for instance, taking a 16-bit sound file and making it into a 24-bit sound file (this is also called more generally *resampling*). Upsampling will not improve the sound quality—and could actually hurt it a little—so there is no reason to do it. The reason upsampling exists is to ensure compatibility. Newer 16- and 24-bit sound cards (or other audio hardware) needs to be able to resample lower bit rate files to conform to their internal 16- or 24-bit operation.

The SoundBlaster Live Value, the new Sound Blaster Audigy, and Turtle Beach Santa Cruz are all very good affordable cards (that again won't really ever be involved in your sound processing, but will serve to output your sound through your speakers a little better). If you don't have a FireWire card already, the Audigy would probably be the best choice, as it includes FireWire on the card.

FireWire Card

The FireWire card is the main thoroughfare of your video editing system. Over the last few years the price has plummeted below $50 for the lowest-priced cards. While many rather high-priced cards offer additional features (above and beyond DV video input), most users will be fine with a simple OHCI FireWire card. Almost every recent Apple computer (with a G3 and up) includes built-in FireWire.

The heart of any FireWire card is the chipset used to process the DV video. I recommend the Texas Instruments chipset. Cards such as the ADS Pyro and Dazzle DV-editor feature this chipset (see Figure 9.10). Most FireWire cards, even the low-end ones, include some type of video editing software.

If you have an older slower computer (300MHz to 450MHz), you can get away with a quality non-OHCI FireWire card for simple cut-and-paste editing. The Pinnacle DV200 is a very good choice.

Figure 9.10

The ADS Pyro was one of the first affordable sub-$100 FireWire cards on the market. It remains one of the most popular consumer cards.

Most of the latest FireWire cards conform to the OHCI standard. OHCI FireWire cards require more CPU horsepower than many non-OHCI cards. Nonetheless, OHCI cards have the best support on the latest Windows operating systems. Just make sure you get a 600MHz+ CPU powered computer. And for faster rendering times, going for 1GHz+ would not hurt.

Power Supply

The power supply is what powers your entire computer—obviously (see Figure 9.11). You need 250 watts minimum. Athlon and Pentium 4 systems require specifically approved power supplies (see http://www.amd.com and http://www.intel.com for a list) of at least 250 watts, preferably 300 watts. However, I had no problem getting a generic power supply to work on one of my Athlon systems. Also, Intel is releasing a new Pentium 4 chipset that does not require a special power supply.

Figure 9.11

The power supply—every computer has one.

DEFINING OVERKILL

If you have followed the computer industry the last few years, you know that technology is evolving at an extremely fast rate. Computer hardware that cost $2000 two years ago can be worth as little as $400 now. This trend is likely to continue.

So the best approach in buying a computer is to only buy what you need. If you decide you really need a super-fast system, go for the highest performance for the money, and not the highest performance regardless of cost; remember that you can always upgrade. Besides excessive prices, the newest and fastest hardware is also the most untested, so buying one notch down saves you from the common reliability and driver performance issues that are all too common in new hardware.

MINIMUM SYSTEM SPECS

- 17-inch monitor
- 700MHz CPU (400MHz Mac)
- 128MB RAM
- 20GB hard drive
- OHCI FireWire card*
- Any sound card*

RECOMMENDED SYSTEM SPECS

- 19-inch monitor
- 1GHz+ CPU (600MHz+ Mac)
- 256MB RAM
- Two 20GB+ 7200RPM hard drives
- OHCI FireWire card*
- Any sound card*

*Sound Blaster Live Audigy (includes sound card and OHCI FireWire)

CHAPTER **10**

UPGRADING OR CHOOSING A NEW COMPUTER SYSTEM

If you are ready to embark on computer video editing, you have a number of options. If your computer is not already equipped for video editing, you have to decide whether to upgrade, buy, or build a new computer. Upgrading is sometimes an option, but if your computer is too slow, it might be time for a whole new system.

If you have the time and energy, I highly recommend building your own computer, as you will end up with the best system and a good understanding of how it works. This knowledge will make your future computer life easier if things ever go wrong—as they occasionally do—as well as making upgrades easier. The second best option is to find a retailer that will allow you to customize your own computer. Failing all that, head to Gateway Country, Dell land, Best Buy, or CompUSA and find a good major-brand PC whose specs and price match your needs.

UPGRADING YOUR COMPUTER

Upgrading your computer is a pretty easy thing to do—I swear. (The Best Buy or CompUSA upgrade center is no Olympian think tank.) However, unless you have at least a 400MHz CPU, it is probably better to just go to the next section and get yourself a whole new computer. Trying to upgrade some of these older systems is just not cost effective, and the only place they will be happy is with their friends at the local landfill, or relegated to a Web browsing computer in your house.

Adding FireWire

A FireWire card, which enables you to import video into your computer, is the only absolute must-have upgrade for digital video editing. Recommended upgrades are RAM (if you have less than 128MB), hard drive (if you have less than 20GB), and a new CPU (if you are experiencing frame dropping during capture). All of these upgrades are safely within the novice learning curve, as long as you can read simple directions.

If you have at least a 400MHz CPU and an open PCI slot, you can simply add any OHCI FireWire card (priced around $50). The card should come with software such as Ulead Video Studio or MGI Videowave, which is sufficient for consumer video editing. You should also ideally upgrade your system RAM to 128MB as well.

While inexpensive OHCI FireWire cards can produce results as good as prosumer models, if you are interested in extra features such as stock number of real-time effects, analog in, or other special features, you will have to choose a prosumer FireWire card.

The top prosumer video capture card companies are Matrox, Cannopus, and Pinnacle. They are all pretty competitive with each other, so no one company has a monopoly on the market. Cannopus and Pinnacle offer more product options, but Matrox's RT2500 is one of the top prosumer video capture cards on the market (see Figure 10.1).

Figure 10.1

The Matrox RT2500 is one of the leading prosumer video capture cards.

If you can afford one of these cards, you can probably afford a nice new system to complement it—unless you have a really fast system already.

Adding RAM

If you have less than 128MB of RAM, you should upgrade to 128MB. If you really like to run your computer hard with lots of applications open at the same time (or are running Windows XP) then go for 256MB. To find out how much RAM you currently have in your computer go to the Start button, Settings, Control Panel, System. This will launch the System Properties window. Your total RAM will be displayed under Computer.

To find out what kind of RAM you have in your system, go to your manufacturer's Web site. Once you find that out, you can buy any RAM of that designated type. RAM prices are very low right now, so this is a very cheap upgrade, not to mention easy. Also make sure you have available RAM slots to add more RAM. If you don't (which is rare), your only recourse is to remove the current stick and put in a larger one.

To install RAM, just power down your computer, open the case, and match the RAM to the RAM slot. The RAM slot has two retention clips on the top and bottom, which should lock tight as you fully insert the stick of RAM.

Adding a Larger and/or Second Hard Drive

Hard drive space is very important when it comes to digital video editing. Five minutes of DV video takes up 1GB of space. So capturing an entire 60-minute tape would take around 12GB of space. Plus, you need space for temp files that your video editing program might create, and you always need to leave your hard drive at least 15% empty for optimal stability.

If you have only one hard drive right now, my recommendation would be to add a second hard drive of at least 20GB (7200RPM speed recommended). The second hard drive should be used exclusively for video capture.

Installing the drive is pretty simple if you don't already have four IDE devices (hard drive, CD-ROM CD writer, DVD-ROM, and so on) installed. Your computer has two IDE channels on the motherboard (each IDE channel will be labeled either IDE1 /primary/ or IDE2 /secondary/ on the motherboard). Each channel can have one IDE cable, which can connect to two devices. So that makes four potential IDE connections.

Each IDE device is designated (by pins on the back of the drive) as either master or slave. Normally, your primary hard drive is the master IDE device on the first IDE channel. However, in my experience, no advantage exists between master and slave. What's important is to have your hard drives on different IDE channels, as this will give them each the full IDE channel bandwidth for moving data. To find out IDE and pin settings for your computer, you will just have to peruse the inside of your case.

Ideally, you will want to make your second hard drive the master (or slave) on the secondary IDE channel (as your hard drive will be on the primary IDE channel). This may require changing IDE connections and pin assignments. Usually, most computers have at least one IDE connection left on the second IDE channel, which will make for an easy installation.

After figuring out the proper pin settings and IDE connections, you can install your drive. Place the drive in any open bay, and then secure with screws. If your computer does not have an open bay (not likely) you can just set the drive on the bottom of the case (add a few pieces of corrugated cardboard under it to prevent vibration transfer between the drive and the case which will cause a buzzing noise).

You then need to format the drive before you will be able to use it. The easiest way to format is to use the software that comes with your drive. Most hard drive manufacturers include easy formatting software. Another easy formatting option is to use a program like Partition Magic (http://www.powerquest.com).

If you are running an older Windows operating system (Win95/95/Me), FAT32 is the only good formatting option. If you are using Windows NT, 2000, or XP, you have another option, NTFS. NTFS is more secure and has one specific advantage for video editing: You have no file size limit. Meaning you can capture 60 minutes of video in one file. FAT32 has a 4GB limit (around 20 minutes). Since it is easy to combine files in video editors, this is not a big advantage. But as DVD authoring becomes more common, you won't be able to work with DVD image files larger that 4GB. If you are starting a Windows 2000 or XP system from scratch, I recommend going with NTFS.

After you have finished formatting your drive, you should see it the next time you boot up in Windows Explorer and My Computer.

For hard drives, IBM, Maxtor, and Western Digital are my favorites (in that order). For RAM, Kingston and Crucial are good. Most brands of RAM will work identically unless you like to overclock your system.

JARGON

Overclocking is when you run your CPU faster than the default speed (normally 10–20% faster). On many CPUs this is difficult or impossible, and usually requires a special motherboard.

Adding a Faster CPU

Your CPU upgrade options for most computers are often more limited, as each motherboard is only compatible with a certain line of processors. Among the CPU models: Athlon, Pentium 4, Celeron, and Duron, there are actually different submodels. Based on recent history, new CPU lines roll out every 12 months, and generally those new lines are incompatible with the previous line of CPUs. So the fastest CPU that will work with your computer will probably have to have been released within a year of when you bought your computer.

Bottom line: Go to your manufacturer and find out specifically what type of processor your computer uses and supports. The good thing is that if your computer does support a faster CPU, installation is about as easy as installing RAM. Make sure if you install a new chip, you also keep the current heatsink and fan or install new ones.

BUILDING A NEW COMPUTER

Computers are made up of a very small number of components: computer case, CPU, RAM, hard drive, floppy drive, CD and/or DVD drive, video card, sound card, and a motherboard that everything plugs into. Add a computer monitor, keyboard, and mouse to that and you have your own custom-built computer system. A computer is, indeed, much less complicated to build than most consumers think.

Advantages

The advantage of building your computer has nothing to do with ease of construction, or even saving money. Building a computer is easy for some, moderately difficult for others. If you can read and follow directions, you can do it. The cost of building your own computer is often comparable to buying a brand new one, so you won't be saving any money.

However, building your computer allows you to choose every single component. This can help you get the fastest, most reliable and stable system, and/or the most compatible for your needs. While some of the computer companies allow you to configure your computer purchase, you are still severely limited in your options. You can maybe choose between two or three video cards, one or two sound cards, and select your hard drive's size. You rarely can choose your motherboard, which is the most crucial component on a computer system in regard to stability.

Computer systems occasionally have problems. The more computer-dependent you are, the more important it is for you to have a mastery of the technology. When you assemble your own computer, all the parts you buy come with warranties like any major-label computer. But if you are going to depend on a warranty entirely, you will hamstring yourself. Warranties will replace defective parts and systems, but they won't replace lost data, or lost productivity time when you were unable to use your computer. If computers are going to become an important part in your productivity, a familiarity with your computer will help you solve any problems that arise without having to wait for a service rep to fix things.

If even after all this you have no intention of building your own system, skip the next section.

Very Basic Assembly Instructions

Obtain all the computer components necessary, and find a big clean table to work on. Follow these steps:

1. Install the CPU with heatsink and fan onto the motherboard.
2. Install the RAM (make sure the stick is not upside down).

3. Install the motherboard into the computer case (remove the stamped metal holes for the mouse, printer, keyboard, and USB ports, or an other ports or jacks).

4. Install the power supply plug onto the motherboard. Install all the other little wires that connect from the cast to the motherboard—your motherboard manual will have a diagram of which cable goes where. The only important cables are the Power ON/OFF, and the Reset button cable. I often leave the other ones—the speaker, hard drive light, and so on—unplugged as they annoy me and are not necessary.

5. Install the floppy drive.

6. Install the hard drives and CD and/or DVD players/writers. Make sure that each is correctly pinned as master or slave. If you have more than one hard drive, put them on different IDE channels.

7. Install the video card.

8. Install any PCI cards you have (sound cards, network cards). You can wait until after you assemble the rest of the computer to do this, but as long as you already have the case open…

9. Connect the monitor to the video card.

10. Power on your computer and monitor.

11. If your hard drives are unformatted, use a boot disk to format them. If you have another computer, it may be easier to format them with a program like PartitionMagic.

12. After formatting, install your operating system of choice.

Important Installation Tips

In the following section, you will find some special installation tips that you should pay special attention to when you are assembling your computer.

CPU

When installing a socket CPU fan/heatsink onto the motherboard, exercise care. It is possible to crack your CPU core if too much force is required to get the heatsink bracket in place. If you find it really hard to get your heatsink to connect to your CPU, try bending the retaining clip so that it will clip on easier.

CPUs come in two forms: socket and slot (see Figure 10.2). Socket CPUs and slot CPUs have the same internal CPU core; they just have a different casing. Slot CPUs can be easier to install, because you don't have the fan/heatsink installation problem to contend with.

Figure 10.2

CPUs come in two form factors: socket and slot. Most newer chips are socket because manufacturing costs are cheaper. Slot CPUs are easier to install—but socket CPUs are not much harder.

If you are using heatsink paste, place only a thin film-like layer on the top of the CPU.

techtv tip

Quality heatsink paste lowers your CPU temperature by about two degrees by filling microscopic grooves and gaps between the CPU and heatsink. This improves the heat transfer between the CPU and heatsink. Two degrees is incidental for most users, but if you are doing some major CPU overclocking it can be helpful.

Multiple Hard Drive Installation

Back in the days of slower CPUs (below 100MHz), we were advised to avoid installing a hard drive and a CD-ROM on the same IDE channel. This tip no longer holds true. In fact, putting both your hard drives on the same IDE channel results in lower performance than if you have them on separate channels. This is because the IDE protocol does not support simultaneous reading and writing (SCSI does though) on the same channel. Having your hard drives on separate IDE channels also allows you to place your CD/DVD drives/burners on separate channels too. This setup is optimal for doing CD-to-CD copying.

The above is a general rule—not an absolute one—because some hard drives and CD burners are finicky and might only work as slave or master. The important thing is to keep your hard drives on separate IDE channels; whether they are set as master and slave is less important. Having your hard drives on the same channel is not the end of the world if doing so is your only alternative, but it will mean slower performance when both are being accessed at the same time. In any case, when each drive is in use independently you won't lose any performance.

Setting the Pins on Your Drives   Hard, CD, and DVD drives all have pins on the back of the drive casing. You have to set the pins to match the arrangement you want them to be in (see Figure 10.3). There should be a sticker or metal etching of the proper pin settings. You ideally want to set your hard drives as masters and the CD and DVD drives as slaves. However, sometimes a certain drive will only work as master or a slave.

Figure 10.3

If you install a new hard drive, DVD, or CD-ROM, you need to set the pins appropriately. You can usually find instructions printed on the back of the drive.

Unrecognized Drives   Sometimes your computer won't recognize one or more of your drives. If this happens, try these steps:

1. If you have an older motherboard upgrade your BIOS.

2. Make sure the pins are set correctly.

3. Switch the drive to another setting—to slave if it is master (change the other drive on the channel to slave).

4. Remove all the pins. I have often found that when none of the pin settings will allow the drive to be recognized, removing all the pins seems to get the drive recognized by the computer. When that happens, see what the computer recognizes the problem drive as—master or slave—and then set the other drive's pins appropriately.

5. Make sure the drive works in another computer—it might be defective or dead.

BUYING A MAJOR BRAND PC

Major brand PCs like Dell, Gateway, HP, Sony, and others have the limitations I discussed previously in regard to component selection (see Figure 10.4). In general, you get a stock model computer. Often, they don't have all the top-end parts. However, most of them are at least going to have mid-range components.

Stock Computer

Most major-brand PC manufacturers give very little information on the contents of their beige boxes. Manufacturers usually only list CPU brand and speed, amount of RAM, size of hard drive, and speed of CD or DVD drive. They are not going to tell who made the hard drive, or what model motherboard is used. Thanks to the technology race, even the slowest new desktop on the market today will perform average digital video editing tasks competently. However, the average computer is not going to compare with the stability and performance of a custom-made system. The difference in performance between a similar speed stock computer and a custom-made one can be as much as 30 percent. Custom systems will also be more stable; by that I mean your computer will crash less. (Of course all computers running a Microsoft OS are going to still crash a little, even though Windows 2000 and XP are far more stable than previous Windows OSes.) However, if phone support is essential to you, buy a Dell or Gateway computer (or comparable major-brand PC) as you generally will not find comparable support at a small computer company.

Figure 10.4

Dell computers and some of the other major PC makers are a good bet if phone support is very important to you.

If you are going with a stock computer, peruse recent issues of *PC Magazine* (www.pcmagazine.com), *PCWORLD* (www.pcworld.com), and *Computer Shopper* (www. computershopper.com) to see which systems have the highest performance in their benchmark reviews (see Figure 10.5). Our own TechTV labs are always putting new computers through rigorous tests, which you can see the results of at http://www.techtv.com. That will reveal which stock computers have the best components, so you at least get the best of what the pre-built world has to offer.

Built to Order

Dell, Gateway, CompUSA, and others allow some built-to-order customization ability (see Figure 10.6). You can choose from a few video cards, hard drive sizes, and sound cards, but you can't select what kind of motherboard or a specific model hard drive. While you can't beat a computer where every part is specifically selected, you can get some solid and reliable computers from the major computer manufacturers. When you add in phone support, a major-brand PC is in all honesty the best choice for many consumers.

Another option is to find a reliable smaller retailer that will allow you to choose every component in your system. (Make sure you check the reputation of any of these establishments before ordering—try a site like ResellerRatings.com.) You will probably pay a little more than you would if you built the system yourself. And you will miss out on the fun and problem solving advantages of being a savvy computer aficionado, but you will end up with a better system than you could get from Dell. However, you will not get the solid phone support that a major PC maker will give you. So you need to weigh the pros and cons of each option.

Figure 10.5

Computer magazines—and their Web sites—are great resources when deciding which computer to buy.

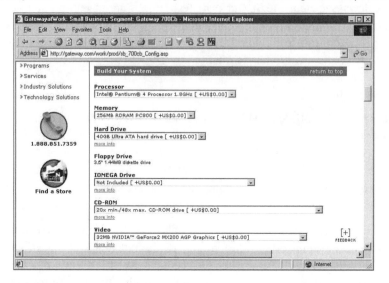

Figure 10.6

Many PC makers now allow you to configure your own PC, within a limited number of options.

BUYING A TURNKEY SOLUTION

If you are willing to spend the extra money, you can buy a system specially designed or equipped for video editing right out of the box. The advantage is that they are guaranteed to work for video editing. These are called turnkey systems. There are two kinds of turnkey systems:

- Regular standard computers—running a consumer OS like Windows—that will operate like a normal computer, but are outfitted and tested with all the proper hardware and software for digital video editing
- A specially designed computer that will only do video editing

Consumer Turnkey

Sony systems are one of the best options in this arena. All new Sony desktops come with FireWire and video editing software built in, and some of the higher-end systems come with Adobe Premiere. Sony is also selling a desktop—called VAIO Digital Studio—with optional DVD-RW drives, as well as a TIVO-like personal video recording system (see Figure 10.7).

Figure 10.7

Sony's VAIO Digital Studio is a nice consumer turnkey video editing system.

More manufacturers are starting to include FireWire and video editing software into their more mainstream home computer systems (see Figure 10.8). In general, they are using standard OHCI FireWire cards, which require a faster CPU speed than non-OHCI, so make sure you have at least 600MHz. These systems are the most affordable, but they tend to have middle of the road software and hardware. They will be fine for simple editing, but will thrive less when it comes to more advanced multimedia creating.

On the Apple end of things, all Apple computers with a G3 processor or better come with a built-in FireWire (I recommend at least 400MHz CPU speed). Coupled with iMovie 2 software, they make very nice consumer video editing solutions (and you'll be seen as different, unique, special) (see Figure 10.9).

Figure 10.8

Compaq (recently bought by HP) was the first major PC maker to release a FireWire-equipped computer under $1,000.

Figure 10.9

The Apple iMac along with iMovie 2 video editing software is one of the best consumer video editing options.

High-End Turnkey

The most famous professional Turnkey system manufacturer is AVID (see Figure 10.10). AVID now makes a number of systems, each geared to different aspects of video editing and production. All of them are top notch, but they all cost a fortune. As consumer technology has blossomed over the last few years, the premium you pay does not really match proportionally with the AVID performance advantage. AVID has responded to this new market reality with lower-cost systems (relative to what they used to charge), but they still are expensive.

Figure 10.10

An AVID is a professional turnkey video editing system.

CHOOSING AN OPERATING SYSTEM

An operating system is the most important piece of software on your system. A good or bad OS will define much of the stability of your computer system. Microsoft has made this important decision easier by monopolizing the OS market. For video editing on the PC, Microsoft operating systems—Win98SE/WinMe/WIN2K/WinXP—are your only realistic options. If you go Apple you really don't have much OS choice either. Luckily the latest OS software is pretty good, so the monopolist side effects have not reached a danger zone level.

Windows 95

The only significant reason to run Windows 95 is that your system can't handle a newer OS, which means it can't handle video editing either. Bottom line: Windows 95 in general is not a workable OS for video editing.

Windows 98/98SE/Me

Windows 98, 98SE, and Me share the same architecture—all of them are evolutions of Windows 95. They work fine for most consumer editing applications. One weakness of these OSes is the 2GB or 4GB file capture limit these operating systems have. This means you can't capture more than 10 or 20 minutes of video in one file.

Since it is not hard to join clips in modern video editing software, this is no big deal. Furthermore, many programs have workarounds for this. More significant is stability problems that plague these OS(s). The most stable of the three is Windows 98SE. Believe it or not, Windows Me, the sequel to Win 98SE, is considered by most to be more unstable. So if you have to run one of these three OS(s), run Windows 98SE.

Why would you want Windows 98SE over Windows 2000 or XP?

If your computer system barely meets my recommendations for hardware performance, you may be better off with Windows 98SE, as it requires less system resources. If not go for 2000 or XP.

Windows 2000 (Windows 2k, WIN2K)

Windows 2000 is the sequel to Windows NT 4.0. Windows NT was an operating system geared for business use. NT offered more stability and security than Microsoft's consumer OS. However, you could not play many new games on NT and the user interface was less friendly. Windows 2000 was built on a whole new kernel, which offered the stability and security of NT with the usability of a consumer OS. So WIN2K was fast and stable, but you could also play Quake 3, and easily install your new printer.

Kernel is the term used to refer to the core code of an operating system.

Windows 2000 is a great operating system for video editing applications (as well as anything else). WIN2K systems have no practical file size limit—if you format your hard drives as NTFS—so you can capture individual clips as large as your free hard drive space.

NOTE

Your computer hard drive has to be formatted with a file system before your computer can read and write data to it. A number of formatting options are available. The two main formatting options are FAT32 and NTFS. FAT32 is the optimal file system for Windows 95/98/Me. For Windows NT, 2000, and XP, you can choose FAT32 or NTFS. The advantage of NTFS is that you have a higher degree of security options and you can capture video clips larger than 4GB. NTFS is not without its drawbacks. If you are running a dual-boot system with Win98/Me, you won't have access to the NTFS formatted data from within Win98/Me. However, you can see FAT32 data from within Win2k or WinXP.

In addition, Windows 2000 requires less system resources than Windows XP. If you don't have the fastest system then you might get more out of WIN2K.

Windows XP (Professional and Home Edition)

Windows XP is the latest (and actually greatest) Microsoft operating system. It is built on the Windows 2000 kernel. Basically, it is an update of Windows 2000 with bug fixes, and an improved, highly configurable user interface (see Figure 10.11). XP comes in both a consumer and professional (business) version. This is the first Windows operating system to base the consumer and professional version on the same architecture.

What sets Windows XP Professional apart from the Home Edition is mainly the dual-processor support and improved security options. So unless you have a dual-processor system, you will get the same basic high performance and stability from the Home Edition.

Figure 10.11

With Windows XP, Microsoft is trying to capture the pretty interface award from Apple.

Windows XP is definitely the best Windows yet and is highly recommended for all new systems. The only drawback of XP is that it requires more system resources than Windows 2000 or 98/Me. If you have a computer slower than 500MHz, you won't be able to run XP as smoothly as an older OS. In that case you are better off with Windows 2000 or 98SE. For optimal performance in XP, make sure you upgrade to 256MB of RAM (RAM is a very inexpensive upgrade).

Apple OS X

OS X, like Windows 2000, is an entirely new operating system based on a new kernel. While OS X is getting very good reviews, all is not good in Macville. The top video editing program on the Mac, Final Cut Pro 2, is not yet optimized for OS X. You will need to run Final Cut Pro 2 in the OS 9 mode included in OS X. As of the end of December 2001, Apple has released Final Cut Pro 3, which is optimized for OS X. Upgrading from version 2 will set you back $299.

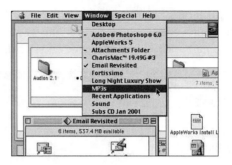

Figure 10.12

If you want to run Final Cut Pro 2, OS 9 is as good as OS X.

Figure 10.13

OS X, Apple's newest operating system is based on Unix.

CHAPTER 11

COMPUTER SETUP AND MAINTENANCE

Tweaking is the term that loosely describes making changes to improve your computer performance. To get your computer working its best will require some level of tweaking, even if your computer is brand new. Making sure you have the newest stable drivers and patches is also very important in keeping your computer working as well as it should.

Computers also don't age entirely well. Even though there is nothing wrong with your hardware, after a while—months, maybe a year after purchase—your computer will operate slower than it once did. The cause and blame goes to inherent failings of the operating system, which allows your data to become messy and disorganized over time. This chapter shows you a few solutions that will renew your system performance until better operating systems are invented.

You never know what computer problem will arise, so it is important to have support and resource avenues on the Internet where you can get answers to your questions, and solutions to your problems. You can use these same resources to find out what the best system optimization settings are, and in general advance your knowledge on the computer.

Patches are software updates that hardware and software companies provide to fix and/or enhance their products. You can download patches and drivers from the companies' Web sites. Sometimes you can choose between the latest stable drivers/patches, and newer beta drivers/patches. Beta means not entirely finished, so avoid these unless you really know what you are doing.

RECOMMENDATIONS FOR OPTIMAL VIDEO EDITING PERFORMANCE

While you may be fortunate enough to already have the perfect video editing system setup, many users might consider some additional hardware and settings customizations to get their systems into ideal position to start crunching video ones and zeroes. The hardware recommendations are recycled from the previous last chapter (as their importance warrants repetition):

1. Install two 7200rpm hard drives, one for your operating system and program files, and the other dedicated to your video files (see Figure 11.1). Run each as the master on a separate IDE channel.

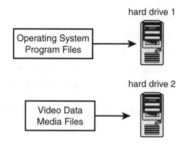

Figure 11.1

A two hard drive system allows capturing video to one drive, while your OS and video editing program run off another drive.

2. Install at least 256MB of RAM.

3. Install the latest stable BIOS and drivers.

4. Go to Control Panel, System, Device Manager and click Disk Drives. Double-click each drive, select the Settings tab, and make sure that DMA is selected (see Figure 11.2). If it's not, select it, click OK, and reboot when prompted.

DMA stands for *direct memory access*. It speeds up hard drive and CD/DVD drive access by using your RAM.

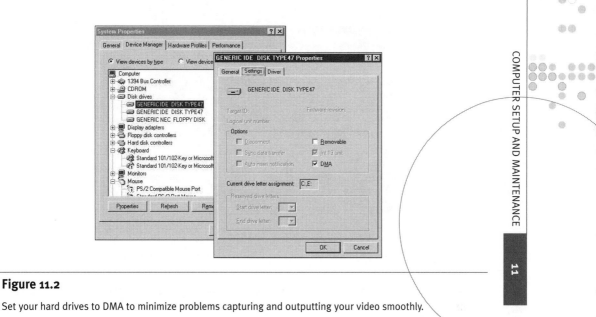

Figure 11.2

Set your hard drives to DMA to minimize problems capturing and outputting your video smoothly.

MEMORY OPTIMIZATION

If you are running Windows 95/98/Me, it is important to adjust the memory settings. Older Windows operating systems have notoriously bad memory management.

Mainly, you should reconfigure the virtual memory settings. Virtual memory is a process that uses some of your hard drive space for system memory when your RAM memory has been exhausted. Follow these steps:

1. Go into your Control Panel.
2. Select System shortcut.
3. Click the Performance tab.
4. Click the Virtual Memory button.
5. Select the radio button that states Let Me Specify My Own Virtual Memory Settings.
6. Set the Minimum to 1.5 times the amount of physical RAM (but no more than 256MB).
7. Set the Maximum to the same number.
8. Click OK, and select Yes when asked if you are sure you want to change the virtual memory settings (see Figure 11.3).
9. Select Yes when it asks you to reboot.

If you have Win2K or WinXP, you can skip this because you already have very good built-in memory management.

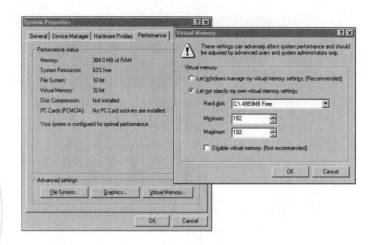

Figure 11.3

If you are using Win95, Win98, or WinMe, make sure you properly configure your virtual memory settings.

DEFRAGGING

As you use your computer over time, your hard drive becomes fragmented. This means that files get moved around from the original location on the physical hard drive, and eventually become randomly scattered. This happens because the Windows operating system repositions files for faster access. This makes things work faster initially, but as data becomes more and more fragmented, it hinders system performance.

Defragging your hard drive reorders your files, ensuring normal system performance. In the days of slower computers and hard drives, a fragmented hard drive was much more likely to cause dropped video frames during capture. Frame dropping is less likely on most new systems even with a fragmented drive, but it is still possible. If you are a power user and you want to be on the safe side, you should defrag your hard drive about every month.

With older versions of Windows (prior to XP), when your computer is defragging, you can't touch it, or the process will have to start all over. Most people schedule defrags for the middle of the night, or you can just manually start it before you go to bed.

Windows Standard Defrag Utility

Windows includes a defrag utility which you can schedule to defrag your hard drives whenever you want (see Figure 11.4). The only problem is that it is really slow—at least the utility that comes with all Microsoft OSes prior to XP. XP actually has an automatic defrag feature that defrags your drives when your computer goes idle for a certain customizable period of time (usually between 5 and 30 minutes). The standalone XP defrag utility appears to work much faster compared to previous Windows operating system defrag utilities. Furthermore, you can run the standalone defragger while you work on other applications.

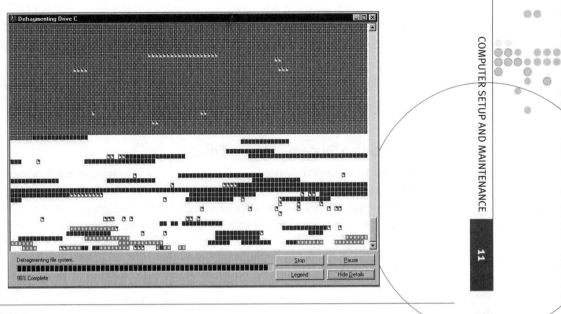

Figure 11.4

Defragging your hard drives reduces the chance of frame drops when inputting and outputting video.

Third-Party Defrag Utilities

If the extremely slow defrag times of the Windows defrag utility bother you and/or you need to be able to defrag FAT32 drives, you can get a third-party defrag utility. Programs like PerfectDisk and Norton Speed Disk speed up the defrag process significantly—up to three times faster (see Figure 11.5).

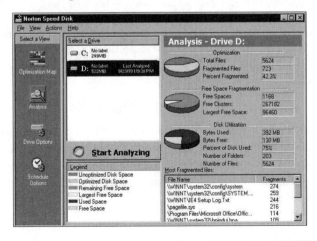

Figure 11.5

Because the Windows defrag utility is rather slow, you may want to use a third party defrag program like Norton Speed Disk.

FIGHTING SYSTEM SLOW DOWN

Every time you install a program on your computer, your system changes a little. Files are added or updated, settings are changed; your OS is just not the same person anymore. As this cycle propagates over time, Windows can start to operate slower. This phenomenon is known as *Windows dry rot* and is most prevalent in Win95/98/Me (it's too early to tell for XP).

Dedicating a System to Video Editing

One way to avoid Windows dry rot is to dedicate a computer solely to video editing. Putting together a system with only a few applications related to video editing will drastically eliminate the dry rot threat. This is undeniably an effective solution, but depending on how often you intend to use your computer for video editing, it can be impractical.

Multi-Boot Operating System

A more practical solution is a multi-boot system. This means you have multiple operating systems on one or more hard drives. This enables you to boot into an OS dedicated just to video editing, or to boot up into a general OS where you can do normal computer things. Programs like PartitionMagic make it easy to set up a multi-boot system (see Figure 11.6). If you have the hard drive space, multi-booting is really the best solution for a user who wants to ensure the highest possible system performance and reliability in the long term, while not limiting the computer's versatility.

JARGON

> *Partitioning* enables you to make one hard drive look like multiple hard drives to your computer. Creating multiple partitions is a good idea when dealing with large hard drives. I usually partition each of my hard drives into three partitions: a small partition for the operating system, around 5GB, and two equal-sized data partitions with the remaining space. I try to avoid having partitions bigger than 30GB because the larger a partition is, the less efficiently it stores data.

Reinstalling Windows and Everything Else Periodically

The final possible way to freshen up system performance is to periodically reformat your hard drive and reinstall your operating system and core applications. This can be time-consuming and requires careful planning and attention, especially in regard to backing up all your essential data. This process will require an extra hard drive or writable media to back up all your data.

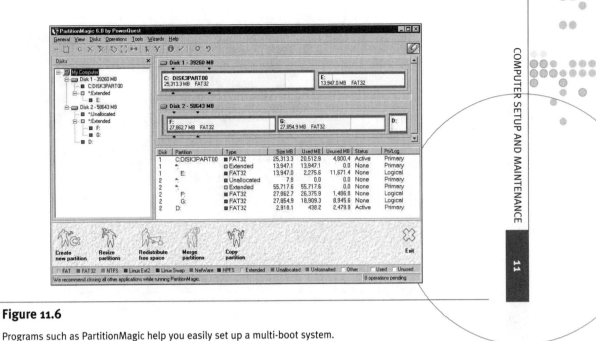

Figure 11.6

Programs such as PartitionMagic help you easily set up a multi-boot system.

FINDING ANSWERS TO INEVITABLE COMPUTER PROBLEMS

You are undoubtedly going to run into problems during your computer-using tenure, problems that are not solved after thorough exploration of the help files or even through reasoned intuition or trial-and-error problem solving. There are probably things in this book that you have questions about. In these situations, you have a huge resource of support known as the Internet, and the millions that use it. I get help all the time from strangers, and as a good netizen on rare occasions I help strangers out too. This is how the Internet works: It is a digitopia.

Your problem-solving Internet friends are very similar to your research friends I discussed earlier. A good search engine like Google, message boards, and newsgroups together will help you find the answer to pretty much any question, or the solution to any problem (see Figures 11.7 and 11.8).

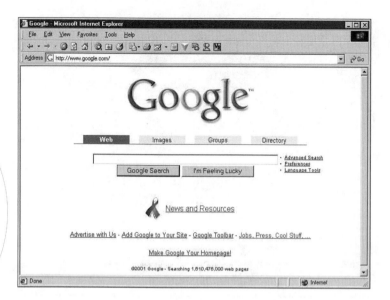

Figure 11.7

Google search engine, oracle of the Internet, can find almost anything.

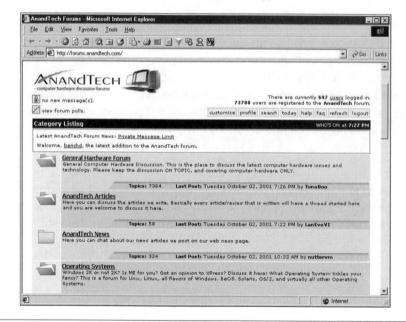

Figure 11.8

AnandTech (Anandtech.com), one of the largest tech Web sites on the Internet, has a very well trafficked message board for getting your tech questions answered.

Make sure you use a free e-mail account like Hotmail when posting questions, or registering for forums or newsgroup sites, because you don't want your personal e-mail address to be posted in public ever (if you learn one thing from this book let it be this) (see Figure 11.9). Spambots troll the Internet 24/7 looking to add any e-mail address they find to their nefarious spam mailing lists.

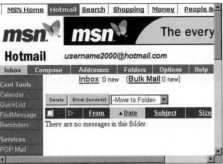

Figure 11.9

Free e-mail accounts like Hotmail are good to have when posting in public areas on the Internet.

Do not be needy either. Only look for help after you have tried your best solving your own problems, by reading the software and/or hardware's help files and applying some common sense, trial and error, and totally random attempts at a solution. This approach is advantageous to you (in raising your level of competence) and to the Web community (who only have so much problem-solving energy in them).

Many Internet users, because they don't have to look you in the face and they have the protection of anonymity, tend to find any occasion available to rip on you—*flame* is the Internet term for it. Sometimes it is justified; sometimes the person has issues. Ignore it and get on with your life. Why waste time in flame wars when you could be making movies?

P R O J E C T **1**

RESEARCHING YOUR CAMCORDER PURCHASE ONLINE

Go online and research—taking notes and bookmarking useful sites—your camcorder purchase using the following resources:

- Search engines (Google.com recommended)
- Newsgroups (Google Groups newsgroup reader recommended)
- Price Search engines (Pricegrabber.com and Shopper.com recommended)

Maintain a summary section at the top of the notes where you periodically summarize the latest status of your research. This keeps you from getting overwhelmed with your recorded data.

P R O J E C T **2**

RESEARCHING YOUR CAMCORDER PURCHASE LOCALLY

Once you find a few camcorders you are interested in, find a local store or stores that carry them so you can test the merchandise in person (see Figure P2.1). When going to the store, bring some of your notes and a pen with you—so you can make more notes.

Figure P2.1

Checking out your camcorder options in person can help finalize your purchasing decision.

CHECKING A RETAILER'S REPUTATION

Once you are ready to purchase your camcorder, visit a retailer rating site to ensure you are buying from a legitimate retailer (see Figure P3.1).

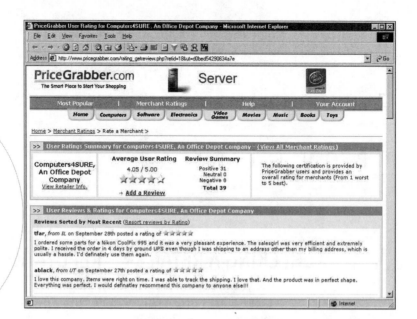

Figure P3.1

You can view retailer ratings, including user comments, at Web sites like Pricegrabber.com.

P R O J E C T **4**

GETTING FAMILIAR WITH ONLINE SUPPORT RESOURCES

Using a search engine like Google.com and a newsgroup search tool like Google Groups, find newsgroups, message boards, and forums where you can get answers to your computer and video editing questions. (I am not getting kickbacks from Google; they just have a good service.) Register to a few of the best, so that you can post questions—and give back by answering others' questions (when you can).

PART III

SHOOTING VIDEO: CAPTURING THE BEST QUALITY FOOTAGE

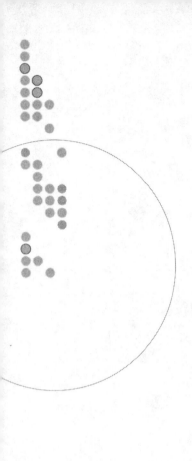

CHAPTER 12

THE LIMITS OF AUTO MODE: WHEN AND HOW TO GO MANUAL

Most of the time you can shoot very good quality video in full automatic mode, at least if you tend to do most of your shooting in average to well-lit areas. However, under some shooting conditions, such as low light or bright light, going manual is the only way to generate adequate picture quality. All camcorders offer some level of manual control; manual focus, exposure, and shutter speeds are some of the most common controls. Only a few of the highest end camcorders allow you to control everything in manual—even sound—if you want to.

The difficulty level varies, but most consumer models only have a handful of manual options to learn. Getting a good idea of what your control options are, and then practicing with your particular camcorder, is the best way to hone your manual skills.

AUTO MODE

All camcorders can be operated in automatic mode, in which the camcorder fully controls focus, exposure, white balance, shutter speed, and sometimes gain (see Figure 12.1). Most camcorders allow you to go manual on one or more of these controls while keeping everything else in auto mode. In fact, even if you want to go full manual, only a few high-end DV models will let you.

Figure 12.1

Most camcorders have a dial or similar control that allows you to operate in full automatic mode, or various other modes.

The advantages of auto mode are obvious; it makes camcorder operation effortless. The disadvantage is that sometimes the auto mode settings fail to produce good image quality. Or perhaps you just want to do something different, such as adding offbeat artistic effects, softening focus, or altering exposure. Furthermore, you may want to go into progressive mode—if your camcorder has that feature—so that you can extract full frame stills from your video. In these cases you need to resort to manual settings. Ideally, you should only go as manual as you need to. For example, if you want to set the focus, just select manual focus, and leave everything else in auto mode. Again, most mid-range and lower-end camcorders will never let you go into full manual mode anyway.

GOING MANUAL

Manual mode is not the solution to everything. For instance, if your camcorder has a small CCD, you won't improve the low-light performance all that much by changing your manual settings. Manual mode is much like computer tweaking; performance gains are noticeable but they are rarely tremendous. Mastering manual settings, in my opinion, results in ten percent better video quality overall. Most of the time, it will not matter, but situations will arise where it will prove beneficial.

If your interest in manual settings is for artistic effects, remember that you are going to get more versatility and control by adding effects within the computer editing environment. One exception would be selective focus, such as when you want the foreground of your video in focus and the background out of focus. Though you could also do this on the computer, it is much easier to do while filming.

MANUAL SETTINGS AND MODES

This section covers all the various manual settings and modes you might find on your digital video camcorder. Try to focus on the ones that you think would be most useful to you. No need to memorize features and settings that you are never going to use.

Progressive Video Mode

Going into progressive video mode (if your camcorder allows it) is ideal if you want to extract full resolution stills from your video later on. Basically, when you are in progressive video mode, it is like taking 30 digital pictures per second (see Figure 12.2). The resolution of these pictures is 720×480, which is perfect for the Web or e-mail, but not good enough for photo quality printing.

Figure 12.2

When shooting in progressive video mode—if your camcorder has this feature—your video doubles as 30 still images per second, each 720×480.

You will also need to change the aspect ratio to 4:3 for any stills taken from a DV camcorder. Any image-editing program can do this. Stills grabbed from interlaced video need to be resized as well. I imagine this sounds confusing, but it's a common issue with digital video formats. The resolution does not reflect the aspect ratio. For instance, SVCD video (which is a video CD format that falls between VCD and DVD quality) is encoded at 480×480, which is a 1:1 aspect. However, SVCD video looks perfectly normal displayed on a 4:3 aspect TV—where it fills the whole 4:3 aspect ratio (see Figure 12.3).

Manual Shutter Speed

Manually lowering your shutter speed brightens your video. This effect occurs because you are increasing the time allotted to capture each frame, allowing more information to be recorded. However, lowering the shutter speed also introduces more motion blur in your picture. For example, if you dropped the shutter speed really low—below 100fps—and filmed a spinning ceiling fan, the video would pick up blurry streaks instead of the fan blades (see Figure 12.4). Nonetheless, a little motion blur is always preferable to video that is too dark to see. Lowering the frame rate (ideally to 1/30 or 1/60) also gives your video a more film-like quality.

Figure 12.3

On the left, SVCD video as it appears in 1:1 aspect ratio. On the right, as it appears when played back at normal TV aspect ratio. Bottom line: Because everything displayed on TV will appear in 4:3 (640×480) aspect ratio, pixel resolution does not have to conform to the 4:3 aspect.

Figure 12.4

If the shutter speed is too low, motion appears blurred. Set the shutter speed higher to avoid this effect.

To capture fast action like sports, raise the shutter speed. For example, if you want to analyze your golf swing, you need the highest shutter speed possible so you can pause any frame and make out your exact form. High shutter speeds will hurt low light performance, but most sporting events usually take place under well-lit circumstances.

Manual White Balance

Automatic white balance varies among camcorders. Many users are not so concerned with exacting white balance. If you need accurate whites, and you are not getting them in auto mode, manual white balance will usually work well. Some camcorders let you point to a white object to set the balance, while other cams offer a less precise *jog dial*–driven range setting (see Figure 12.5). If your shooting environment changes, you will have to reset your white balance settings.

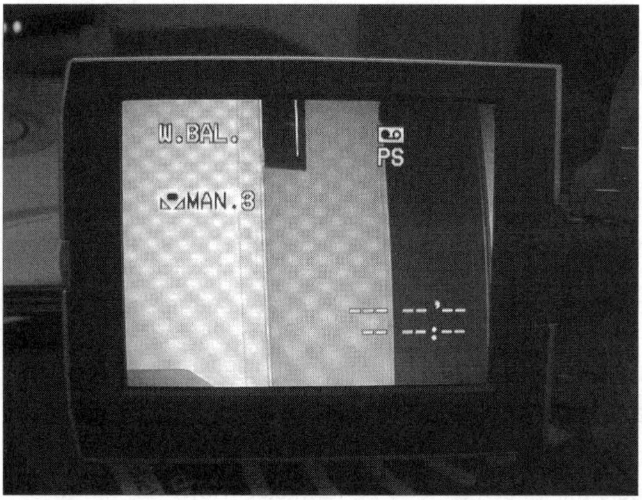

Figure 12.5

Most camcorders allow you to adjust your white balance. The figure above is the manual white balance control screen from my JVC camcorder.

Manual Exposure

Exposure controls the aperture of the camera, allowing more or less picture information into your camcorder's CCD. This affects how bright your picture is, as well as the depth of field.

The depth of field determines what is in focus and not in focus in your video field. A wide depth of field results in everything being in focus; a narrow depth of field results in just the foreground being in focus (see Figure 12.6). If you set the exposure high, which means the aperture is wide open, you will get a brighter picture with a wide depth of field. If you set it low, you will get a dimmer picture with a shallow depth of field.

Figure 12.6

The picture on the left demonstrates a shallow depth of field where the flower is in focus, but the background is out of focus. The picture on the right demonstrates a large depth of field where everything is in focus.

Exposure is useful to control the lighting of your video and for creative focus control. However, mastering focus control takes a lot of practice. Camcorders vary in their exposure controls—most just have a numbered plus/minus range. A few of the top models use F-stops, which is the standard for exposure measurement in the film camera world.

Most camcorders also come with a number of easily selectable auto exposure modes (AE), each of which is optimized for certain shooting conditions. For instance, the Sony DCR-TRV900 has five modes: Aperture priority, Shutter Speed priority, Sports Lesson, Sunset & Moon, and Low Lux. This gives users who are squeamish about controlling the exposure five easy options, which match five of the more common exposure-trying shooting situations.

Image Stabilization

Image stabilization systems compensate for mild camera shaking by the camera user. In old camcorders this affected video performance. However, the most recent stabilization technology has no deleterious effect on picture quality (see Figure 12.7). Most users should probably use it when not using a tripod (although I find a subtly unsteady picture to look more natural sometimes).

Figure 12.7

Disabling image stabilization will cause you to have a shakier picture, unless you have an incredibly steady hand or are using a tripod.

Manual Focus

Manual focus is probably the most commonly used of the manual settings. Many automatic focus systems fail in poor lighting. If the lighting is too low, the focus system will just keep focusing in and out *ad infinitum*. The only solution is to disable the automatic focus and focus manually.

Furthermore, you can use the manual focus to create artistic effects, such as to soften the picture (see Figure 12.8). However, this effect is easy to achieve digitally in most video editing software, where you have more control. I advise against using manual focus like this unless you feel the digital effect does not look as authentic to you. However, if you want something that is off center in focus (remember, the auto focus mechanism is based on the center of the frame), then you need to use the manual focus. Also, if you are altering exposure to focus only on an object in the foreground, you will need to use manual focus.

Figure 12.8

The two split screen images show the difference between altering focus in camera (the first picture), or adding a digital out of focus effect with your computer (the second picture).

Special Effects

All camcorders come with a number of special effects that you can apply to your footage in real-time. While it can be fun to shoot in black and white, or using other special effects, again, applying effects should wait for the computer video editing environment. On your computer you can add an effect and then eliminate it if you don't like it (see Figure 12.9). You can't do that if you add the effects in camera.

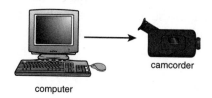

camcorder

computer

Figure 12.9

You can add in-camera effects to your footage while exporting from or into the computer on many camcorders.

I do, however, advocate using on-camera special effects in another way. If you edit a video on your computer and decide you want it to be in black and white, rendering it in black and white on your computer can be time consuming—depending on the speed of your system. A potentially quicker option is to turn on your camcorder's built-in black and white special effect and output the video to your camcorder. This will turn all the footage you import into your camera into black and white on-the-fly. You can also add in-camera video effects when outputting your video on many camcorders. So make sure you know all your camcorder's built-in effects, as you may be able to use them in post editing.

Manual Gain Settings

Most camcorders have some sort of gain control, usually referred to in the manual as AGC (Auto Gain Control). AGC digitally brightens your picture in low-light conditions. A side effect of AGC is reduced picture quality. Your picture is brighter, but contains digital arti-facts (see Figure 12.10). Video noise (also known as digital snow) is the most common side effect of AGC. Most camcorders allow you to enable or disable AGC. You can also manu-ally adjust the gain so as to find the best compromise between picture visibility and reduc-tion of digital artifacts. I usually prefer to disable AGC and use other means of brightening my video, but with some camcorders, you need it if you want any picture at all in some low-light environments.

Figure 12.10

On the left with no AGC, the picture is very dim. On the right with AGC enabled, visibility is improved but artifacts (digital snow) are also introduced.

BEST SETTINGS FOR VARIOUS SHOOTING CONDITIONS

In the next few sections, you will find recommended settings for obtaining the best picture in different shooting environments. Use them as the basis for manually setting your own camcorder. Every camcorder is different, so you will have to find your own perfect settings for your rig.

Low-Light/Night Shooting

Low-light and night shooting are the most trying environments for your digital camcorder. Mastering the following manual settings for these situations is the most important skill you can develop:

- Lower shutter speeds
- Increase exposure settings
- Turn your Auto Video Gain (AGC) on, off, or manually adjust it
- Use special night shot settings
- Manual focus

All of the above settings will increase the brightness of your picture, but each has drawbacks. I prefer lowering the shutter speeds to around 1/30 or 1/60 (30 or 60 shutter openings per second) and setting exposure to the maximum (see Figure 12.11). Manually adjusting shutter speeds makes the biggest difference without sacrificing video resolution.

Figure 12.11

On the left, shutter speed is left on auto, resulting in a very dim picture. On the right I manually lowered shutter speed to 1/15, resulting in a much lighter picture.

 Lowering shutter rate below 1/60 in regular video mode and 1/30 in progressive video mode will lower your video resolution. However, often you may find this a necessary compromise to get a brighter picture.

Some camcorders feature special low-light shooting modes. Most of these low-light modes just utilize optimized shutter, exposure, and gain settings. Sony has a special mode called NightShot, which projects an invisible infrared light about ten feet forward, allowing you to shoot video in absolute darkness (within a range of ten feet) (see Figure 12.12). The resulting picture is a green-hued black and white.

Figure 12.12

Sony NightShot allows you to shoot video in total darkness at distances of up to ten feet. NightShot works by emitting an infrared beam and recording the reflection.

If things get too dark, you usually have to go to manual focus, as your auto focus will often fail.

Bright Sunlight or Excessive Indoor Light

Bright sunlight or excessive indoor lighting is the second most common difficult shooting situation. The following manual settings will help:

- Increase shutter speeds (see Figure 12.13)
- Lower exposure
- Try one of the Auto Exposure settings related to sunlight if your camcorder has them
- Try to keep bright sun-filled windows out of your shots

Figure 12.13

The left image depicts video with the shutter speed set low (1/30): The sky is too bright and washed out. The right image depicts video with the shutter speed set high (1/300): The sky and clouds are now clearly visible.

Too much light can lead to overexposure, which causes an overly bright picture and/or washed out color.

Sports and High-Speed Shooting

If you want the best quality video of high-speed action subjects, you need to go manual. The following manual settings will help:

- Increase shutter speed
- Raise exposure

The shutter speed setting is the most important manual setting when shooting fast action. Exposure settings are less important—and can probably be left on auto—though manually setting them can ensure that everything remains in focus (large depth of field), ideal if you are shooting a large playing field.

Mixed Locations

In totally mixed locations, you are going to have to decide between trying to get the best picture in manual, or just accepting what auto mode delivers and saving yourself the headache. Try the following:

- Full manual
- Full auto

For most users, I would advise sticking with auto settings in environments like this, but the discriminating videographer might go full manual.

CHAPTER 13

A PRIMER ON LIGHTING

Lighting can be one of the most important aspects of your video quality. Too much or too little light can result in very poor and sometimes zero picture quality. Besides getting the best low-light performing camcorder possible, you can take advantage of many devices and techniques to tame the forces of light and dark. Some of these devices and techniques, such as an external camcorder light or manual settings, can be employed when shooting home video. However, some of the more advanced and elaborate options explained in this chapter are best used only for professional video production and amateur filmmaking.

Home video should always be easy, recreational, and most importantly, transparent. If you try to break out a professional light kit for your family videos, or stress over manual settings, your family will hate you, you will miss shots, and your videos will look odd. Home movies are supposed to look unprofessional. As long as the video quality is there, and the moment is captured, no viewer cares about little flaws—in fact those flaws are endearing.

DV UNDERPERFORMANCE IN LOW LIGHT

As we've stressed in previous chapters, DV camcorders often perform poorly in low light. The low light weakness results from putting more pixels on ever-smaller CCDs, which yields less light pick-up capability. Realize that most home shooting environments would qualify as being low light, so this problem will affect most users.

If you have ever been to a TV studio, you know how brightly they light everything. Excessive set lighting is what it takes just to achieve an effect of normal lighting. Some TV shows shoot with film, which requires more light, but major lighting is used with video cameras, too.

Poor lighting is actually why many soap operas (especially older ones) look so bad compared to a prime time show. Because of low budgets and faster shooting schedules, they skimp on lighting, so everything appears darker in the final print.

If low-light performance is important to you, the best solution is to get a camcorder that performs competently in low light. Ideally, most models listed below will give you the option of never having to worry about lighting, at least for general home video footage. If you want your home video to look like a prime time sitcom, you are going to have to employ some external lighting solutions. However, if you just want to be able to shoot video in low light as good as your human eye can see, many of the camcorders listed below will come close. Keep in mind though, the majority of DV camcorders will not.

The following are the best low-light camcorders (in order of performance):

1. Sony DCR-VX2000 ($2400) (the best by far)
2. Canon GL-1 ($1700)
3. Sony TRV-900 ($1500)
4. Canon Optura 100MC ($1500)
5. Canon Optura Pi ($900)
6. Panasonic DV201/401/601/701/801 ($500–$800)
7. JVC 9800u ($900)

The VX2000 is a step above every camcorder listed in terms of its low-light performance (see Figure 13.1). So if you can handle the size and cost, nothing else compares to the VX2000 in terms of low-light performance (or image quality for that matter).

Figure 13.1

The Sony VX2000 performs better than any other sub-$5000 camcorder in low light.

LIGHTING OPTIONS

The next step is to learn the options available and techniques involved in lighting your video. If you grew up in the days of film cameras (8mm and Super 8mm), you might actually feel spoiled by an average performing DV camcorder, as film cameras in general require more lighting than even some of the worst low-light performing DV models (see Figure 13.2). However, if you grew up more recently, you are probably not as forgiving.

Figure 13.2

Back in the day of Super 8mm film cameras you could not shoot indoors without using some type of external lighting. Handheld spotlights like this were common.

Making Use of Available Light

Before resorting to an external option, you should take full advantage of all the light sources already present in your shooting environment. If you are shooting at home and the picture is too dark, make sure all the lights in the room are turned on. Moreover, try to get your subjects close to any available light.

You could also move lamps in from other rooms. Cheap halogen lights are a pretty good non-directional light source.

Camcorder Light

Camcorder lights are the most convenient external lighting option. If your camcorder has a hot accessory shoe, you can get a model that will operate off the battery of your camcorder (see Figure 13.3). If you need a brighter light, you will need to get a light that operates off its own battery source. Sony and Canon make external lights that use the same rechargeable batteries used in their camcorders.

Figure 13.3

Many camcorders include an accessory shoe where you can add an external light.

These lights will enable you to shoot in situations where you otherwise would not get any picture, as well as brighten your picture in mildly low-lit situations. However, they are not the most natural lighting solution. Limited by size, they can display a relatively narrow and flashlight-esque beam, which is better for shooting close-up scenes with a few people in the frame as opposed to wider shots. For home video, and even documentary work, they are a good choice. If you are doing amateur filmmaking, however, you should probably choose a more natural-looking solution.

Lighting Kit

A *lighting kit* is a generic term originating in the film world. Professional lighting kits usually consist of an arsenal of special high-powered lights and accessories such as barn doors and scrims, which allow you to control your light sources (see Figure 13.4). An amateur film kit, on the other hand, could be anything you can think of that does some of the same things. A professional light kit costs thousands; a good do-it-yourself (DIY) can cost well under two hundred (see Figure 13.5).

Figure 13.4

Gels, barn doors, and scrims are advanced lighting tools useful for amateur filmmaking and professional video applications.

Figure 13.5

Professional light kits run well over a thousand dollars, and are not appropriate for home video applications.

Light Kit Terminology

Scrim—A filter made of semi-transparent fabric or wire mesh used to control the intensity of the light source.

Scrim—A filter made of semi-transparent fabric or wire mesh used to control the intensity of the light source.

Barn doors—Metal flaps that fit over film lights and allow you to control the direction and throw size of the light.

Colored gels—Colored film sheets that can be used to change the color of light.

Diffusers—Large white surfaces (such as a sheet), which are used to reflect direct light into wider, softer (more diffuse) rays.

DIY Light Kit Options

The easiest DIY light kit can be picked up at Home Depot or a similar store (see Figure 13.6). They have a 1000-watt Dual Head telescoping tripod worklight (composed of two 500-watt lights) for $50.

Figure 13.6

This portable light from Home Depot makes a great starter light kit for an amateur filmmaker.

Each 500-watt halogen light can be turned on and off separately. If you are just doing home video, you don't need more than one. If you are an amateur filmmaker, two would be great. If you really want to add functionality to this light you can buy inline dimmers ($5–$40). Inline dimmers allow you to precisely adjust the intensity of the light. To install an inline dimmer, you need to splice the power cord, so make sure you can handle this task before buying the dimmers. And make sure after installing that you reinsulate the power cord with serious amounts of electric tape.

If you are an amateur filmmaker, you need to buy or improvise your own scrims, barn doors, colored gels, and diffusers. You will probably have to improvise or modify anything you buy from a professional film supplier, as it won't fit out of the box on a Home Depot purchased light.

You should be able to fashion your own diffuser with a sheet, and barn doors with black painted sheet metal, or even really dense cardboard. As far as scrims and colored gels go, while you could probably fashion your own I think it is better to buy them, as they are not tremendously expensive. You can also buy additional incandescent clip-on lights that attach to your light stand, for more lighting options.

If you prefer or own clip-on lights, you can build your own lighting stands. For each stand, use a five-gallon plastic bucket, plumbing pipes, and concrete. Pour a half bag of concrete in the bucket (about 25lbs) and then mix with water per the directions on the bag. Then take a two-foot-long (or 18 inches), one-inch threaded galvanized pipe and place it in the middle of the concrete. Let it set. Then add any arrangement of pipes to get whatever size (6 feet, 8 feet) and shape (straight, or t-shaped) stand you want. The great thing about using the threaded modular pipes is that you can do different things, and you can quickly disassemble everything for easy transport.

FILM AND VIDEO LIGHTING

Film and video lighting has developed into a rather exacting science. Moviemakers usually hire a director just for lighting. Lighting is important because film, and to a lesser degree video, does not have the low-light sensitivity that the human eye has, so external lighting is required to brighten things up and make them look normal to the viewer. (I think in general the industry overcompensates, causing most TV and film indoor shots to be lit brighter than reality.)

The main terms in lighting are color temperature, back light, fill light, and key light. Color temperature has to do with lighting intensity; the other terms have to do with how the light is positioned on the subject.

Color Temperature

We look at light in terms of brightness, cinematographers, videographers, and even photographers look at light in terms of color temperature. Every kind of light emits a certain color, and this is called the color temperature (see Figure 13.7). Color temperature is measured in degrees Kelvin. Most light (both electric and natural) ranges from 2000 degrees Kelvin up to 7500 degrees (see Figure 13.7). The higher the color temperature, the more bluish things are; the lower the color temperature, the more orange. This rule is easy to remember as everyone knows a blue flame is hotter than an orange flame.

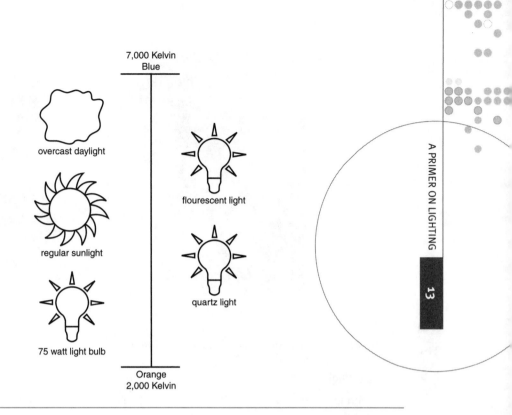

Figure 13.7

This diagram illustrates the different color temperatures of common light sources.

We don't notice the different color temperatures so much because the human optic system has built-in white balance, like most camcorders. Except that the human white balance works better.

Knowing color temperature is important, as it makes it easier to adjust your manual white balance correctly. However, because many camcorders now allow you to set white balance to something white in the frame, this skill is not essential.

Positioning Your Lighting

Knowing how to position your lights is crucial in achieving natural well-lit footage. Every movie and TV studio uses three main kinds of light: the key light, the backlight, and the fill light. They are often used together, hence the term *three-point lighting*.

Key Light

The key light is aptly named, as it is the main, most direct, and most prominent of the three types of lights. Key lights are generally pointed toward the subject, slightly off axis so as to not be too severe and obvious (see Figure 13.8). The key light should match the light level of the scene (it should not be obviously brighter).

Figure 13.8

The key light brightens your subject, but it also adds excessive contrast and shadows.

Backlight

With just one light source (the key light), the subject looks one-dimensional and shadowy. If they have a wall behind them, it might as well be a mug shot—not exactly natural lighting. A back light eliminates the back wall shadowing and lightens areas from behind (see Figure 13.9). Though subtle, the back light also helps to add three dimensionality to the subject.

Figure 13.9

A back light eliminates any wall shadows, as well as illuminating the back of the subject, which adds depth.

Fill Light

With both the key light and back light in action, the subject still suffers from excessive contrast—some places on the face are light and shiny, while other places have dark shadows. A fill light softens the shadows and lowers the contrast (see Figure 13.10). A fill light is softer than a backlight and key light, and literally fills in all the harsh shadows with soft highlights. A fill light is achieved by using a diffused light source positioned on the opposite axis of the key light in front of the subject. You can achieve a diffused light source in a number of ways. Try shining a light on a sheet, or using one of those Chinese paper globe lights.

Figure 13.10

The addition of a fill light further softens the shadows and contrast, providing for a more natural lighting effect.

OUTDOOR LIGHTING

Morning and late afternoon are the best times to shoot outdoors, as the sun is at the most optimal angle at those times and delivers more of a muted light (see Figure 13.11). If you can't shoot outdoors at these times then try using shade—under a tree, or better yet under many trees—in any way you can.

The most important lighting tool when shooting outdoors is some type of reflection and diffusion material to neutralize the contrast-producing light source of the sun. You can get something like this from any photo store, but one of the more popular DIY solutions is to obtain foam core from the hardware store. It usually has a shiny side for more light reflection, and a matte side for more diffuse light reflection.

Figure 13.11

The golden hour occurs an hour before sunset, and is one of the best times of the day to shoot. It's also naptime for my dog.

You can also use bedsheets as diffusion filters for excessive sunlight. This requires some sort of framing, which can get rather involved. If you have anything nearby that you can hook a clothesline to then using a sheet is an easier solution. Ultimately, I think using a neutral density filter on your camcorder or just shooting in the shade is a much easier and still effective solution compared to trying to erect a bedsheet superstructure.

CHAPTER 14

CAMCORDER SOUND

Video is important, but so is sound quality. DV camcorders have clearly improved the video quality consumers are able to achieve in their home movies. However, sound quality has not made as great of an improvement, at least not yet. Often, sound quality is not even as good as older analog camcorders. One of the disadvantages of DV technology so far has been an increased amount of motor noise being picked up during video recording. This problem has improved to some degree, but it continues to be an issue across the whole DV camcorder industry.

This chapter presents a few solutions that can correct or minimize this problem. The most obvious and ideal for most users is to make sure you buy a camcorder that overcomes these sound issues entirely. However, popular models like pocket camcorders all have this problem to some degree. Purchasing an external microphone is sometimes your only alternative. While this will usually not eliminate 100% of the problem, it will often significantly improve things.

THE PROBLEM WITH MOTOR NOISE

The tape drive on DV camcorders operates at twice the speed of previous analog camcorders. This results in greater friction and consequently more audible noise. This motor noise is often picked up to some degree by your camcorder's microphone. The fact that DV camcorders are often ultra-compact only makes the problem worse, as the microphone is closer to the source of the noise.

The automatic audio gain control found on most camcorders further complicates the problem. This feature raises the audio gain in a quiet room, so you can pick up silent voices, but you also tend to pick up the hum or whine of your tape drive motor.

Motor Noise Solutions

The following solutions can help reduce and even eliminate motor noise from your video:

- Better hardware engineering of the tape drive to reduce noise
- Built-in audio DSP (digital signal processor) chips, which are programmed to remove tape drive noise from your audio
- Larger camcorders and/or better mic placement to isolate the microphone from the tape drive
- Manual audio gain controls
- Use of an external microphone

Most manufacturers are working on the first solution. Audio DSP chips are only available on a few of the higher model camcorders like the Sony DCR-TRV900. Manual audio gain is found on even fewer models. Most camcorders allow you to use an external microphone (as long as they have an external microphone input). So at the very least, you want a camcorder with an external mic jack.

Camcorders Providing Good Sound Quality

The following are good options if sound quality is important to you:

- **Sony DCR-VX2000**—Large body camcorder with high quality mic in a position well removed from tape drive.
- **Canon XL1**—Professionally neutral sound quality.
- **Sony DCR-TRV900**—Audio DSP chip eliminates all tape drive noise.
- **Canon Optura Pi or 100MC with DM-50 external hot shoe microphone**—One of the best consumer-oriented hot shoe microphones gives these camcorders good quality audio (see Figure 14.1).

Figure 14.1

The DM-50 external microphone added to the Optura 100MC makes a great camcorder even better.

AN EXTERNAL MICROPHONE PRIMER

Using an external microphone almost always raises your sound quality. If you are not sat-isfied with your onboard sound then your only real solution is an external mic. If you are happy with your onboard sound, and you are just shooting home video, count yourself lucky, and don't bother with an external microphone and its inconveniences.

If you decide you want to try an external microphone, consider your options before you buy. If your camcorder comes with a hot shoe (also called an intelligent accessory shoe), you'll probably find an external microphone option by the same manufacturer. If you have an accessory shoe, but it is not hot, your choices all involve having a cable between the mic and the external sound input jack. If you don't have a shoe, but you do have a micro-phone input jack, then you can purchase an accessory shoe adapter ($15) that mounts to the bottom of your camcorder (see Figure 14.2).

Figure 14.2

If your camcorder lacks an accessory shoe you can buy a shoe adapter that will attach to the bottom of your camcorder.

Hot Shoe Microphones

These microphones are made to operate with your camcorder conveniently, transmitting the sound through the accessory shoe of your camcorder—no need for a dangling mic cable. The only con is that you usually have limited options, as most companies only make one hot shoe microphone model. So if the microphone offered does not have high qual-ity sound (and many don't) then the convenience is lost. For instance, Sony only has one hot shoe mic—the ECM-HS1—and the quality is bad (see Figure 14.3).

Figure 14.3

The Sony ECM-HS1 mic is a hot shoe zoom mic, which picks up sound in line with the zoom control of the camcorder. However, the sound quality is disappointing.

The only hot shoe mic I have found that has good sound quality is the Canon DM-50, which works on the newer Canon Camcorders like the Optura Pi and 100MC. The DM-50 is nice and compact and has a switchable pickup pattern, stereo mode for normal recording situations, and shotgun mono, which is ideal for picking up directional sound sources like a distant speaker (see Figure 14.4).

Figure 14.4

The DM-50 external microphone only works on newer Canon camcorders with a compatible hot shoe; the sound quality is very good.

Universal Camcorder Microphones

If you don't have a hot shoe or don't like the hot shoe mics available, don't fret. The non–hot shoe microphone options are far more diverse. Before you buy, determine your desired applications. If you just want better sound quality for your home video then you probably should get a good quality stereo camcorder mic. For professional applications and amateur filmmaking, you might be better served with a shotgun mic. Keep in mind that most shotgun microphones record in mono, but this is better for picking up voices.

Stereo Microphones

For home video applications, a good stereo microphone is probably your best external mic solution. News crews and filmmakers use mono (non-stereo) shotguns because they are looking to capture and control specific sound sources such as a single actor or interviewee, and they don't want peripheral noise.

Home video is totally different because you need to cover wider areas, and you only have one microphone to do it (see Figure 14.5). If you were making a serious film you would mic each person, but that is not a realistic setup for home video. Moreover, I think if you are just starting with amateur filmmaking, a good quality stereo mic might be better to work with in the beginning because it will keep things simpler.

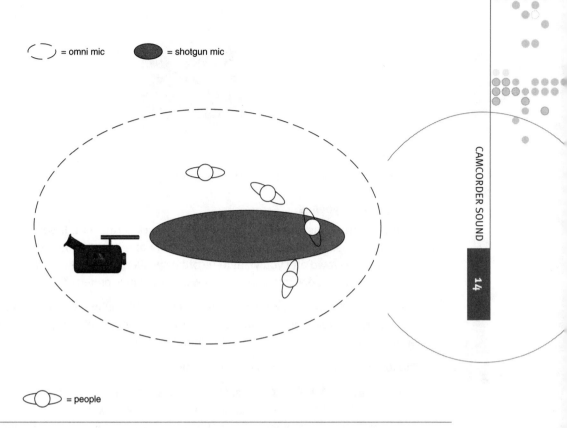

= omni mic   = shotgun mic

= people

Figure 14.5

This diagram shows the different mic pickup patterns. The dotted circle represents the average built-in stereo camcorder mic, and the shaded circle represents a shotgun mic.

The following are recommended stereo microphones:

- **Sony ECM-MS908C (price: $100)**—Very good quality stereo camcorder mic, highly recommended (see Figure 14.6).

Figure 14.6

The Sony ECM-MS908C is a high quality stereo camcorder mic that will work with any camcorder with a microphone input jack.

- **Audio Technica ATR-25 (price: $40-60)**—Average quality, but inexpensive (see Figure 14.7).

Figure 14.7

The Audio Technica ATR-25 is a low-cost external stereo mic.

Shotgun Microphones

Shotgun microphones have a long and narrow pick up pattern. If you need to pick up sound from specific areas, rejecting all peripheral noise, buy a shotgun mic. For instance, if you are in a crowd and you want to record a speaker, you want a shotgun microphone. Or if you are doing documentary interviews, a shotgun is preferred.

The two main types of shotgun mics are supercardioid and hypercardioid. The distinction is that a hypercardioid mic has an even narrower and longer pickup pattern than a super-cardioid. Supercardioids are the more common of the two.

The following are recommended shotgun mics:

- **Sennheiser ME-66/K6 (price: $600)**—Professional news videographers use this mic. The ME-66/K6 is a very long mic, so it won't fit very well on smaller camcorders. I would only recommend this for professional applications and serious filmmaking (see Figure 14.8).

Figure 14.8

The Sennheiser ME-66/K6 is a professional shotgun mic of excellent quality.

- **Sennheiser MKE 300 (price: $200)**—A compact and affordable shotgun mic that still delivers good quality, recommended for smaller camcorders (see Figure 14.9).

Figure 14.9

The Sennheiser MKE 300 is a good quality compact shotgun mic for smaller camcorders.

Wireless Microphones

Wireless microphone systems are great for applications where you need to record one or more distant sound sources. If it was not for the high cost, I would be more inclined to recommend them. Prices on pro-end wireless systems (Sennheiser, Telex, Lectrosonics, Shure, Sony, Vega) can run over a thousand dollars per component.

Some reasonable wireless options are available. Azden and Samson make competent UHF wireless systems that sell for less than $500. A receiver that can control one (or in some cases two microphones) mounts on the accessory shoe of the camcorder (or attaches with Velcro tape), and then you can place lapel mics on your sound sources—you can also use handheld mics. If you are making a film, and don't have enough personnel for sound, this can be an effective solution.

Because wireless mics are not a mass consumer product, users pay a premium. With wireless mics, the more money you are willing to spend, the more quality you can expect to get. Every little increase in quality, however, is usually matched by a big jump in price.

The following are camcorder-mounted wireless systems worth considering:

- **Sennheiser EW112p (price: $500)**—A very good quality camera-mountable UHF receiver; includes one lav mic and transmitter (see Figure 14.10).

Figure 14.10

Sennheiser EW112p is a high quality wireless microphone system.

- **Shure VPL/93 (price: $400)**—VP3 VHF camcorder mountable receiver; includes microphone and transmitter.
- **Samson UHF (price: $300–$500)**—Camcorder mounted, several different models (see Figure 14.11).

Figure 14.11

Samson makes a pretty good quality camcorder mountable UHF mic system.

- **Azden IRR20 (price: $300)**—Camcorder mountable system that lets you use two mics simultaneously.
- **Sony WCS-999 (price: <$150)**—Affordable wireless lav system sold at consumer electronics stores like Best Buy, with good quality for the price (see Figure 14.12).

Figure 14.12

The Sony WCS-999 wireless system is small and cheap, and for the price it performs well.

WIND GUARDS

If you are shooting outside under windy circumstances, and you need to maintain pristine sound quality—for a professional application or film—you will need a professional wind guard. Most camcorders come with a wind cut switch, which enables an in-camera digital filter eliminating certain frequencies. Since this is invasive to your sound quality, it is not an ideal wind elimination solution.

Many external microphones include some sort of foam wind guard. While fine for light breezes, a wind guard is not effective for anything stronger. The two main wind screen types used in the professional field are the fur windscreen (see Figure 14.13) and the capsule windscreen. If you have ever seen a news camera team shooting outdoors, you probably have seen one of these guards in action.

Figure 14.13

Fur wind guards are used by field videographers to eliminate wind distortion.

The fur guard works well because the fur's non-uniform surface disperses any wind that hits it. A capsule guard—also called a Rycote—is a bit different, entirely encasing your microphone, leaving significant buffer space between itself and the microphone (see Figure 14.14). Wind hits the capsule guard, and deflects or is absorbed. The buffer space then makes sure the microphone stays isolated from any energy/sound transference. A capsule guard is more effective, but it is also larger and more expensive.

Figure 14.14

Capsule wind guards, called Rycotes, are the best way to neutralize the effect of wind on a microphone.

MASTERING LOW-LIGHT ENVIRONMENTS

The following four projects will help you hone your video skills. While filming in the various modes, talk out loud to the microphone intermittently, specifying what your settings are. This will help you figure out, when you watch the tape, what settings work best for your camcorder.

Make sure you disable AGC (Auto Gain Control) for all the shooting experiments (unless the step specifies enabling it). Try these steps:

1. Take a video in a low-light environment in auto mode.

2. Take a video in a low-light environment in the following various manual modes:

   a. Altering just the shutter speed

   b. Altering just the exposure

   c. Turning on just the AGC (Auto Gain Control)

   d. Manually setting the AGC

   e. Disabling the AGC

   f. Enabling any special low light mode that your camcorder may have

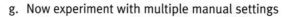

g. Now experiment with multiple manual settings

h. When you find settings you like, try manually setting the white balance and experimenting with the manual focus

3. If you have a video light, go through the above steps again with the light on.

4. Watch your recorded footage and then redo the entire project until you have found the best settings for your camcorder.

P R O J E C T **6**

MASTERING BRIGHTLY LIT ENVIRONMENTS

Take a video in a brightly lit environment—for example, outdoors on a sunny afternoon—going through all the steps listed in Project #5, except for the video light/ low-light setting mode steps.

P R O J E C T **7**

MASTERING FAST ACTION VIDEO

Take a video of a fast action scene (sports, fast moving cars, and so on) with the following settings:

- In Auto mode
- Alter just the shutter speed
- Alter just the exposure
- Alter both exposure and shutter speed

Review footage and repeat if necessary.

SELECTIVE FOCUS/EXPOSURE

The point of this project is to learn how to place an object/subject in the foreground in focus and the background out of focus, or to have everything in focus. Follow these steps:

1. Shoot a subject or object at close range. Make sure you have enough of the background in the picture, and the zoom is at 1x power.

2. Disable the auto focus.

3. Manually focus on your object/subject.

4. Lower the exposure as much as possible without making your picture too dim.

5. Lower the shutter speed as low as possible without introducing motion blur. If the object/subject is stationary, I would recommend 1/30 or 1/60, but you can experiment with lower. This should raise the light level of your picture.

6. Review footage and repeat if necessary.

7. Experiment with putting the midfield in focus or the entire field in focus.

PART **IV**

EDITING VIDEO: TURNING YOUR FOOTAGE INTO A MOVIE

ADVANCED PRIMER ON VIDEO/FILMMAKING: THE SCIENCE BEHIND THE ART OF CAPTURING GOOD FOOTAGE

We live in the age of science; as a result we tend to systemize how things are done. Believe it or not, a science to the world of video and film exists. To people that are naturally gifted at taking good video, some of these systems can seem obvious, but for the most part, they enable anyone (regardless of natural ability) to get an understanding of how to capture at least adequate-looking video. These systems are merely frameworks, and are constantly being improved upon, so don't take them as canon law. Use them merely as a reference point, and build up your own style from them.

EXPERIENCE-BASED SCIENCE OF VIDEOGRAPHY

While I think the best thing to do for home movies is often to just break out that camera and start shooting, some other options and steps can enhance your work. Furthermore, if you are making an amateur film or professional production, you should go through some preshoot planning steps before you can say action.

The textbook approach to anything tries to encompass the best of all available proven systems and truths. Experiential learning—what you pick up in the field—is the other spectrum of knowledge that is also very important. I gleaned the following tips from my own videography field experience.

Employing Multiple Camera Operators in Your Home Video

The one winning technique I have discovered in my video taking days is this: Employ your friends and family members to shoot some of the video. For example, if you are filming a party, and you are the sole operator of the camcorder, the footage is always going to reflect your subjective view. This makes for monotonous footage in the long run, no matter how talented and funny you are.

However, if you let two or three of your friends and family do some filming, you will end up with a far more well-rounded and interesting video that a wider audience will appreciate. In your choice of camera operators, I suggest this—the weirder the friend/family member, the better (however, also factor in competence). The attention of the viewer is intensified when your video has an offbeat character, as opposed to something that looks ordinary. This makes the difference between memorable and forgettable.

Employing Multiple Camcorders for Special Events

If you can afford it, buy a few inexpensive DV camcorders with long-life batteries for your wedding or other landmark events (you can sell the camcorders on eBay afterward) (see Figure 15.1). Just commission the camcorders to a few chosen friends and relatives through the ceremony and after events. Make sure they know how to use them, and pick people that are entertaining, or have good artistic senses, or ideally both. You will often end up with unforgettably authentic footage that no professional videographer could ever deliver.

Figure 15.1

The Panasonic PV-DV201 is an inexpensive basic DV camcorder that delivers on quality: a great budget choice.

THE TEXTBOOK SCIENCE OF SHOOTING GOOD VIDEO

The following sections discuss the currently accepted techniques of proper video taking. Use them as an absolute guide or merely as a base for developing your own unique video taking style.

Storyboarding

Storyboarding has been a part of motion pictures since the silent era. A storyboard is kind of like a cartoon version of your film; it also serves as an overall outline for your film. Each shot of a movie usually has its own cartoon. Each storyboard frame depicts how the director wants that shot to appear. This helps the director and cameraman visualize each film shot before actually filming. It also helps the cast and crew know what's going on in each shot, as well as where each shot fits into the entire film.

You don't have to be a talented artist to create your own storyboards. Stick figure artistry can be more than enough to convey the desired shot (see Figure 15.2). If you can't even handle that, you can use computer software that helps you to create your own storyboards (see Figure 15.3). Or you could just use a general computer art program like Paint Shop Pro. Some people use a character animation program called Poser to create storyboards.

Figure 15.2

Your storyboards don't have to be works of art.

Figure 15.3

Computer storyboarding software like Storyboard Quick makes creating storyboards easy.

While I would not recommend anyone storyboarding their family videos, you could assemble a shot list before a big event or trip (see Figure 15.4). This is just a list of things you want to get video of: Grandma Hilda, your children water skiing, or whatever you think is important that you don't want to forget.

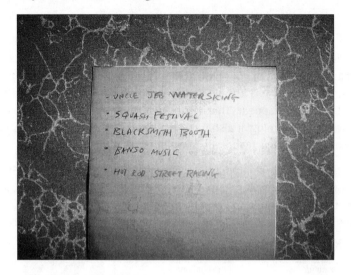

Figure 15.4

Creating a shot list can help you ensure you won't forget important video moments.

Video Technique Primer

Video techniques, like film lighting, have evolved into somewhat of a science. If you have good aesthetic senses, you probably already employ many of the techniques I am about to explain by instinct.

Proper Framing

The most fundamental shooting technique is proper framing of your object/subject. This universal technique can be applied in all shooting applications—home movies, amateur films, or professional applications. For instance, if you are shooting video of a subject, you need to have the right amount of headroom. No exact formula exists, but having half the video frame filled with empty space above their head is too much. Cutting their head in half is too little. The last frame of Figure 15.5 might be considered just right.

Advanced Framing

If your subject is looking at something toward the right of the picture, the proper way to frame them would be to have them over on the left of the frame, as opposed to the right or middle of the frame (see Figure 15.6). This framing method conveys to the viewer that the subject is looking at something. Trust me on this—it has been proven scientifically. If they are looking to the left, you would frame things exactly the opposite way.

Figure 15.5

Too much headroom; too little headroom; just right.

Figure 15.6

If your subject is looking at something, the film textbooks suggest framing them all the way to the left if they are looking right.

Shot Angles

Shooting at a downward angle, upward angle, or at eye level can all achieve different visual effects (see Figure 15.7). Shooting up at a villain is a common cinematography technique used to make the villain more menacing—larger than life. The viewer is made to feel small and overwhelmed. This technique is sometimes used by filmmakers to make Tom Cruise look taller, when in fact he is actually three feet tall (we're kidding here...).

Shooting at a downward angle makes the subject look less significant, possibly weaker, and child-like. A flat shooting angle would be neutral, denoting equality.

Figure 15.7

Shooting at a downward angle gives the audience a sense of superiority. Shooting at an upward angle can inspire fear or weakness in the viewer.

Correct Eye Lines

Whether shooting an amateur film or professional production, learning to shoot correct eye lines is important. Basically, your footage needs to convey whatever reality you want to present to the viewer. This seems easy, but if you shoot things incorrectly, the resulting video footage might look entirely different. For instance, if the script calls for your actors to be looking into each other's eyes, you don't want one actor appearing to look into space instead because you have the camera at a bad angle. The eyelines need to match. Mastering this takes practice. The general rule in achieving direct eyelines is to tell the actor to treat the camera like the other person. This means you will need to shoot each actor separately.

Most scenes are shot slightly off axis, which allows you to shoot an entire scene full of actors without having the cameras show up in the frame (see Figure 15.8). This technique, among others, was used to shoot the famous coffee shop scenes on *Seinfeld*.

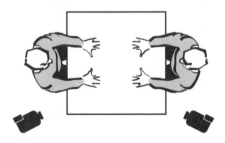

Figure 15.8

This diagram illustrates using two cameras to shoot a dialogue scene similar to the famous *Seinfeld* coffee shop scenes.

Another technique used to shoot dialogue scenes is the two shot, where you see both actors in the same frame. Another common technique is the over-the-shoulder shot, which is similar to a two shot except that the camera is positioned over one of the actors' shoulders (see Figure 15.9).

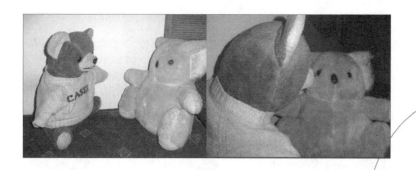

Figure 15.9

The two shot and over-the-shoulder shot allow you to use one camera to shoot two people talking.

Wide Shot, Medium Shot, Close Up, Extreme Close Up

Depending on the position of the subject/object, how close or far away you shoot is defined as a wide shot, medium shot, close up, or extreme close up (the last popularized by *Wayne's World*). These shots are all fairly self-explanatory; consult the figure examples (see Figure 15.10). It is important in home video, as with amateur filmmaking, to get a variety of shots to keep things interesting to the audience. If everything is a close up in your videos, the audience will experience perceptual claustrophobia, so mix it up.

Figure 15.10

In clockwise order: wide shot, medium shot, close up, extreme close up.

Depth of Field

Depth of field relates to how much of the frame is in focus (see Figure 15.11). A wide depth of field means everything is in focus. A medium depth of field means the foreground and middle are in focus. A shallow depth of field means that just the foreground is in focus. Depth of field is achieved by altering the exposure of your camcorder. Mastering this also takes practice.

Figure 15.11

Depth of field examples: shallow depth of field, medium depth of field, wide depth of field.

Movement Shots

If you are filming someone walking, and you want to move with them, you usually set it up as a dolly shot. A professional dolly shot utilizes some sort of track—much like train track—called a *dolly* (see Figure 15.12). You affix the camera to that track so it can move smoothly. Steadicams are an option if you don't want a dolly, as they afford more movement options, but they are not as steady.

Figure 15.12

Picture of a professional dolly manufactured by Danny Boy services.

Build Your Own Dolly

techtv tip

Most amateur filmmakers are in no position to buy their own dolly. However, it is easy to improvise alternatives. Using a skateboard, remote control car, real car, or some sort of wheelchair can all give you the ability to achieve your own dolly shots (see Figure 15.13).

Figure 15.13

Introducing the practical and affordable Tony Hawk model skateboard dolly.

Other Types of Shots

The following are some other common camera shots:

- **Master Shot**—A shot that shows the entire scene, often used as a backup in case other shots go wrong.
- **Aerial**—A shot taken from far above the scene.
- **Subjective View**—A shot taken to represent the perspective of one of the actors—that is, what they see through their eyes.
- **Periscope**—A shot that emulates a periscope; the frame moves up, usually to reveal something.

The swiveling LCD screens included on most new camcorders afford you great shooting versatility. You can adjust the LCD to all sorts of angles to get previously difficult-to-capture shots.

CHAPTER 16

CONSUMER AND PROSUMER VIDEO EDITING SOFTWARE OPTIONS

If you are a novice, uncertain, or don't expect to do much video editing, investing in a inexpensive consumer video editor—or using whatever program comes with your FireWire card—is going to the wisest approach. However, if this is something you start spending a lot of time on, prosumer editors offer significant advantages both in terms of speeding up the editing process, and also in terms of giving you significantly greater video editing options.

My own experience has been that working with most consumer editors rides the line between enjoyment and tedium—due to rendering delays and feature/user interface limitations. However, using a prosumer editor like Premiere 6 video editing is just plain fun much of the time.

VIDEO EDITING SOFTWARE OVERVIEW

Computer video software varies in terms of user interface, speed, stability, and features. Nevertheless, some basic commonalities exist:

- All video editing programs include an interface, which allows you to control your camcorder and capture video into your computer.
- All allow you to edit those clips in various ways and put those edited clips together into a movie.
- All allow you to add transitions between clips (such as fades, dissolves, and wipes).
- All allow you to output your created videos back to your camcorder, and/or to encode in various other video formats (VCD, Web video, video e-mail, and so on).
- Most let you add titles and text to your video.
- Many allow you to add special effects and filters.

VIDEO EDITING SOFTWARE FEATURES

Most budget/consumer video editing programs have a storyboard editing structure (see Figure 16.1). With storyboard interfaces, you order your clips on some type of horizontal grid, sometimes resembling a filmstrip. Each square of the grid shows the first frame of the clip residing there. Sometimes smaller boxes appear in between storyboard frames where you can drag transition effects. This editing structure works fine for simple home movies, but if you are into anything more elaborate, like special effects or complex soundtracks, you will need a more versatile prosumer editor.

Figure 16.1

The storyboard interface is commonly used in budget video editors.

With the exception of iMovie 2—only available on Apple computers—all budget video editors require you to rerender your movies before outputting back to camcorders, which can as much as double the time it takes to output your video (see Figure 16.2).

Figure 16.2

If you like implementing special effects or are using a budget editor, meet your new friend: the rendering delay window.

Professional and prosumer video editing programs use a multi-track timeline interface, which allows multiple audio and video tracks (see Figure 16.3). For example, you can add a dialogue track, a sound effects track, and a background music track to a multi-track timeline interface. If you have used a multi-track audio program, this interface works the same except with the addition of video tracks. Having more track options really opens up your creative possibilities, and allows you far more control over your video and sound. Many prosumer editors feature instant timeline playback, which means you can output your video back to your camcorder without delay.

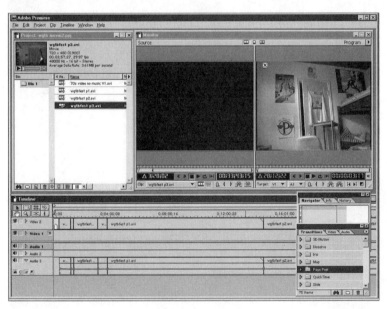

Figure 16.3

Most prosumer video editors and a few budget editors use the timeline interface.

Batch Capture

The batch capture function, which is available on some video editing programs, enables you to go through your video and select the portions you want to be captured. Once you finish marking the scenes, you just engage the batch capture, and the program will take control of your camcorder and transfer the selected clips. This function often did not work very well in older programs that featured it, but I have had greater success with newer software. However, batch capture—even if it works—has a lot of negatives. Going through your video to mark scenes and then having the batch capture function go through and get those scenes puts more wear and tear on your camcorder. Unless you have limited disk space, it is much easier to transfer all your footage to your computer—or just what scenes you want—and then edit out selected smaller clips with the software.

Video Filters

Video filters are special effects that enable you to alter your footage (see Figure 16.4). Most prosumer video editors include them, as do a few of the budget programs. For instance, if you want fog in a scene, you need to add a video filter. Video filters can also do more elaborate (and arguably unusable) things like make your video look like rippling water. Depending on the complexity of the filter, it can take a long time to render your video.

Figure 16.4

Video filters allow you to alter the look of your video, which can make your video look more professional, or in some cases obnoxiously amateur.

Most of the higher priced video cards (Matrox RT2500, Pinnacle DV500, Cannopus Raptor RT) allow a certain number of real-time filters, but only on analog video output. While great for previewing your editing possibilities, if you need to output to DV (which most of us do), you will have to do a final time-consuming render. The Cannopus DVStorm, however, does output DV (including filters) in real-time—as long you don't employ too many effects/transitions (see Figure 16.5).

Figure 16.5

The Cannopus DV Storm is one of the only prosumer video capture cards that can render DV filters and transitions in real time.

Transitions

Transitions are effects that go in between video clips. The most common transition is a dissolve, where the old clip dissolves into the new clip. All of these programs have numerous obnoxious transitions such as page turns, which in general look tacky, but this allows software companies to add another digit to their feature set numbers (see Figure 16.6). Keep in mind that most movies have very few transitions, if any.

Figure 16.6

The page turn transition is one of many transitions I find to be pretty useless.

Instant Timeline Playback/Play Thru Capability

Instant timeline playback is the most important video editing feature and is generally only found on prosumer video editors. This feature means that any DV video you play inside the software will output to your camera, or better yet, a TV hooked up to your camera, in full resolution (see Figure 16.7). The exception is if you add effects (video filter, titles) you will have to render them, but only the footage affected by the filter needs to be rendered.

Figure 16.7

With instant timeline playback capability, you can view anything playing in your video editor on a large consumer television.

Most other software programs force you to deal with little monitor windows inside the software interface, and you have to render the whole movie before you can output it to your camcorder. This makes video editing take up to twice as long. The following are some programs that offer real instant timeline playback:

- Adobe Premiere 6
- Apple iMovie 2
- Apple Final Cut Pro 3

Many programs that offered instant timeline playback in the past such as Edit DV required a small buffer delay, so it was not exactly instant (still much better than most programs though). Some of the newer prosumer editors that still have this limitation are Cinestream and Ulead Media Studio Pro 6.5.

Storyboard Editing

Storyboard editing enables you to take your clips and assemble a movie with them. You place each clip on some type of horizontal grid strip, in whatever order you choose (see Figure 16.8). Most consumer video editors employ some type of the storyboard interface. This makes editing very easy, but it limits your editing options, as you don't have additional sound or video track areas. Some prosumer editors enable you to edit in both storyboard and timeline multi-track mode.

Figure 16.8

The storyboard interface makes video editing a simple affair, ideal for novice users.

Timeline Multi-track Editing

The timeline interface is the preferred choice for prosumer video editing software, as it offers far more options than the storyboard interface. With multitracking you have multiple audio and video tracks at your disposal (see Figure 16.9). Multi-track editing makes adding additional sound and video tracks incredibly easy. If you are going to do anything more than simple editing, you need a program that offers this interface.

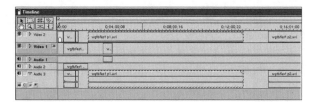

Figure 16.9

The timeline interface allows the user control over multiple audio and video tracks, ideal for more complex movies.

Output Options

Most video editing programs offer you a number of output options for your edited movies (see Figure 16.10). All of them let you output DV video back to your camcorder. You can create streaming video for the Web in Real Video format or Windows Media format—some offer QuickTime as well. You can also usually create video e-mail and VCDs. Some of the newer model video editors are starting to include DVD authoring capabilities.

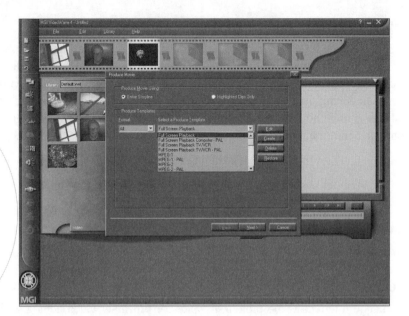

Figure 16.10

All video editors offer multiple output options for your video projects, from regular DV video to several
Web video formats.

Transparency and Layering

Many video editing programs allow you to superimpose one video over another (see
Figure 16.11). With this feature, you can create one of those TV news–style windows in the
footage. Most programs allow you to resize the video window and then select the transparency level. The more transparent you make a video layer, the more the video underneath will show through it (see Figure 16.12). The transparency setting would be useful for
creating a ghost effect.

Figure 16.11

Most prosumer video editors and a few budget editors allow you to create picture-in-picture effects as
shown here.

Figure 16.12

The transparency effect allows you to blend two different video files together, useful for some special effects.

Advanced Video Compositing Features

Video compositing is a term relating to advanced video effects editing (covered in Chapter 22). Compositing refers to taking multiple elements—video clips, sound effects, static pictures—and putting them together, usually in some sort of animated way.

Video compositing enables you to animate multiple layers of video, as well as static images, allowing you to create complex animations.

Take a shot of a horizon plus a jet plane plus some cool sound effects, and you can add some expensive looking realism to your action movie.

Keep in mind that most video editors are limited—or altogether barren—in their compositing capabilities. So if you are going to be doing compositing to professional levels of complexity, you are going to need a standalone video composition program like Adobe After Effects (see Figure 16.13).

Figure 16.13

Adobe After Effects is the premiere video compositing program, but it costs $649 just for the standard version.

CONSUMER VIDEO EDITORS

Consumer video editors offer a tremendous value of performance for what they cost (most under $100). They enable you to easily capture video from your camcorder, edit into clips, arrange a movie, and even add titles, effects, and music. For the casual video editor, they are the perfect compromise between cost and performance.

Ulead Video Studio 5

Ulead Video Studio (UVS5) often comes bundled with OHCI FireWire cards like ADS Pyro and Dazzle DV-editor (see Figure 16.14). UVS5 definitely used to be one of the better consumer video editors. However, while the competition made advances in their offerings, the latest version of Video Studio was somewhat disappointing. Nonetheless, UVS is still one of the simpler budget video editing programs currently on the market. The program is very easy to use and includes the ability to add transitions, video effects, titling, and outputs in pretty much any video format available.

The best aspect of UVS5 is that it is one of the few consumer video editors that have a timeline interface. With only one video track, it does not really help on the video end. However, you get two audio timeline tracks in addition to the audio of your movie clips. This makes it easy to add background music or narration throughout your movie.

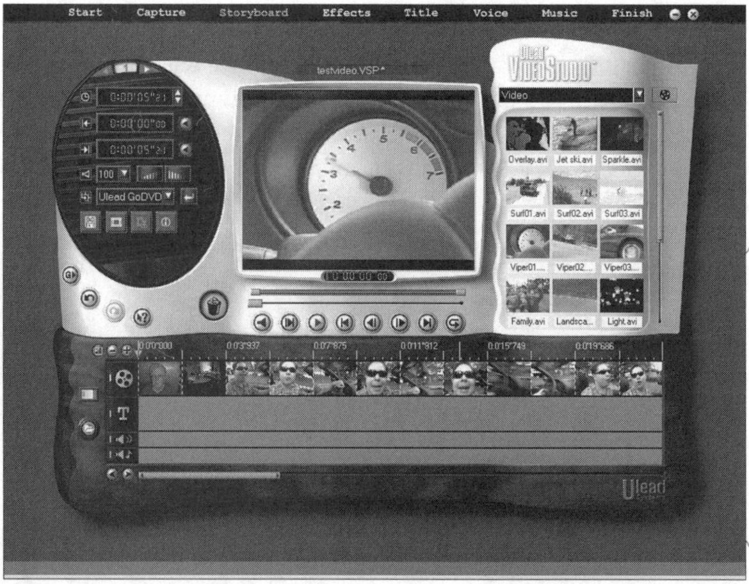

Figure 16.14

Ulead Video Studio is the most popular budget digital video editor because it comes bundled with most FireWire cards.

UVS5 is compatible with an optional authoring plug-in for creating your own VCD/SVCD/DVD discs. The plug-in enables you to easily create your own menu-driven DVDs. You can get the plug-in separately or bundled with UVS5; either way you pay about $50 more for it.

UVS5 has a timeline playback feature, but it is not instant. When I exported the timeline (my movie) directly to tape, it took 22 seconds to render per one minute of video on an 800MHz computer system. So by those numbers a 60-minute movie would take 22 minutes to render, and then an additional 60 minutes to output to tape.

The downside of UVS5 is that the video window is fixed at 320×240, which is pretty small. The small size window was acceptable in the days of slower computers and monitors, but not any more. Most of the other budget editors enable you to customize the size of your video window—up to full DV size, 720×480. You can preview all effects and transitions in real-time in UVS5, which is great, but if you want to watch your whole movie or more than one clip, you have to render a preview of the entire movie. This can make the editing process tiresome and is the major weakness of this program. Bottom line: UVS5 is not perfect but good enough for beginners and casual users.

MGI Videowave 4

MGI Videowave 4, for the most part, has a better interface and feature set when compared to UVS5 (see Figure 16.15). Videowave 4 has all the features of UVS5 plus the ability to customize the size of the video preview window, a feature lacking in most consumer video editors. It also includes a TV tuner so you can record video if you have a TV card in your computer.

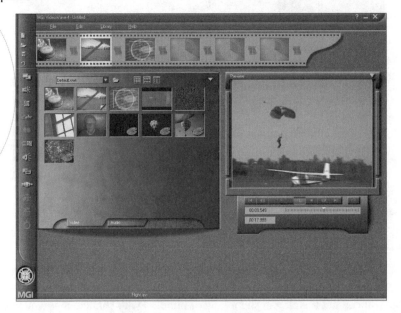

Figure 16.15

Videowave 4 is a very well-featured budget video editor that couples an attractive, easy-to-use interface with some advanced bells and whistles.

The Achilles heel of this program is the lack of a timeline interface. Videowave 4 has the aforementioned storyboard interface. While fine for simple home movies, if you want to add sound or music tracks, your job can get complicated. If you can learn to adapt around the lack of the timeline and MGI's peculiar sound interface, I think Videowave is one of the best consumer video editors, especially for beginners. Compared to UVS5, the interface is laid out better, it offers more effects, and the preview window size can be customized.

Pinnacle Studio 7 (Formerly Studio DV)

Studio 7 is a software/hardware package sold by Pinnacle, one of the leading manufacturers of prosumer video capture cards (see Figure 16.16). The Studio 7 software has a beautiful timeline interface, which is one of the best you will find for less than $100. As far as design layout, this is also perfect for beginner DV video editors as all functions are very sensibly laid out. Unfortunately, this software—and the FireWire card included—doesn't always work very well. The Studio 7 package has a reputation for software bugginess, instability, and hardware incompatibility. Pinnacle is a small company, with limited support.

Figure 16.16

If it works with your computer, Studio 7 is a great intro level video editor that closely resembles iMovie 2.

If you can get it to work, Studio 7 is the one of the best budget DV packages on the market right now because it includes the FireWire card, but this is a *big IF*. Studio DV is probably the closest thing to iMovie 2 you can get on a PC, but it does not allow instant timeline playback, which iMovie 2 does.

Sonic Foundry Video Factory 2

Sonic Foundry is one of the leading manufacturers of prosumer sound editing software (Sound Forge and Vegas Audio software). Over the last few years, Sonic Foundry has expanded into all aspects of multimedia production. Video Factory is their entry-level video editor with a professional edge (see Figure 16.17). Video Factory 2 packages prosumer aspects like timeline multi-track editing and DirectX sound plug-ins in an easy-to-use consumer video editor with well-designed built-in tutorials. The result is the most powerfully featured editor for less than $100 on the PC.

Sonic Foundry allows two video tracks and three audio tracks. Everything is easily placed, moved, or removed from a timeline multi-track interface. Another great aspect of this program and many other Sonic Foundry products is the built-in file explorer, which makes finding and adding video, graphic, and audio files incredibly easy. All effects and transitions can be previewed in real-time for the entire movie.

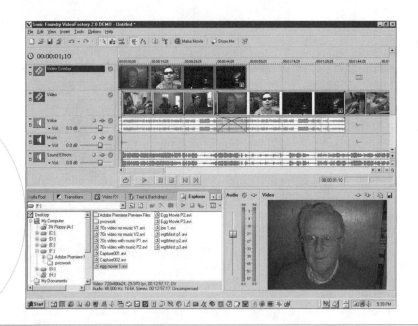

Figure 16.17

Sonic Foundry Video Factory features a timeline interface, built-in file explorer, and real-time effects preview.

The only downside of Video Factory is that the video preview window is limited to 320×240, and like most of the other budget editors, it lacks instant timeline playback. Given all the options currently available for the PC, Video Factory is my consumer video editor of choice.

iMovie 2

If you are interested in going for an Apple computer, iMovie 2 is the best consumer video editor on the market. It is supremely easy to use and has a beautiful interface (see Figure 16.18). You also are freed from hardware incompatibility problems as all Apple computers (G3 and above) have the same FireWire hardware built in to the computer, so things are guaranteed to work smoothly.

iMovie 2 is currently the only budget video editor that features instant timeline playback— Apple calls this feature *play thru*. So you won't have to rerender your video before outputting to your camcorder, essentially cutting your editing time in half. You can also preview your timeline video or clips at full resolution on your camcorder LCD, or better yet, on a television hooked up to your camcorder. Basically, anything playing in the program plays out to your camcorder and/or TV.

iMovie 2 still does not compare to prosumer programs like Adobe Premiere or Final Cut Pro (Mac only). iMovie 2 is designed for home movie editing. If you need to do more complicated things, you are going to need a more advanced program.

Figure 16.18

iMovie 2, attractive and functional, is currently the best budget video editor, but it is only available on the Mac.

For instance, if you capture a ten-minute clip, you can't take specific parts of it and drop it on the timeline, like you can in the clip editor of a prosumer video editor. All iMovie lets you do is split and/or trim clips. However, the video quality in iMovie or any of the aforementioned basic video editors is the same as you will get in high-end programs. So ultimately, the difference between prosumer video editors and consumer video editors is features—and sometimes speed—not video quality.

Rating the Consumer Video Editors

To help you narrow your choices, here is a concise breakdown of the best consumer video editors:

1. **iMovie 2**—Only available on the Mac, this program is a winner because it's the only budget editor to offer instant timeline playback, and the interface is drop-dead easy.
2. **(tie) MGI Videowave 4**—This program has customizable video monitor size, video filters, and is very easy to use, but no timeline.

   Sonic Foundry Video Factory 2—Offers a more professional level of control over your video and audio with a multi-track timeline interface, but the video monitor is limited to 320×240.
3. **Ulead Video Studio**—Easy to use, timeline interface, and features optional SVCD/DVD authoring plug-in. Cons: intrusive rendering delays during the editing process, and video monitor is limited to 320×240.
4. **Studio 7 (formerly StudioDV)**—Kind of like the PC version of iMovie 2, but it has stability/compatibility problems.

PROSUMER VIDEO EDITORS

If you can handle a little bit of a learning curve (it's not much) or are going to be editing a lot of video, forget about budget editors all together. Prosumer video editors feature multi-track timeline-based video editing. The interface centers around two video monitors instead of one. The monitor setup is customizable, but generally one monitor is devoted to individual clip editing, and the other monitor reflects what you have on the timeline (the whole movie).

Prosumer video editors feature more effects and better sound options. They offer a significant step up from their consumer counterparts. With a more feature-rich interface, the editing is much quicker, and you have significantly greater options. You can usually get limited edition versions of some of the better video editors such as Premiere and Media Studio Pro for around $200, which is not much more than some of the consumer programs that offer much less.

Adobe Premiere 6

Adobe Premiere was one of the first prosumer video editors and helped start the computer video editing revolution. For much of this period, Premiere has been the video editor of choice among professionals. However, things started to slide with the release of Version 5. Premiere 5 reflected the intermediate state of computer technology at the time, where sleek graphical user interfaces presented a lot of creative possibility, but the hardware limitations of the computer often made the reality something entirely different.

The whole process was slow, as video had to render before you could output things. Video editing was definitely a chore. As hardware capabilities improved, other companies released applications that took advantage of them and Premiere 5 just did not compare well anymore. As a result Adobe lost significant market share. Many users fled to Final Cut Pro.

With Premiere 6, Adobe played more than catch up. Premiere 6 is a huge improvement, an evolution over the unimpressive version 5. Premiere 6 was the first video editor on the PC to offer real no-delay instant timeline playback (see Figure 16.19). This made editing and outputting to tape incredibly fast. It also made it easy to set up a preview monitor, so you could preview your timeline or clips on a regular TV monitor. All you have to do is hook up a regular TV to the A/V output on your camcorder, and anything that is played on the Premiere monitors gets output to your TV instantly at full resolution. Premiere 6 was the first program that actually made computer video editing as fun and easy as I had imagined it could be when I originally became interested in editing on a computer years ago—the reality had always been very different.

Another huge improvement of Premiere 6 is the sound capabilities. Premiere 6 includes an audio mixer control, which enables you to control as many audio tracks as you see fit to add to your videos. Furthermore, you can adjust the levels while you preview your video, and Premiere remembers those level changes. If you are working with complicated soundtracks, or just like to get the sound absolutely perfect, you will be very pleased with Premiere 6. You can also use DirectX sound plug-ins in Premiere—though in my experience not all of them work.

Figure 16.19

Adobe Premiere 6—featuring instant timeline playback, After Effects filters, and new audio mixer controls—is one of the best prosumer video editors.

Premiere 6 has a storyboard feature, which enables you to arrange clips on a storyboard. You can then select *automate to timeline*, which automatically adds all those scenes to the timeline, saving considerable time. You can also take a bunch of still photos and apply the *automate to timeline* command—a default transition is added between each picture. This enables you to create a cool photo montages, which, with the addition of some music tracks—Premiere supports MP3 files—looks impressive.

You can use After Effects filters in Premiere—25 are included. Although they are not technically supported, After Effects plug-ins appear to work as well.

Final Cut Pro 3

Prior to the release of Premier 6, professional video editors were fleeing Adobe Premiere 5 and migrating to a program called Final Cut Pro. Final Cut Pro is for the Mac only, so it involves buying a new computer if you are currently using a PC.

Final Cut Pro (now in version 3) has become somewhat of a standard in the professional video editing community (see Figure 16.20). FCP shares many of the advantages of Premiere 6, like real instant timeline playback, but it had these features before Premiere 6 hit the market.

Figure 16.20

The top prosumer editor on the Mac, Final Cut Pro 2 has caused many video professionals to choose an Apple computer.

A big advantage Final Cut Pro still has over Premiere 6 is that you can have multiple sequences (timelines) in one project. With Premiere, you can only have one timeline per project. Many users think FCP has a more intuitive user interface as well, with larger buttons, and a less complicated and cluttered layout.

Final Cut Pro also includes a built-in compositing/animation module, which is probably the biggest advantage it has over Premiere, as it is included and integrated quite well into the program. If you need advanced compositing/animation in Premiere, you will have to buy another program, Adobe After Effects, which is not cheap. While After Effects (AE) is considered the best compositing/animation program on the market (and many die-hard FCP users also use AE), you get a pretty good compositor within FCP for free. As Napster proved, everyone loves free.

Ulead Media Studio Pro 6.5

Media Studio Pro is a PC-only prosumer video editor meant to compete with Premiere (see Figure 16.21). The advantage of MSP is that it incorporates some advanced composition features, which Premiere and other prosumer editors do not have. However, the program fails to compete as strongly on a basic level as a video editor.

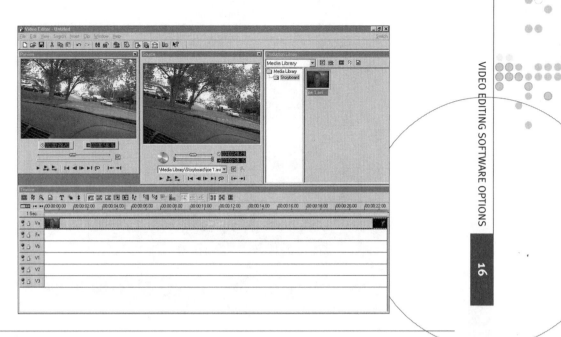

Figure 16.21

Media Studio Pro 6.5 is an affordable prosumer video editor that includes extra features not found in Premiere and FCP; however, it lacks real instant timeline playback.

MSP is composed of 5 modules: Audio Editor, CG Infinity, Video Capture, Video Editor, and Video Paint. CG Infinity is a vector-based compositing/animation program, which enables you to add text and image animation to your video, or merely to create animations. Video Paint allows you to paint on top of video frames, which enables you to achieve rotoscoping effects (see Figure 16.22). The other modules are self-explanatory.

JARGON

Rotoscoping is a technical term that basically means doctoring video frame by frame. Rotoscoping is used in those commercials and movies where dogs appear to talk, as well as all sorts of other special effects. The light saber effects in Star Wars were drawn in or rotoscoped frame by frame.

Released after Premiere 6, the newest version of MSP still has no real instant timeline playback as you get with Premiere and Final Cut Pro. You can output to the timeline with only a small delay, but you have to select Export to do so. Video played within the program monitors or timeline won't play out to your camcorder or TV monitor as it does in Premiere and FCP on-the-fly. The interface has changed little from the previous version; it is just not as slick and refined as Premiere or FCP.

Figure 16.22

This primitive rotoscoping example will not win any awards, but you get the idea.

However, despite these shortcomings, MSP has one big advantage over Premiere. You can preview effects in real-time (albeit at reduced frame rates) using the Instant Play mode. For users that are really into effects, this is a strong selling point.

MSP also includes one of the best MPEG encoders, ideal for creating VCDs, SVCDs, and DVDs. Furthermore, MSP includes a DVD authoring plug-in for burning your own VCDs, SVCDs, and DVDs to CD or DVD. If I were not addicted to being able to preview my video project with a 20-inch television, I would use MSP a lot more.

Cinestream

Cinestream (formerly Edit DV) is another prosumer video editor available on both the PC and Mac (see Figure 16.23). MEDIA 100 bought the company that created EditDV and renamed the new version Cinestream.

When called Edit DV about a year or so ago, Cinestream had a lot of market momentum behind it as another alternative to the disappointing Premiere 5. At that time, it had the closest thing to instant timeline playback—with a very small delay for buffering before output—and had a pretty good user interface. However, the newest version has stability problems and is outgunned in terms of features when compared to Premiere 6 or Final Cut Pro 3. Whether this program was a casualty of new personnel or a more competitive market, it does appear to have a questionable future.

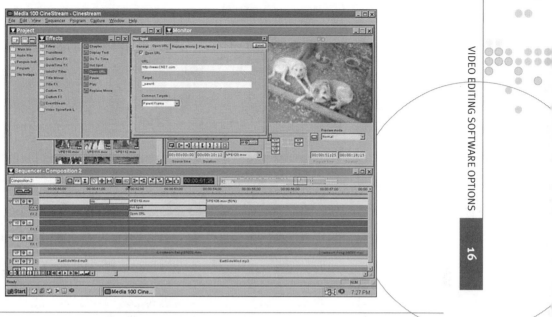

Figure 16.23

Cinestream is the latest version of Edit DV.

SETTING UP YOUR COMPUTER FOR EDITING

Once you have decided on a video-editing program and installed it, and you have your FireWire installed on your computer, you are ready to begin editing. If you are using Premiere 6, iMovie 2, or Final Cut Pro, all of which allow you to preview all your video clips and project timeline instantly, I highly suggest adding a TV monitor next to your computer. This will greatly enhance your video editing setup (see Figure 16.24).

Be forewarned that some monitors are not very well magnetically shielded, so you may experience interference with a TV or second monitor next to your computer. This interference will be manifested on your computer monitor as flickering. If you have this problem, moving them farther apart or lowering the resolution on your monitor often fixes or greatly minimizes this problem.

Then all you need to do is hook up the composite or S-video output of your camcorder—preferably S-video. Then when you have your camcorder hooked up via FireWire to you computer, all the video playing in your video editing software window will play out in full resolution on your TV. This makes for an amazingly immersive video editing setup, which is worth the small cost of a TV ($100–$300). I am using a 21-inch Panasonic television, but you could use a 13-inch TV as well. I don't think it's wise to go bigger than 21 inches unless you want to set the TV farther away from you. After six months with this cathode ray bombarding setup, I remain brain tumor free.

Figure 16.24

If you are using Premiere, iMovie 2, or Final Cut Pro, adding a TV to your editing setup enables you to preview anything playing inside your software on your TV at full resolution.

Go through the following optimization checklist before you start video editing:

1. If you have not defragged your PC's hard drive recently, defrag. If you use a Mac, optimize your hard drive.

2. Make sure your hard drives are set to DMA in the System properties.

3. If you have two hard drives, make sure they are on different IDE channels.

IMPORTING VIDEO INTO YOUR COMPUTER

If your camcorder is powered on and the FireWire cable is plugged into the FireWire ports on both your computer and camcorder, you are ready to import video (see Figure 16.25). You can plug the FireWire cable into your camcorder while you computer is on. Nevertheless, you should exit your video editing software before unplugging the FireWire cable if you want to be on the safe side. With some software, disconnecting the FireWire can cause the computer to freeze or do other weird things. This will not harm your computer in any way; it just might require a reboot.

Figure 16.25

All new DV camcorders—and most older models—include a FireWire jack for inputting and outputting your video digitally.

CHAPTER 17

CONSUMER VIDEO EDITING BASICS

Ulead VideoStudio (UVS) is the most common video editor on most PCs (which make up more than 90% of computers), so it makes sense to use it as the software for my basic consumer-editing tutorial. Better consumer editors are available on the PC, but none has such a huge advantage that I would feel comfortable recommending everyone to go out and buy it.

This chapter will take you through all the basic digital video editing techniques necessary to make a movie out of your DV video, from clip editing, adding transitions and effects, creating rolling credits, to finally outputting back to your camcorder.

SIMPLE EDITING IN ULEAD VIDEOSTUDIO 5

Ulead VideoStudio 5 (UVS5) is divided into seven parts, each selectable on the top of the program's interface screen. They are Capture, Storyboard, Effects, Title, Voice, Music, and Finish (see Figure 17.1).

Figure 17.1

The top of the UVS5 interface shows your seven main options.

Capture mode is for importing your video. Storyboard mode is where most of the video editing takes place. Effects mode is where you can add transitions to your video clips. Title mode is where you can add text over your video. Voice mode is where you can add a narration track to your video. Music mode is where you can add music tracks. Finally, Finish mode is where you can finalize your movie and choose from various output options—back to your camcorder, Web video, video e-mail, or DVD/VCD/SVCD.

STARTING YOUR PROJECT AND CAPTURING VIDEO FROM YOUR CAMCORDER

To start the editing process, follow these steps:

1. Make sure that your camcorder is on and is in VCR mode—also called VTR or Play mode. This mode allows you to replay your video (see Figure 17.2).

Figure 17.2

When connecting your camcorder to your computer, make sure you set your camcorder to PLAY mode—also called VTR or VCR mode on some camcorders.

2. Open UVS5 by going to the start icon at the bottom of your screen. Click Programs and Ulead Video Studio.

If you are going to be using the program often, you may want to add a shortcut to the program on your desktop or to the bottom toolbar. To do this, just repeat the above step and when you get to the Ulead VideoStudio link, right-click it and select Create Shortcut. Then you will see a new shortcut; drag that to the desktop or the bottom toolbar (or both). You can even rename it if you want by right-clicking and selecting Rename.

3. Select New Project. This will prompt a window to pop up, which allows you to select your project template (see Figure 17.3). Project templates encompass all the settings of your video editing project: the video size, frame rate, the codec (DV, MPEG, AVI), audio sample rate. Every program includes the more commonly used templates such as NTSC DV or PAL DV. Also you will often see Video E-mail, Web Video, and VCD templates. If you live in a country with the NTSC video format, then you will usually want to select NTSC DV. You can also create your own templates (discussed later in this chapter). This feature is handy if you can't find a profile that matches your needs.

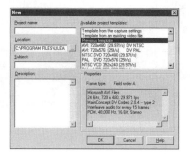

Figure 17.3

Via the Template selection window you choose a template with the appropriate settings for the video you want to produce.

Caution

If you are customizing your own templates, be diligent in choosing your settings. If you select the wrong frame size or audio sample rate, your camcorder won't be able to read the output. For DV camcorder output, always make sure that the video size is 720×480 NTSC or 720×576 for PAL, and make sure the audio sample rate is 48kHz. If you have problems outputting video to your camcorder, the likely culprit is incorrect template settings.

4. Fill in Project Name. Subject and Description fields are optional.

5. Select AVI 720×480 (29.97f/s) DV NTSC from the template window. Or if you have a PAL camcorder, select the PAL template.

Eliminating the Pop-Up Help Windows

There are pop-up help windows that you will find somewhat annoying after awhile. To disable them, click the global project settings button and select preferences. Then uncheck Enable Ulead VideoStudio Guide and click OK.

Figure 17.4

The Global Preferences button—marked by the letter G—is where you can access all the advanced program settings. In this figure, I used it to get to the Preferences screen to disable the pop-up help screens.

6. Select Capture. This option is located on top of the program's interface.

This will bring up the part of the program that enables you to control your camcorder and capture footage (see Figure 17.5). On the top left of the interface—to the left of the video monitor—are the Camcorder and Camera buttons. The Camcorder button engages video capturing of whatever you have playing in the video monitor. The camera button captures stills of whatever video frame is currently displayed in the video monitor.

Below the video monitor your will find the control buttons for controlling your camcorder playback. From left to right, the buttons are: Volume (controls your preview sound, but has no effect on the levels of sound captured), Stop, Pause, Play, Rewind, Previous Frame (to reverse frame-by-frame; remember that there are 30 frames per second in DV video), Next Frame, and Fast Forward.

The camcorder controls are pretty much self-explanatory. If you want to fast forward through the tape, click the Fast Forward button on the screen. If you want to scan around slower (and more precisely), use the Next Frame or Previous Frame buttons.

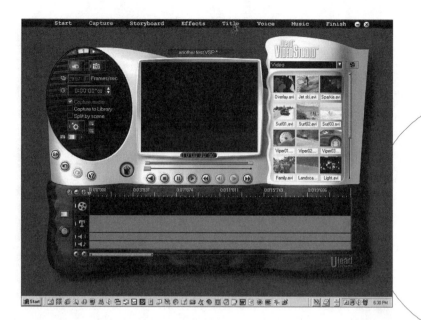

Figure 17.5

Capture mode is where you import video clips from your camcorder; the VCR-like control buttons enable you to control your camcorder.

7. If you are going to be making a lot of different movies at the same time, you should learn how to use the media Library. The media Library is located on the right side of the user interface. The media Library enables you to capture clips into custom named folders. To create your own folders for any type of video, sound effects, or images, click the drop-down menu and select Library Manager (see Figure 17.6).

Figure 17.6

The Library window is where all the media files are organized and accessed.

8. Select New and type any name you want. I will type *Dog Movie* (see Figure 17.7).

Figure 17.7

You can create custom library folders for organizing your own media files.

9. Select your new folder from the drop-down menu.

10. On the left side of the user interface, click the Capture to Library check box.

    Now all clips I capture will go to the Dog Movie folder unless I manually change to another folder in the drop-down list.

    If you don't want to create folders then all captured movies will be added by default to the storyboard or video timeline. Make sure the Capture To Library check box remains unchecked.

11. Below the monitor window you will find the video editing area. You have two interface options here: Storyboard or Timeline. You can select either by clicking the green LED switch on the bottom left of the interface (see Figure 17.8). You are not locked into either mode; you can switch from Storyboard to Timeline throughout the editing process without problems. Storyboard mode is preferable for some beginners who just want to edit a few simple video clips. If you want to add photos, narration, sound effects, or video, Timeline mode is better.

Figure 17.8

UVS5 allows you to operate in both Storyboard (top) and Timeline (bottom) mode. You can switch between the two at any point in your project by clicking the switch on the left.

12. Once you are ready to edit, use the camcorder controls under the monitor window to find the scenes you want captured. When you find a scene you want, click the Play button and then click the Camcorder button, and the capture will start. Make sure you err on the side of capturing more of the scene rather than less of the scene—you can make precise edits and trims later.

While capturing to the right of the video monitor you will see a display of frames captured and dropped frames (see Figure 17.9). You should never have dropped frames; if you do your computer is either misconfigured or not fast enough. To stop capture press Escape or click the Camcorder button. The next step is to trim the clip.

Figure 17.9

Immediately to the lower left of the video monitor you will see the stats of frames captured and dropped during the video capture process; in this case 799 frames captured, 0 frames dropped.

TRIMMING YOUR CAPTURED VIDEO CLIPS

Below the monitor window are two sliders (which the program refers to as *bars*). One is the Trim bar; the other is the Preview bar. The Preview bar lets you move around anywhere in the captured clip. The Trim bar enables you to exactly specify which part of the clip you want to include in your movie (see Figure 17.10). The Trim bar has two gold sliders that you position to indicate the starting and ending point of the clip.

Figure 17.10

The trim bars allow you to trim your captured video into smaller and/or more precise clips.

To trim your clips, follow these steps:

1. Select the starting point by positioning the first Trim slider.
2. Select the ending point by positioning the second Trim slider.
3. Select the Checkmark button on the left side of the user interface to finalize things.
4. Then drag the clip into the Storyboard or Timeline.

If you need to edit multiple scenes from one clip, you have to capture your clips to the Library. While not exactly sensible, you can grab multiple scenes from clips in the library, but anything you capture direct to the timeline can only be trimmed once. However, you can get around this by dragging clips you have captured to the Timeline into the Library.

To trim multiple scenes from one clip, just keep dragging the clip from the Library and follow the above trimming steps.

UVS5 has no batch capture mode, so you just have to find the scenes you want and capture them using the above method. Whether you prefer to capture one large clip and trim multiple scenes from it, or to capture smaller scenes, is up to you. I prefer to capture one large clip—or a few medium-sized clips.

DV VIDEO TIME CODE

Between the video monitor and the Trim bar is the time code window. If you double click the time code window, you can specify the exact time code—and the video monitor will display that frame (see Figure 17.11). You will find this essential if you need absolutely precise editing, especially since the frame fast forward button does not advance in increments of one.

Figure 17.11

The time code window is helpful when you need to make very precise edits.

Once you are done capturing video, click the Storyboard link at the top of the screen. This will remove the camcorder and video capture controls, but most of the interface will remain the same.

PUTTING YOUR CLIPS TOGETHER INTO A MOVIE

In the Storyboard mode, a few new options are available to the left of the video monitor (see Figure 17.12). The first is an arrow button that will advance you into the video filter portion of the program. Below that is a time window (marked the clock icon) denoting the duration of the currently selected video clip on the Timeline or Storyboard. Below that is another scene editing option that works in collaboration with the Trim bar, enabling you to set the beginning (marked by the left arrow icon) and end points (marked by the right arrow icon) of the selected video clip.

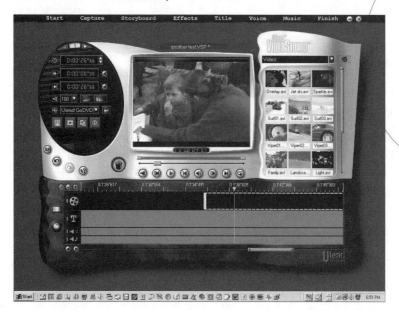

Figure 17.12

Storyboard mode in UVS5 is where you will do most of your video editing.

Below that you will see a sound control feature that lets you set the overall volume of the selected video clip (marked by the speaker icon). To the right of that are two buttons that look like ramps, which allow you to make the sound of the video clip fade in, and fade out. Below that you will find an export control feature, useful if you want to export a selected clip from the Timeline as an e-mail video clip (or any other format available in the drop-down box).

Remember that once you make your changes, you have to click the Checkmark button to finalize things. Finally, there are four buttons; from left to right, the first saves a static picture of whatever is in the current video monitor, perfect for extracting stills from your video (see Figure 17.13). The second button saves the selected video clip as a separate file. The third button enables you to cut the selected video clip at whatever point you have the Preview bar set at. The final button just pops up a window with information about what kind of video clip it is.

Figure 17.13

In storyboard mode these four buttons allow you to extract stills, save video clips, make cuts, and obtain file info.

ADVANCED EDITING

Simple arrangement of clips alone can make for very well done movies. However, Videostudio enables you to add transitions, video filters, titles, narration, music, and sound effects, which when used correctly can make for an even more exciting movie.

However, be conservative, as using every bell and whistle can often make a movie look less professional, and more importantly less entertaining.

Adding Transitions

Most video editing programs are loaded with transitions. However, transitions are seldom used in professional movies. While some of them can be fun, they often make your video look like a novelty. Use transitions and effects to add to your video, not to distract from it.

The most common transitions in professional film editing are fade to black, fade from black, and cross dissolve. A cross dissolve is when the video of the previous scene fades into the video of the incoming scene. Though more often than not, a simple cut is used, which means no transition.

To add transitions in UVS5, select the Effects link at the top of the program interface (see Figure 17.14). In the Library area you will now see a large amount of available transition effects; select the drop-down box and you will see even more. To preview a transition, double-click on it and you will see a preview of it in the monitor window. When you find a transition you want to use, drag it to the Timeline or Storyboard and place it in between your desired clips. Then click the Play button and you will see your transition preview in real-time. On the left side of the screen you will also see a few options available to tweak the transition. If you change any settings, make sure to select the Checkmark button to finalize your changes.

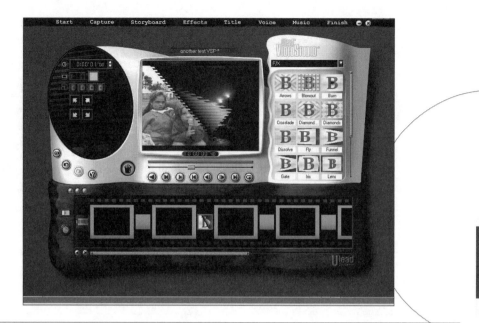

Figure 17.14

The UVS5 transition mode is accessible via the Effects link at the top of the UVS5 interface.

Adding Video Filters

To add video filters—black and white, film grain, fog effects, and so on—click Storyboard at the top of the screen. Then click the Library drop-down box and select Video filters. The other, more complicated way to do this is to click on the right arrow button next to the green number one (on top of the left interface menu area). This will also take you to the video filters area. You have about 30 video filters at your disposal (see Figure 17.15). My experiences suggest that adding multiple filters to your clips often causes the program to crash—so make sure you save your project often when working with video filters.

To add a filter, drag the desired filter and drop it on any clip. You can add multiple effects to each video clip. You can also alter the settings of each effect by choosing from a number of thumbnail templates that will show up to the left of the video monitor. An advanced settings button right below the thumbnail window will open up a menu with more advanced filter settings (see Figure 17.16).

If you click a clip in the Timeline or Storyboard when in this mode, you will see all the effects currently applied to each clip in a scrollable menu to the left of the video monitor. Just click the effect to alter the settings, or to delete the effect select the X labeled button.

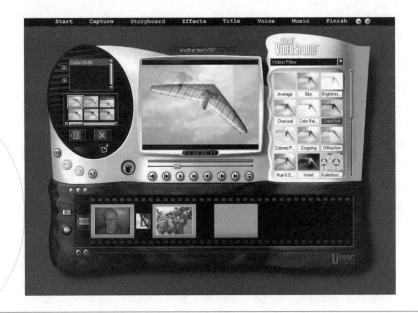

Figure 17.15

UVS5 enables you to add 30 video filters—and preview them in real-time—to your video clips.

Figure 17.16

Advanced video filters settings are accessible via the arrow buttons on the top right of the video monitor.

Adding Titles

UVS—as well as every other video editor—enables you to add titles to the movies you create. To add a title to your movie, click Title at the top of the screen (see Figure 17.17).

Adding a title to UVS is as easy as clicking a clip or moving the Preview bar to where you want the title. Then click the monitor window, and a text frame will appear enabling you to type in your desired title. In the Library window a number of prefab titles are available to get you started—but they're just select greetings in different colored fonts.

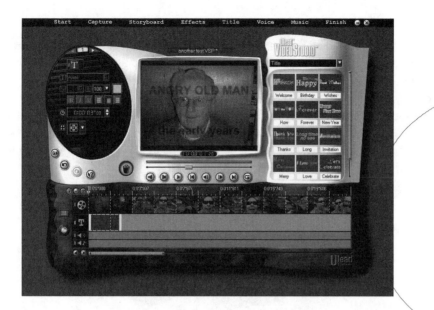

Figure 17.17

Title mode allows you to easily add text to your video clips, setting the font type, size, and title duration.

To the left of the video monitor you will see all the customizable title/text settings: font type, size, color, bold, italics, underline, align left, center, align right. Below this feature is a window (marked by a clock icon) which specifies the length of time the title will appear onscreen.

Scrollable Titles

UVS5 also enables you to employ several types of scrollable text options, so you can create your own ending credits in a movie or whatever else you might want. Right below the title duration window is the text scroll settings drop-down button (see Figure 17.18). This allows you to choose the direction of scrolling animation.

Figure 17.18

When in title mode you can select up to 16 different title scrolling animations, useful when creating rolling credits.

Advanced Title Settings

At the top of the Title interface, click the right arrow adjacent to the green button to get to more advanced title editing capabilities (see Figure 17.19). Page 2 of the Title interface enables you to set the transparency of your titles, as well as the sharpness or smoothness of the font edges. Page 3 of the Title interface enables you to add different shadow and glow effects to your titles. Again, make sure you click the Checkmark when you want to apply your changes. These effects can make your text look a lot cooler and more professional, so experiment with them. I prefer the transparency and font edge softening settings myself.

Figure 17.19

You can add various transparency and font edge softening effects to your text and titles via the advanced title menus.

Adding Sounds

It is really easy to add any type of sound file (WAV or MP3) to UVS5. If you are already in Timeline mode, you have access to the sound tracks; just click on either speaker icon in the Timeline (see Figure 17.20). If not, switch to Timeline mode or click Voice or Music on the top of the screen; either one will activate the Timeline mode.

Figure 17.20

The audio tracks on the timeline interface allow you to add MP3 music tracks, sound effects, or voice narration to your movies.

After selecting Voice or Music, the Library window will show the Audio folder. You can add new sounds to the Audio folder or create a new folder. You can fill either with any sound files you want to add to your movie, including MP3 sound files.

JARGON

MP3 is a very efficient audio compression format used mostly to encode music files.

Adding Narration

If you click on the first optional sound track or the Voice link at the top of the UVS5 interface, you will get new controls to the left of the video monitor (see Figure 17.21). These controls enable you to record a narration track while watching your video. The top button with the circle icon on it starts the recording. You need to have a mic attached to the sound card of your computer to record a narration track.

Figure 17.21

The Voice mode of UVS5 allows you to add and also record your own narration tracks to your movie.

Once you are ready to record—mic in place, witty remarks in head—click the record button. A pop-up screen will appear with a horizontal LED meter on it to show you what your microphone audio levels are (see Figure 17.22). Start talking in the mic. If you see lights flashing, you are set up properly. You want to make sure when talking that you don't go into the red—which means your mic signal is too high; this can cause distortion. If your signal is too hot or you are not getting any LED activity, you will need to follow the directions below.

Figure 17.22

The LED window displays the recording levels of your microphone; it is important to keep them out of the red.

The pop-up screen will also direct you to use the Windows Media Mixer to set your audio levels. Follow these steps:

1. Open the Windows Audio Mixer, also called Volume Control.

2. Go to Options, Properties.

3. Click the Recording radio button, and select OK (see Figure 17.23).

4. A mixer will pop up. Make sure that Microphone is selected, and then adjust the volume level of the Microphone mixer section so that at the loudest level you plan to speak the LED stays under the red (see Figure 17.24).

5. If you have headphones plugged into the speaker out jack of your sound card, you can monitor your recording—but you can't monitor the recording with speakers because that will cause feedback. If you are going to use headphones to monitor your recording, go to Options, Properties in the Volume Control Mixer and select the Playback radio button. In the Playback mixer, unmute the Microphone and set it to whatever level you want.

Once you are finished with the track, you can trim it as you would a video file, as well as move it around in the timeline. The other controls to the left of the audio menu enable you to trim and/or set the level of your newly recorded track, as well as fade the track in and out. You can record multiple tracks through the movie as long as they don't overlap. You can also trim any of your recorded tracks the same way you trim a video track with the Trim bar.

Figure 17.23

Select the Recording radio button to get to the recording mixer.

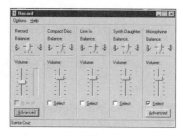

Figure 17.24

In the recording mixer screen, make sure that the microphone check box is selected, and alter the microphone volume to appropriate levels.

Adding Sound Effects and Music

You can add sound effects and/or music tracks to the Voice or the Music track as long as open space on the timeline is available where you want them. However, you need to be in Music mode to add to the Music track or Voice mode to add files to the Voice track (don't ask me why). Just drag and drop desired tracks from the Library window.

If you select the Music mode—selectable by clicking Music on the top of the UVS5 interface, or by clicking the bottom speaker icon—there are controls to record music tracks directly off your music CDs (see Figure 17.25).

Figure 17.25

UVS5 Music mode enables you to add MP3 tracks to your movie, as well as add music tracks directly from an audio CD.

The problem is while the program records from CD digitally—which is good—it previews via analog. Meaning if you don't have your CD-ROM hooked up to your sound card—which many newer computer owners don't—you can't hear what is being recorded until after you have recorded the track.

As long as you know exactly what track you want off a CD—and need or are willing to trim the whole track to fit your movie—then you will not have any problems. Otherwise you are better off using an external MP3 encoder/ripper like MusicMatch that will digitize your music into MP3s which you can then import into UVS5, and place on the Timeline (see MusicMatch tutorial in Chapter 21).

FINALIZING AND OUTPUTTING YOUR MOVIE

Once you are finished editing your movie, you are ready to finalize things. Click Finish at the top of the screen, which will bring up another new set of options to the left of the video monitor (see Figure 17.26).

If you are going to output your movie back to a DV camcorder, select the Timeline playback button, which is marked by a square icon with four arrows. After clicking, a pop-up screen will appear with a check box for device control (see Figure 17.27).

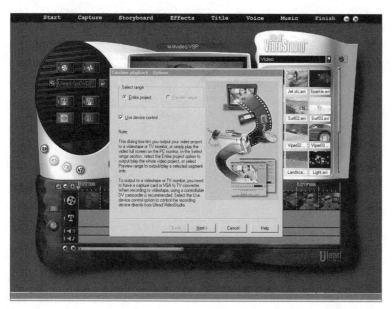

Figure 17.26

UVS5 Finish mode is the final step in the movie making process. From this mode you can output to a DV camcorder or encode your movie into Web format.

Figure 17.27

The timeline playback screen gives you the option of outputting your entire movie or just part of it, and you can also output with or without the device control interface.

If you selected the device control interface option, this opens a small control screen with a video monitor that allows you to remotely start the capture to your camcorder (see Figure 17.28). Otherwise you can start the timeline playback without checking the device control box, and you will have to manually press record on your camcorder.

Figure 17.28

The device control interface allows you to precisely control your camcorder during the movie output process.

If you are interested in rendering the movie into one of the many available video file formats—for Web video, video e-mail, QuickTime, VCD, SVCD, or DVD—select the Make a movie button (marked by a movie reel icon). Clicking that will bring up a pop-up menu of all your output options (see Figure 17.29).

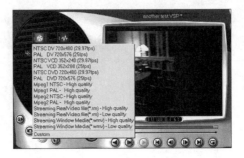

Figure 17.29

Clicking the movie reel button opens up your movie output options.

The Windows Media and RealMedia formats look as good as if you used a Microsoft or Real encoder, because they use the same codecs. However, the built-in MPEG-1 and 2 codecs in UVS5 are not very good. If you want custom settings, you have to select *Custom* at the bottom of the pop-up menu, as you can't customize any of the profiles they offer. You can save your newly created profiles to use again in the future. I found that all the offered profiles are so limited, most people are better off creating their own.

To create an output profile, follow these steps:

1. Select the Make movie icon button.

2. Select Custom from the pop-up menu options; it is the last entry.

3. Choose what kind of format you want by selecting from the file type drop-down box. Your main options are AVI, QuickTime, RealMedia, Windows Media, and MPEG.

4. Select the options button to specify the exact settings you want for the format you chose. The main options are going to be the video size, the frame rate, and the bit rate.

NOTE

When selecting your format settings, you should know that larger video size, frame rate, and bit rate—while delivering better quality—will also result in much larger file sizes. Experiment with different settings until you find the right formula for your outputted video, and then save that as an output profile. Experiment with a short one minute or less movie so that you don't have to wait forever for rendering.

RENDERING TIMES (TESTED ON AN 800MHZ AMD ATHLON COMPUTER)

With a test file of one minute, the following numbers reflect the amount of rendering time before UVS starts to output video to your camcorder:

- No effects—0min 33sec

- One second transition—adds 0min 09sec

- Adding five-second Title sequence—adds 0min 17sec

- One minute Black and White effect—adds 2min 47sec

Based on these results, a 20-minute movie with five transitions, two five-second title sequences, and two minutes of effects filters would take around 16 minutes to render (and then another 20 minutes to output to tape).

CHAPTER 18

BASIC OVERVIEW OF ADOBE PREMIERE

Because Premiere is a far more involved program than Ulead Video Studio, I am going to devote one chapter to an overview of the entire program, and in the next chapter I will take you through a simple video-editing tutorial as I did in the UVS basic editing chapter. So, if you are in a hurry, you can skip to the next chapter for that tutorial. A demo of Premiere is included on the program CD.

Adobe Premiere 6 is the top prosumer video editor on the PC platform right now, both in user base and in features. The program is loaded with functionality, and yet fairly easy to use.

Adobe Premiere does not have an immense learning curve. Most users can pretty much figure out how it works without ever looking at the manual by using trial and error, and occasionally conferring with the included help screen—accessible via Help, Contents.

However, if you are going to do lots of editing, it helps to have a good understanding of all the available controls in the Timeline, Monitor, and Audio Mixer interfaces. The following chapter should give you a handle of everything you need to know in this program.

Because I can't devote the entire book to Premiere, I did not cover features that most users don't use or that I consider useless. Nonetheless, I was able to cover most of the program's features and controls in a fairly small space.

GETTING STARTED IN PREMIERE 6

When you first open the program, you are faced with the Load Project Settings window (see Figure 18.1). The Project Settings window is composed of assorted settings templates that conform to the numerous different video types an average user might use. Most users should select DV - NTSC Standard 48kHz or PAL if they have a PAL camcorder. Even if you want to output to Web video or video e-mail, you still should choose a normal DV template. Otherwise, you won't be able to work in instant timeline playback mode and use a full-screen TV preview monitor during the editing process.

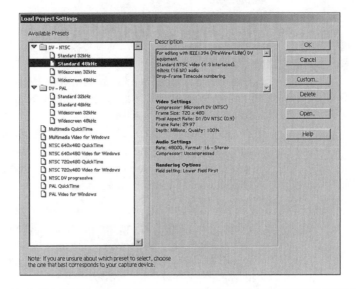

Figure 18.1

When you open Premiere you need to choose a project template; for most people DV – NTSC Standard 48kHz is the preferred template.

If you have a progressive video–capable camcorder and you shot in progressive mode, you will have to create a custom template, which will be discussed further in the editing tutorial.

Once you select a template, if this is your first time using Premiere, you will get another screen asking you if you want to do A/B editing or Single-Track editing.

A/B Editing

A/B editing is the old system of editing used in previous versions of Premiere. Basically, you have your video on one track—the A track—and your transitions on a second track—the B track (see Figure 18.2). Like most other users, I don't like this system. Final Cut Pro drew many Premiere users away because it used the more sensible single-track editing. In the program literature, Adobe suggests that A/B editing is probably easier for novice users, but you can decide that for yourself.

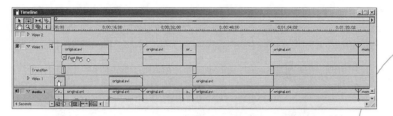

Figure 18.2

A/B editing allows you to see your video clips and transitions on two separate lines.

Single-Track Editing

Single-Track is a new and much welcomed addition to Adobe Premiere 6. With Single-Track editing all of your video, transitions, and effects exist within one track (see Figure 18.3). Single-Track editing from my viewpoint makes for much less clutter in your editing environment. While A/B Editing mode displays all transitions on a separate track, making it easier to keep tabs on your transitions, having two tracks of information devoted to one actual video track is not very efficient.

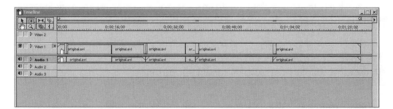

Figure 18.3

Single-Track editing features transitions and video clips on the same track. Most people prefer Single-Track editing.

Regardless, Premiere lets you choose either type of interface style. In fact, you can jump between the two throughout the editing process. This approach makes Premiere accessible to users of older versions, while also pleasing users who prefer Single-Track editing—and users who like to work in both modes alternately.

OVERVIEW OF THE USER INTERFACE

The user interface of Premiere consists of three main elements: Monitor Window, Project Window, and Timeline Window. The Monitor Window is the eyes of Premiere, enabling you to view your media files. The Project Window is the library of Premiere, where all media files are organized. Finally, the Timeline Window is the canvas where you create your movie.

Monitor Window

The Monitor Window houses Premiere's virtual preview monitors. These virtual monitors enable you to preview your individual video files as well as the entire timeline. Users often operate in dual virtual monitor mode using one virtual monitor—the Source monitor—for clip previews, and the other virtual monitor—the Program monitor—to preview the entire timeline (your movie). Premiere calls this Dual View (see Figure 18.4).

Figure 18.4

In Dual View, the Source monitor enables you to preview clips, while the Program monitor enables you to preview the entire content of your movie on the timeline.

> Premiere is sort of confusing because the timeline is called the Timeline, but the content of the Timeline (otherwise known as your movie) is called the Program.

You can also operate with just one virtual monitor—called Single View (see Figure 18.5). Trim View, a third option, features two virtual monitors and is used for exact trimming between adjoining clips. The left monitor shows the preceding clip, while the right monitor shows the following clip.

The most essential part of the editing process in Premiere, as well as most other prosumer editors, is taking raw video clips and editing them more precisely by marking in and out cut points. You can then add the newly edited clip to the Timeline. The controls necessary to do this are all located under the monitors in Premiere (see Figure 18.6).

Figure 18.5

Single View provides a single Program monitor, which can only view the content of your timeline.

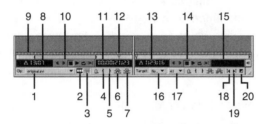

1. Select clip	11. Current clip location
2. Take Video	12. Shuttle
3. Take Audio	13. Program duration
4. Mark In	14. Program control buttons
5. Mark Out	15. Program location
6. Insert	16. Target Video track
7. Overlay	17. Target Audio track
8. Clip duration	18. Previous edit
9. Frame jog	19. Next edit
10. Clip control buttons	20. Add default transition

Figure 18.6

Most of your clip editing will take place in the Monitor window.

Frame Jog

The first control you will find beneath the video preview part of the monitor is a thin striped line called the Frame Jog. The Frame Jog is useful for navigating around small areas of a clip with precision. For instance, if you are trying to decide where to make a cut in a one-to-two second range, you will find the Frame Jog useful. If you need to move around a clip faster, use one of the other controls.

Shuttle Slider Area

Underneath the Frame Jog is the Shuttle Slider Area. The shuttle is a blue upside-down triangle that you can drag back and forth to navigate within a clip or timeline, depending on which monitor you are using.

Clip Duration and Time

Two time windows are positioned underneath the Shuttle area. The left window shows clip duration and the right window shows the location of the shuttle in the clip.

If you have marked in and out points, the duration time window reflects the total length of the selected portion of the clip.

VCR Buttons

In between the time windows, you will see a bunch of VCR-like buttons for controlling the clip or timeline, depending on whether you are in the Source or Program monitor. From left to right, you will see a Frame Back button—for going back one frame at a time—followed by a Frame Forward button, then Stop, Play, Loop, and finally a Play In and Out. The Play In and Out button plays the green area of the clip, which is the area of the clip that is marked with in and out points. If you have not set any in and out points, that button will play the whole clip.

Mark In and Out Buttons and Marker Menu

Located under the right time window, the Mark In and Out buttons are probably the most important editing buttons in any prosumer interface, and Premiere is no exception. After adding a clip to the Source Monitor (by dragging it in or double-clicking it), you can set a specific part of the clip, or even several parts, to be added to the timeline. For example, if you select a clip of someone catching a pass in the end zone and then doing a touchdown dance, and you only want to add the touchdown dance to your movie, you mark in and out points around the dance part of the clip.

Just use the shuttle, Frame Jog, and/or VCR buttons to find desired in and out points in your video clip and click the Mark In or Out button. You will see that the Shuttle area now is green between the in and out points you selected.

To the left of the Mark In and Out buttons, you will see the Marker Menu, which affords you more advanced marking options   (see Figure 18.7). I have not found it very useful.

Now once you are finished marking a clip, you can right-click on the monitor and drag the newly edited clip anywhere in the timeline (see Figure 18.8). Then, if you want, you can set new in an out points of the same original clip and drag that to the timeline as well. Using this process, you can create a large number of scenes from one long DV movie file.

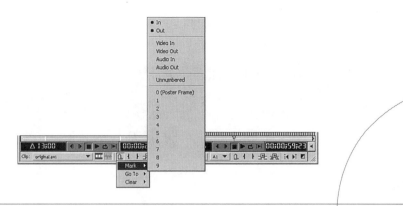

Figure 18.7

The Marker Menu—which I rarely use—gives you more options in marking off your video.

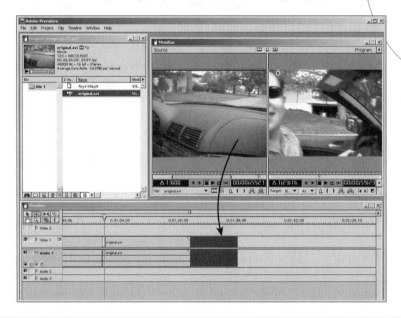

Figure 18.8

Once you are finished editing a clip, you can drag it anywhere you want in the timeline.

Insert and Overlay Buttons

Another way of adding your clips is to use the Insert and Overlay Buttons. The Insert button takes the created clip and adds it to the timeline at whatever point the timeline edit line marker is positioned. The timeline edit line marker is the needle that shows the current program position on the timeline (see Figure 18.9). If the edit line marker is positioned in the middle of a clip on the timeline, this function will cut that clip in half, insert the new clip, and move the other half of the cut clip on the other side of the added clip. No footage is ever lost using the insert method, but you can accidentally cut clips in half if you don't pay attention to the position of the edit line marker.

Figure 18.9

The timeline edit line marker reflects the current location displayed in the Program monitor.

If you position the edit line marker in an empty area between two clips and click Insert, the new clip will be placed correctly in between the adjacent clips, moving the following clip ahead enough to accommodate for the size of the new clip.

The Overlay button also adds clips to the timeline at whatever point the edit line marker is located. However, if there is not enough room for the clip, any clips that are in the way will get overlaid. In other words, if you are adding a 2-minute clip and there is only 1.5 minutes of room after the edit line marker before the next clip, the next clip will lose the first 30 seconds.

I rarely use the Insert and Overlay buttons. Of the two, I only find the Insert button useful, and only when I want to add a bunch of consecutive clips to the timeline.

Clip and Target Drop-Down Menu

Below the left time window, you will see the Clip drop-down menu. This drop-down menu enables you to select which clip you want showing in the monitor.

The clip drop-down menu is obviously for selecting clips. The drop-down window will show a list of all the previous clips you have worked on in the current project. Selecting any of one of them from the drop-down list will bring that clip into the Source monitor, for editing or previewing.

The Target drop-down menu consists of all the available tracks on the Timeline window. You have two Target drop-down menus, one for video tracks and one for audio tracks. The Target drop-down window determines the destination of clips you add to the timeline from within the Source window (see Figure 18.10). If you have the Target set to V2 (video track 2), A2 (audio track 2), and you add a clip from the Source window to the timeline—with the Insert or Overlay buttons—then the video of that clip will go to V2 and the audio will go to A2.

Figure 18.10

The Target drop-down menu enables you to specify which tracks you want to be the destination of video clips you add to the timeline with the Insert and Overlay buttons.

Take Audio and Take Video Buttons

The final two buttons in the Monitor window interface are Take Audio and Take Video. These buttons allow you to disable the audio or video in case you just want to add a clip of only the audio or video to the timeline.

Right-Click Options

Right-clicking either monitor will open up a pop-up menu of options (see Figure 18.11). Most of these options are alternative controls to functions already covered in this section.

Figure 18.11

Right-clicking on either monitor will open a pop-up menu of additional/alternate options.

The most unique and useful of these options is Open in Clip Window. This feature will open a larger resizable floating window of the Source movie that has the same identical control interface as the Source window, but has a larger screen. If you are not editing with the aid of an external TV, or just want a bigger look at your movie file, this feature can make editing easier.

Project Window

The Project window organizes all your media files—video, images, sounds (see Figure 18.12). The project window works like a file explorer program most users are probably already familiar with. Right-clicking will engage a pop-up window with several options. The main options are New and Import (see Figure 18.13).

Figure 18.12

The Project window holds all your media files for your movie.

The New function enables you to create new bins (which is Premiere's name for a folder), new storyboards, new titles, and so on. Import enables you to import video, graphics, and sound files that you can then use in your video project.

Figure 18.13

Right-clicking in the Project window will open a pop-up menu of additional/alternate options.

Storyboarding

The new Storyboard feature in Premiere 6 enables you to arrange your video clips on a storyboard where each clip is represented by a frame—the first frame of the respective video clip (see Figure 18.14). Each storyboard frame has a box beneath it where you can add info about that particular scene. Best of all, you can open each clip from the storyboard—by double-clicking clips—and edit the in and out points of that scene in the Source monitor.

Figure 18.14

The Storyboard window enables you to assemble a sequence of clips, and later automatically add them to the timeline.

Once you have completed your storyboard, you simply select the Automate to Timeline feature—right-click to get to this command—and your storyboarded movie will be added automatically to the timeline (see Figure 18.15). In general, the storyboard feature works great as a quick starting point or shortcut for getting your clips together into a movie. You will still need to eventually switch to the timeline mode, where you can then add effects, transitions, and, of course, do more editing if necessary.

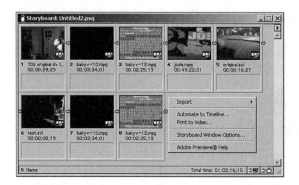

Figure 18.15

By right-clicking on the Storyboard, you can select Automate to Timeline, which will add the contents of the Storyboard to the timeline.

Adding Titles

The built-in title functionality of Premiere is the only weak part of the program (see Figure 18.16). Right-clicking in the Project window and selecting New, Title will open the Title interface.

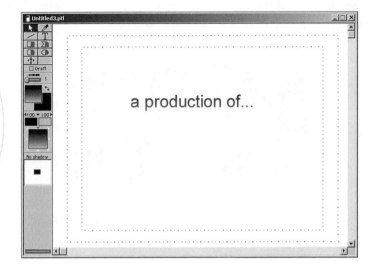

Figure 18.16

Premiere's title creation module offers a pretty simple interface with limited advanced options.

The Title interface is about as simple, and as limited, as it appears. The basic controls are on the left toolbar; the more advanced controls—font type, size, style, shadow—are accessible by right-clicking (see Figure 18.17). The title animation effects are also accessible by right-clicking. If you want your text to look smoother, you will have to add a video effect onto the timeline over the title clip.

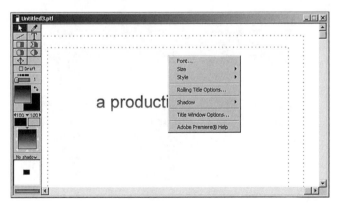

Figure 18.17

Right-clicking the Title window will open a pop-up menu of additional/alternate options.

Premiere 6 comes bundled with TitleDeko, which is a more advanced title creation plug-in that many users prefer (see Figure 18.18). If you don't like the built-in title creator in Premiere, you should install TitleDeko. Some other title creation plug-ins are also available for Premiere. For example, one of the highest-end products is Inscriber Title CG.

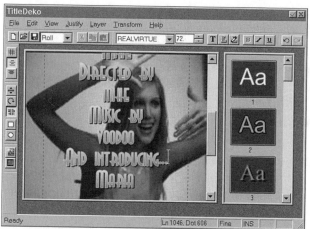

Figure 18.18

TitleDeko, which is included on the Premiere CD, offers more advanced title creation options than Premiere's Title module.

Universal Counting Leader

Right-clicking in the Project window and selecting New, Universal Counting Leader will enable you to create one of those old-school countdown windows as you may have seen in old film clips (see Figure 18.19). This is actually useful for video destined for broadcast television as it helps broadcasters cue the video up precisely.

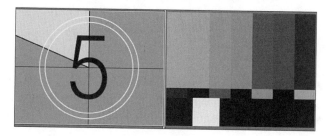

Figure 18.19

By right-clicking in the project window and selecting New, Universal Counting Leader you can create a Universal Counting Leader (old-school countdown animation) and Bars and Tone (color bar).

Bars and Tone

Right-clicking in the Project window and selecting New, Bars and Tone will allow you to create a Color Bar screen with Tone sound (see Figure 18.19). Die-hard videophiles and broadcasters use Bars and Tone to make sure their equipment is calibrated correctly for the video.

Black Video, Color Matte

Right-clicking in the Project window and selecting New, Black Video or Color Matte enables you to create a black or colored screen effect in your movie.

Timeline Window

The Timeline window is the blueprint of your movie. The Timeline window houses all the audio and video tracks of your movie on an expandable and collapsible multi-track timeline (see Figure 18.20). From this timeline interface, you can move audio and video tracks around, add and control effects and transitions, and control audio levels. Generally speaking, the more complicated the project, the more time you will spend in the Timeline window. The Timeline window controls are also the least easy to learn—but they're not that bad.

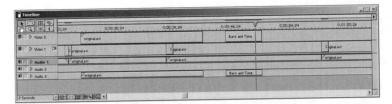

Figure 18.20

The Timeline window is where you arrange the sequence of your clips, as well as add effects and transitions.

Choosing an Interface

As discussed before, Premiere offers two kinds of interfaces, A/B Editing interface or Single-Track Editing interface. All of the tutorials in this book will be done within Single-Track interface mode because most people prefer it. To select either interface, go to Window, Workspace and you will be able to choose either A/B Editing or Single-Track (see Figure 18.21).

Main Timeline Controls

The main timeline controls are located in the top left side of the Timeline window. At first glance, there are only eight, but five of them are pop-up buttons that reveal still more buttons (see Figure 18.22).

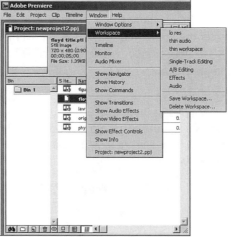

Figure 18.21

By clicking Window, Workspace you can select an A/B editing style interface or Single-Track editing inter-face.

Figure 18.22

The main Timeline control buttons are located on the top left of the Timeline window.

Selection Tool   The first and most commonly used control—which is always selected by default on program startup—is the Selection tool (see Figure 18.23). This tool looks and works like a cursor; use it for clicking, selecting, and controlling things throughout Premiere.

Custom Select Tools   The second button is a specialized set of Select Tools. The Select Tools are used for selecting multiple audio and/or video clips on the timeline far quicker than if you used the regular Selection Tool. You have the option of four different Select Tools: Range Select Tool, Block Select Tool, Track Select Tool, Multitrack Select Tool—each selects clips in a different way.

Figure 18.23

The Selection Tool is the generic cursor/pointer/selector tool in the Timeline interface.

The Range Select Tool enables you to drag a rectangle over clips you want to select. Any clip even partially inside that rectangle gets selected. The Block Select Tool works like the Range Select Tool except only the portions of the clip within the draggable rectangle are selected. The Track Select Tool enables you to click a clip and select the clip and everything on that track following it. The Multitrack Select Tool works the same way except that every track is selected.

Edit Tools   Edit tools—all five of them—are used to control special edits on the timeline (see Figure 18.24). When using each tool, you can change the size of your clips on the timeline. This clip shortening or lengthening affects the clips around it in different ways, depending on which tool you use.

Figure 18.24

The arsenal of Edit tools offers you a number of ways of editing your clips on the Timeline.

If the clip you are customizing on the timeline is from a larger movie file, when you lengthen the clip on the timeline, you are essentially adding more time from the original movie file. However, if you try to lengthen a 10-second clip which came from a 10-second movie file, by lengthening it you will just be stretching it, which will create a slow motion effect. I really don't use these particular tools much because I prefer to just use the Mark In and Out controls in the Monitor window for all my clip editing.

Rolling Edit Tool   When you lengthen a selected clip in the timeline with the Rolling Edit Tool—the adjacent clip becomes precisely that much shorter, in whichever direction you lengthened the clip (see Figure 18.25). So if you have 10 seconds of a video of the night sky next to 10 seconds of a sunset, and you lengthen the night sky scene to 12 seconds, the adjacent sunset clip will now be 8 seconds. When moving the starting or ending point of a clip, you will see a double-screen view in the Source monitor of the clip you are adjusting and the adjacent clip you are affecting. You may want to switch into Single View monitor mode to get a larger view of things. I personally find the Rolling Edit tool to be less useful than other Edit tools, but as Premiere saw fit to put it first, maybe you will decide otherwise.

Ripple Edit Tool   When you lengthen or shorten clips with the Ripple Edit Tool, no adjacent clips are themselves affected; instead the entire movie just gets longer or shorter to accommodate for the clip size change. In contrast to my opinion on the Rolling Edit tool, I think the Ripple Edit tool can be useful.

Rate Stretch Tool The Rate Stretch tool time stretches your clip so it plays slower or faster, a useful feature for introducing a high-speed or slow-motion video effect. This tool has no effect on the adjacent clips. (An easier way of changing clip speed is to right-click on the clip and select Speed.)

Figure 18.25

When using the Rolling Edit Tool you will be able to preview clip changes in the Program monitor.

Slip Tool The Slip Tool maintains the length of your movie, but enables you to change the in and out points of the selected clip without affecting the adjacent clips. When you select the Slip Tool and click on any link, you will see in the Source monitor the last frame of the preceding adjacent clip, and the first frame of the selected clip (see Figure 18.26). If no preceding clip exists, you will just see the first frame of the selected video clip. The Program monitor will display the last frame of the selected clip and first frame of the following clip. By moving the mouse left or right, you will be able to change the in and out points of the selected clip by whatever number of frames is displayed in the small white boxes inset in the monitors.

Slide Tool The Slide Tool works much like the Slip Tool except you change the adjacent clips' in and out points, while the selected clip and the entire movie length remain unchanged.

Clip Cutting Tools The clip cutting tools enable various methods of cutting up your timeline video and sound clips (see Figure 18.27).

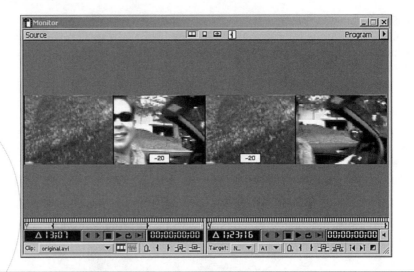

Figure 18.26

When using the Slip Tool you will be able to preview clip changes in the Source and Program Monitor.

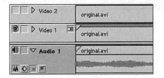

Figure 18.27

The Clip Cutting tools allow you various methods of cutting up (or splitting) your clips on the timeline.

Razor Tool and Multiple Razor Tool The Razor Tool will split a track anywhere on the timeline that you engage it (see Figure 18.28). However, it will only split that specific track of audio and video. If you want to split all of the tracks on the timeline at that point, you need to use the Multiple Razor Tool.

Figure 18.28

The razor tool enables you to cut (split) one track of linked audio and video, at whatever point you engage (left-click) the razor.

Fade Scissors Tool The Fade Scissors Tool is used to cut audio or video event rubber-bands (see Figure 18.29).

Rubberbands are a key component of the Premiere timeline interface. They are used to control video transparency (opacity), video effects, and most commonly audio levels. Handles are square nodes that you can add to a rubberband to alter the level at that point.

Figure 18.29

Rubberbands are used to control the levels of various settings in Premiere, such as audio volume, panning, and video opacity.

The magic of the Fade Scissors Tool is that it puts two handles at the same point so you can create fades more precisely. In general though, most handle creation and manipulation is done with the generic Selection Tool.

Hand Tool The Hand Tool is useful for moving around the timeline quickly, but with so many other ways to move around the timeline you may never feel the need to use the Hand tool.

Zoom Tool and Time Zoom Level Menu The Zoom Tool magnifies your audio and video tracks on the timeline in ever smaller time increments. You can achieve the same effect, usually quicker, by using the pop-up time menu—also called the Time Zoom Level—which enables you to simply choose what time increment to view your movie in (see Figure 18.30).

Figure 18.30

The Time Zoom Level pop-up menu enables you to quickly change how much or little of your movie project is displayed on the timeline.

Fade Tools Two different fade buttons are available among the main timeline controls: Cross Fade and Fade Adjustment (see Figure 18.31).

Figure 18.31

The Fade Tools afford you additional levels of control over your audio tracks.

The Cross Fade Tool is very useful if you are mixing lots of sound files into your movie. The Cross Fade Tool enables you to click on any two audio tracks that are on separate tracks but overlap in the same time area, creating an automatic cross fade between the two (see Figure 18.32). A cross fade is when the previous audio track fades out in sound volume, and the new audio track fades in. I use this feature often when I add music to my movies and need one song to cross fade into the next.

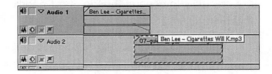

Figure 18.32

The Cross Fade Tool allows you to quickly create a cross fade between two overlapping audio tracks.

The Fade Adjustment Tool (FAT) enables you to adjust the level between two adjacent rubberband handles for quicker editing of video or audio events. FAT works faster than altering each handle, because it moves the whole line from between any two handles (see Figure 18.33).

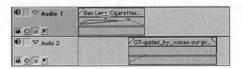

Figure 18.33

The Fade Adjustment Tool enables you to lower the level between two adjacent rubberband handles at the same time.

Link/Unlink Tool Hidden as the last button under the Fade tools is the Link/Unlink Tool. The Link/Unlink Tool (LUT) enables you to unlink or link audio and video files (see Figure 18.34). For example, when you add a clip you have captured from your camcorder, the audio and video will be linked on the timeline.

So, if you move the video file, the audio file will move with it; if you use the Razor Tool to split one, both will split; if you delete the video file, you will lose the sound file too. If you need them separate, because maybe you just need the video file or audio file for your movie, you need to unlink them. The LUT tool will allow you to unlink them; all you have to do is click on one clip and then the other. To relink them or to link together other audio and video clips, just do the same thing, click on one and then the other. You will notice that linked files are green on the timeline by default, and unlinked audio and video files are blue and yellow, respectively.

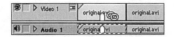

Figure 18.34

The Link/Unlink Tool allows you to link or unlink audio and video tracks. By default any tracks you add to the timeline with sound and video are linked.

Mark In and Out Tools   The final main buttons in the Timeline window are the In Point Tool and Out Point Tool buttons. By using these buttons, you are able to click on any clip and select a new in point or out point. I think these buttons are not very useful, as it is far easier to double-click any clip and set new in and out points from within the confines of the Source window interface. If you do set new in and out points via the Source window, you have to click the Apply button at the top of the Source monitor for the new changes to be applied on the timeline (see Figure 18.35).

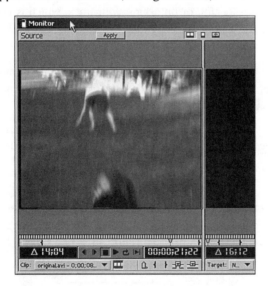

Figure 18.35

When you edit a clip on the timeline in the Source monitor, you need to click Apply to finalize your changes.

Track Controls and Interface Overview

Each track is listed as Video or Audio with a number specifying which track it is (see Figure 18.36). Every new track gets the next consecutive number assigned: Audio 2, Audio 3, Audio 4, and so on.

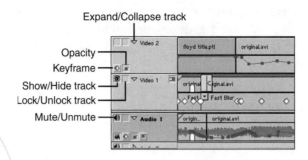

Expand/Collapse track

Opacity

Keyframe

Show/Hide track

Lock/Unlock track

Mute/Unmute

Figure 18.36

The Track interface is where you control your whole movie. You can expand/collapse tracks, hide tracks, lock tracks, mute audio tracks, control opacity, and add keyframe effects.

The first three controls are an Eye icon box, empty box, and a triangle. The Eye icon shows that this track is viewable on timeline playback and movie output. If you want to make a track invisible, click on the eye, which will remove it and leave an empty box, disabling video playback from this track.

The second box is for locking or unlocking your track, which is useful if you have things perfect and you don't want to accidentally change the settings. If you work with lots of idiots, this feature can be useful.

The final control is a triangle, which if selected will expand your track, revealing extra track information. When working with video opacity, video effects, or setting audio levels, you need to be in expanded track mode.

techtv
tip

The lower the opacity, the more see-through or transparent a video track appears.

The controls on expanded Video 1 tracks will be different than all other video tracks because all the secondary video tracks—Video 2, Video 3, and so forth—include opacity controls but Video track 1 does not (see Figure 18.37).

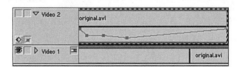

Figure 18.37

Video 1 track is the only track that has no opacity (transparency) controls. Video 2 (and all the secondary video tracks Video 3, 4, 5...) have rubberband-controlled video opacity.

If you want a video clip to be transparent, you need to place it in any video track other than Video 1.

Expanded Video Tracks and Keyframes If you add a video effect to a clip on the time-line and you are in the expanded track mode, you will see a rubberband area with the name of the effect above it. You can add keyframes anywhere along this rubberband area by clicking on the check mark (see Figure 18.38).

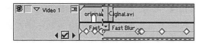

Figure 18.38

Keyframes are displayed as white diamond-shaped icons wherever they are placed along a clip.

By adding a keyframe, you will be able to add a modification to the effect at that point on the timeline. So if you were creating a scene where an actor is just getting up, you might want to create that blurry early morning vision effect. Adding several keyframes to a Blur effect, where the video blurs in and out along the timeline of the clip, would be an effective use of keyframing.

If you are in any video track—other than Video 1—you will have two extra buttons, a diamond-shaped button, which will reveal the keyframing controls, and a red handle button, which will reveal the opacity controls. Selecting either mode will hide the controls of the other mode.

Expanded Audio Tracks If you expand any audio track, you will see a rubberband that when altered affects your audio levels. Double-clicking anywhere on the rubberband creates a handle which, if moved up or down, alters the volume of the track at that point up or down (see Figure 18.39).

Figure 18.39

To manipulate a rubberband you need to create handles (by clicking at any point on the rubberband with the Selection Tool).

Final Timeline Window Controls

To the left of the timeline scrollbar are five buttons (see Figure 18.40):

- **Track Options Dialog**—allows you to name your audio and video tracks, as well as add new ones.
- **Toggle Snap to Edges**—turning this function on makes your clips snap to the edge of adjacent clips when you are moving them around in the timeline; turning this off disables that.
- **Toggle Edge Viewing**—this function allows you to view—in the Program monitor—the edge frame of any clip you resize on the timeline. The edge frame is the first or last frame at the beginning or end of your clip. As you resize a clip, the edge frame is obviously going to change. Engaging Toggle Edge View will enable you to see

the new edge frame in the Program monitor. By default, Toggle Edge Viewing is turned off, so you will need to click the Toggle Edge View button to enable it.

- **Toggle Shift Tracks Option**—this function controls how the timeline reacts to added clips. If you want clips on all the tracks to move over when you insert a clip on the timeline, click on this button so that two arrows are showing. However, if you want only clips in the Target track to be moved, click this button until a single arrow is showing. Any locked tracks will not be affected by this setting.

- **Toggle Sync Mode**—while this mode is on, which is the default, when you move linked audio and video clips they move together. But if you disable Sync Mode, your linked audio and video clips will no longer move together. This feature is an alternative to unlinking audio and video files using the Link / Unlink Tool to move them. However, unless you need to move numerous linked audio and video files separately, you are better off sticking with the Link / Unlink Tool as it is safer. Indeed, if you forget to re-enable the Sync Mode, you might accidentally move apart linked audio and video clips.

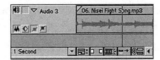

Figure 18.40

The toggle controls at the bottom of the Timeline window enable you to control major aspects of the time-line editing interface.

Timeline Markers, Time Data

At the top of the timeline you will find time markings that show the clip's location within the movie. The time increments displayed will vary depending on what level of Time Zoom you have selected.

Above the time markings is a status bar or thin strip, which is either standard gray or filled in with red indicating the rendering state of the video (Premiere calls this the Preview indicator area) (see Figure 18.41). Any area marked red needs to be rendered.

Figure 18.41

At the top of the Timeline window are the Preview indicator area, Work area bar, and time markings.

Finally, above the status bar, you will see a thicker bar, which is usually yellow, and has a gray-colored handle at the beginning and end of it. This resizable bar marks the active area of the project (also called the Work area bar), determining what can be previewed in the Program monitor and/or output to a movie file or your camcorder. The default setting of this bar is your entire movie.

Edit Line Marker

The Edit line marker is an upside-down blue triangle with a line attached to it. The Edit line marker shows the current location on the timeline within your video as displayed in the Program monitor.

OVERVIEW OF THE EFFECTS INTERFACE

The Effects interface consists of two floating windows: one that contains all of the audio and video effects as well as video transition options, and another that contains information about currently implemented effects. If you don't see these windows on your current Premiere screen, go to Window, Workspace and choose Effects.

Audio and Video Effects Palettes

The floating window storing all the video and audio effects is known in Premiere as the Audio and Video Effects palette. There are 21 built-in audio effects, 74 video effects, and 75 transitions (see Figure 18.42). The effects are divided into subfolders. You can create your own subfolders, which is useful for storing often-used effects.

Figure 18.42

The Video effects palette in Premiere includes 74 video effects. Create your own effects folder for quick access to your favorite effects.

To add an effect to your audio or video clip, just select the effect and drag it onto the timeline, placing it on top of the clip (see Figure 18.43). For transitions, drag them between clips, unless you are in A/B editing mode, in which case you would drag them to the B line of the video clip.

Effect Controls Window

The Effects Controls window is where you can see a list of all currently applied effects and where you can control those effects (see Figure 18.44).

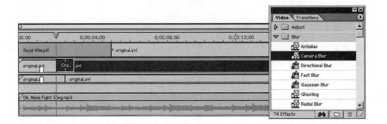

Figure 18.43

To add an effect, just left-click and drag it over your desired destination clip in the timeline.

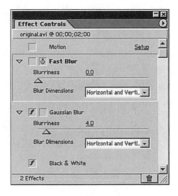

Figure 18.44

The Effects Controls window is where you can tweak your added effects.

Each effect is listed in the order applied; if you want to change the order just drag the clip higher in the order. When you have multiple effects on a clip, the timeline will show a downward arrow icon, which when clicked will show a list of all the applied effects.

Each effect can be collapsed or expanded in Effects Controls palette by clicking the triangle button to reveal the effect controls. To the right of the triangle button you'll see two buttons: the Enable Effect button and the Enable Keyframe button.

The Enable Effect button allows you to see what the effect will look like on an individual frame of the clip you applied it to. This preview will appear in the Program Monitor. To see the effect on the entire video, you have to render (see Figure 18.45). So I recommend trying to go on just the static preview; otherwise you will waste a lot of time rendering (or you can pay $1,000 for a real-time effects capture card).

NOTE

If you really are going to be using a lot of effects, are pressed for time, and have the money, consider buying the Matrox RT2500 or the Cannopus DV Storm. Both show real-time previews of most of the built-in Premiere Effects and Transitions. The DV Storm will also render them to your DV camcorder in real-time (as long as you have a fast computer and don't use too many effects simultaneously).

Figure 18.45

Premiere gives you a static preview of added video effects in the Program monitor.

The Enable Keyframe button allows you to add keyframes to your video clip. Make sure you have the video track expanded so you can see the effects rubberband. To add a keyframe, just move the edit timeline to the point where you want the keyframe and click the checkmark. You will see a diamond symbol added at that point. Click the keyframe and make any changes you want in the effects menu. Now when you render your movie, your effects will change at the point of that keyframe. If you have multiple effects on a particular video file, make sure that you have selected the right effect to add keyframes to.

AUDIO MIXER

One of the coolest new features to Premiere 6 is the audio mixer. The audio mixer enables you to control multiple audio tracks using a common mixer interface (see Figure 18.46). The magic of this mixer is that you can alter your sound levels while previewing your movie, and Premiere remembers all those changes. This allows for easy and exact audio level control.

Basic Mixer Overview

Outside of the common mixer controls—volume level, pan control (how much volume goes to the right or left speaker), mute, solo (just plays back the track selected), stop, and play—the top three timeline buttons control the mixer's level of automation. The first button, marked by the glasses icon, engages Automation Read mode. In this mode, the volume slider position moves to reflect the volume settings on the timeline. The second button, marked by the pencil icon, engages Automation Write mode. In Automation Write mode, any changes you make to the mixer during playback are saved to the timeline. The final button, marked by the circle slash icon, disables automated mixer mode. Disabling mixer automation is a good idea if you just want to experiment with the sound levels, or merely get used to the mixer controls.

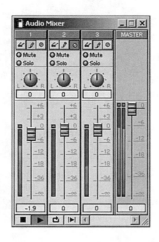

Figure 18.46

The audio mixer allows you greater control over your audio tracks on the timeline.

Advanced Mixer Controls

If you right-click the mixer, you will be able to get into the Audio Mixer Window Options (see Figure 18.47). These options contain four variables relating to Automation Write mode: Touch, Latch, Write, Write/Touch.

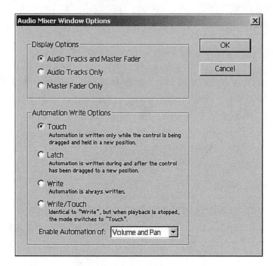

Figure 18.47

Right-clicking the audio mixer will enable you to access the Audio Mixer Window Options menu.

Touch mode is the default. In Touch mode, if you ever stop controlling the volume, the mixer goes back to the volume level of the remaining audio track. So if you wanted to lower the volume of an entire audio track, you would have to hold down the volume slider during the entire track's playback.

Latch maintains your last volume position. So if you lowered the volume on a track 12db and then let go of the mouse, the volume slider would stay in that position, changing the rest of the audio track to that level as long as you continued to play the timeline. However, when you stop playing the timeline, the volume slider goes to the volume level of the remaining audio track.

Write mode is identical to Latch except when you stop playing the timeline, the volume slider does not reset; it remains wherever you had it last.

Write/Touch mode works just like Write mode except when you stop playing, the timeline reverts to Touch mode. So when you restart timeline playback, you will be in Touch mode.

If you like to add additional audio tracks to your movies, you will probably use all of these modes; each one is useful depending on the situation. Used in conjunction with manual audio rubberband alteration, the automated mixer gives Premiere a real edge over most other prosumer editors when it comes to audio control.

Audio Effects

Audio effects are located in the same palette as video effects, and they work the same way. Just choose an effect and drag it over the desired audio clip. 21 audio effects—EQ, compression, reverb, echo, flanger, and more—come included in Premiere, but Premiere is also compatible with DirectX effects (see Figure 18.48).

DirectX Audio Plug-Ins 101

DirectX audio plug-ins are non-proprietary audio effects used and supported by most prosumer audio software. Hundreds of commercial and freeware DirectX effects are available. Unfortunately, my experience is that some work in Premiere and some don't, so not all DirectX effects will work for you. In general, I have found the simpler the plug-in, the better chance of it working. Of course, most of my favorite plug-ins are not simple and consequently don't work.

Figure 18.48

Premiere is compatible with some DirectX audio plug-ins.

An obvious instance where an audio effect would be useful would be if you have a lot of motor noise on your tape. The Hi and Low Pass filters included in Premiere may be helpful with this, but results are not that effective. Some really good noise reducing DirectX plug-ins exist, but none of them appear to work in Premiere. (You can, however, export your audio from Premiere and work on it in another sound program, and then later import it back into Premiere.)

Info Palette

The Info palette window displays clip info on any currently selected file; that's all it does (see Figure 18.49).

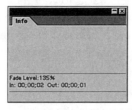

Figure 18.49

The Info palette displays clip info.

NAVIGATOR, HISTORY, COMMANDS PALETTES

The final interfacewindow in Premiere contains three palettes: Navigator, History, and Commands.

The Navigator palette provides a quick way to alter the zoom level of the timeline and a quick way to move around the timeline (see Figure 18.50). You can also manually enter exactly where you need to be in the lower left–positioned timecode window.

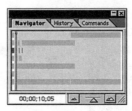

Figure 18.50

The Navigator palette allows quick movement around the timeline.

The History palette shows a list of all recent changes. Clicking any one of them will undo all changes made after that point (see Figure 18.51).

Figure 18.51

The History palette displays a list of previous event actions.

The Commands palette shows a list of all the recent commands that you have used (see Figure 18.52).

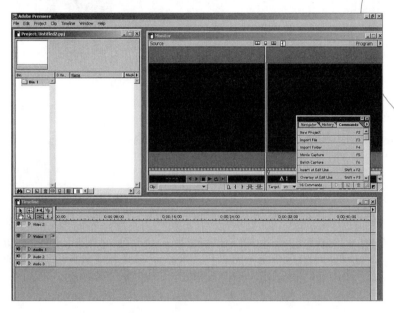

Figure 18.52

The Commands palette displays a list of previous commands.

MAIN MENU OPTIONS IN PREMIERE

Seven drop-down menus are at the top of the Premiere interface. Each contains a number of controls—some not available anywhere else in the interface. Some just offer more ways to do things already covered in this chapter. So I will mostly focus on the unique menu commands.

File Menu Options

The File menu, like in most programs, includes the more important program functions. Saving, creating new projects, outputting video, all these functions are accessible via the File menu (see Figure 18.53).

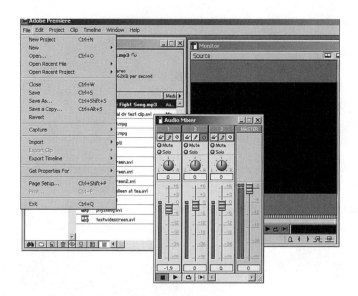

Figure 18.53

The File drop-down menu houses the more important Premiere functions.

Common File Menu Options

The following is a list of the most commonly used File menu functions:

- **New Project**—whenever you want to start a new movie project, select this.
- **Open Recent Project**—saves you time looking for where you saved your last project file. Premiere remembers the last few projects you worked on in this space.
- **Save and Save As**—self explanatory.

Capture Settings

To import video and/or audio from your camcorder, select File, Capture, Movie Capture. A monitor-based interface will pop up with VCR-like controls and a timecode window (see Figure 18.54). With this interface you can control your camcorder and capture video clips.

To the right of the monitor, you will see a settings palette which shows the current capture settings and preferences. If you want to change either, just click the Edit button.

Camcorder Settings

Premiere supports a long list of specific DV camcorders, but often the Generic DV Device Control, which is the default, works fine (see Figure 18.55). So you don't have to go into preferences and specify your exact model of camcorder if the generic controls work for you.

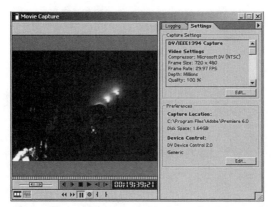

Figure 18.54

Premiere's camcorder control module allows you to take control over your camcorder and capture video.

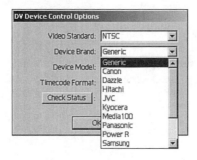

Figure 18.55

Premiere allows you to select your exact camcorder model, for better camcorder control compatibility.

By editing the Preferences, you can select where you want all the video files written (see Figure 18.56). If you have two hard drives, you will definitely want to go into Preferences and set everything to work off your secondary hard drive. With this setup, the program and operating system work off one drive, and all your captured media files will work off a second drive.

Capture Preferences

The Capture preferences should be edited if for some reason you don't want to capture to DV, or if you are getting dropped frames. Clicking Edit, DV Settings will launch a pop-up screen that lets you disable audio and/or video preview during capture (see Figure 18.57). Disabling preview will lower system resource usage and will help eliminate dropped frame issues if you have a slower computer system.

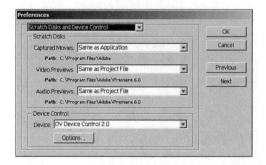

Figure 18.56

In Preferences, you can specify where you want your captured video to go—I recommend pointing everything to a second drive.

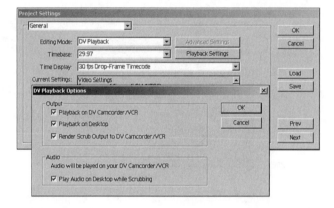

Figure 18.57

If you are having problems capturing video, you may want to alter the DV capture settings.

Batch Capture If you click the Logging palette next to the monitor, you can access the Batch Capture functions of Premiere (see Figure 18.58). As you play your video, just click the Set In and Set Out buttons, and then click Log In/Out to add the marked scene to the Batch Capture list, or Capture In/Out to immediately capture that clip. After you are done logging files, just open the Batch Capture menu and click the red record button to start the Batch Capture process.

The other Capture options in the file menu are Stop Motion Capture and Audio Capture. Audio Capture is hardly a feature, as it just launches an external audio recording program that you specify—which means you need to have an audio recording program installed on your system.

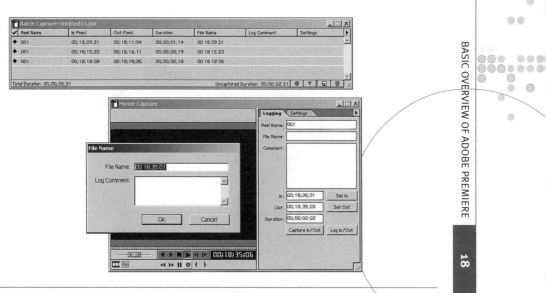

Figure 18.58

The Batch capture interface enables you to log exactly what scenes you want captured, and have Premiere automatically capture them.

Stop Motion Capture   Stop Motion Capture enables you to capture individual still video frames from your connected video devices. Right-clicking the Stop Motion interface will open up an advanced menu, where you can alter Stop Motion capture settings. One of the cooler options is time lapse capture (see Figure 18.59). For instance, if you have an hour-long video of a sunset, you can capture a frame of the video every three seconds, creating a time-lapse sunset effect. (A few higher-end camcorders like the Sony TRV900 include a time-lapse recording mode in camera.)

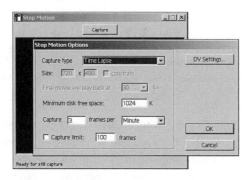

Figure 18.59

Premiere has a Stop Motion interface that allows you to create stop motion animation, as well as time lapse video sequences.

Exporting Your Clip or Movie

When you are ready to output a file or the entire movie on the timeline, go to File, Export Clip or Export Timeline (see Figure 18.60). At this point, you will be confronted with all of Premiere's Export Options. The main export options are Movie, Frame, Audio, Print To Video, Export To Tape.

Figure 18.60

Once you are ready to output your movie, select File, Export Timeline.

Since Premiere renders DV out to FireWire in real-time whenever you play anything in the Premiere interface, you can theoretically manually press record on your DV camcorder and just play the entire timeline. The advantage of using the File, Export Timeline method is that you have a status window that will alert you if frames are dropped.

The Movie Export option, along with Cleaner Export, Advanced Windows Media, and Advanced RealMedia Export options, enable you to create a movie file of selected clips or the entire timeline in a wide range of formats. If you are creating video for a VCD, you might want to use Cleaner. If you were creating a video file for the Web, you could use Cleaner, Windows Media, or RealMedia.

The Export to Movie option enables you to save your video in AVI, DV AVI, QuickTime, animated GIF, and a few other formats (see Figure 18.61). All you do is select which file format you want from the drop-down box of the export movie dialog window. Most formats have advanced settings that can be tweaked. You can access these settings by clicking the Settings button. If you install third-party encoding plug-ins (which you will need to do if you want quality MPEG-1 and MPEG-2–encoded video in Premiere), they will usually show up in this drop down-box unless they integrate themselves into the Premiere menu interface (similar to Cleaner, Windows Media, and RealMedia encoders).

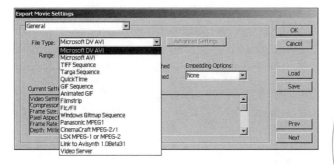

Figure 18.61

Premiere offers many different file format output options.

Project Menu Options

The two important functions accessible from the Project drop-down menu are Project Settings and Automate to Timeline. Automate to Timeline was already covered. This function allows you to add your Storyboard files to the timeline, or if you have a bunch of images, you can add them all to the timeline for a nice photo montage.

Project Settings resembles program preferences for each individual project. If you select Project, Projects settings, a window will pop up allowing you to access various settings in five categories (see Figure 18.62). The categories—General, Video, Audio, Keyframe and Rendering, Capture—are selectable from a drop-down box.

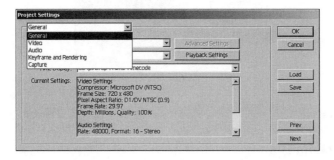

Figure 18.62

Project settings are like program preferences for each movie project.

The only Project Settings that I might recommend altering are the Playback Settings—accessible under General. Click the Playback Settings button, and a dialog window will appear called DV Playback options (see Figure 18.63). If you are using an external TV, you may want to deselect the Playback on Desktop box as it will save processor power, especially if you are having playback problems. Furthermore, if you are not previewing on your camcorder's LCD or an external TV, you can deselect the Playback on DV Camcorder/VCR box, as it will also save processor power, improving your on-screen playback.

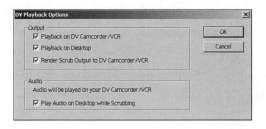

Figure 18.63

If you are having problems smoothly outputting your video to tape altering the DV playback settings often helps.

Timeline Menu Options

On the Timeline drop-down menu, you can access the render options—Render Work Area and Render Audio (see Figure 18.64). If you have added effects to your movie, you will need to render them before you can preview them. To do this, you will need to select Render Work Area for audio and video, or if you have only added audio effects, Render Audio. Depending on the number of effects you have added to your movie, and the length of those effects, you may be in for a wait.

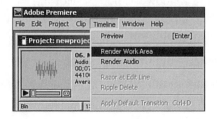

Figure 18.64

If you added any effects or transitions, you will need to render them before you can output your movie.

Window Menu Options

The Window drop-down menu is where you can go to choose or change the look of the program. If you go to Window, Workspace, you can choose from four prefab editing interfaces or you can customize your own—highly recommended—and save your newly created interface for future use (see Figure 18.65). You can also reveal or hide various windows—audio mixer, effects, monitor, and so on—from this drop-down menu.

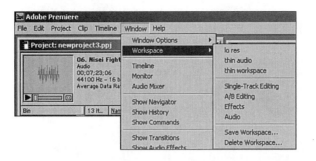

Figure 18.65

To change the layout of your workspace or create a custom workspace, go to Window, Workspace and choose from one of the options.

Alternatives to the Main Menus

Besides the regular Premiere interface controls and the drop-down menu controls, there is a tremendous number of keyboard shortcuts. The most common of these is the spacebar, which starts and stops timeline video playback. The main keyboard shortcuts are listed on the Premiere Quick Reference Card, in the Help files, and of course your Premiere manual (which I am sure you have already read).

CHAPTER 19

BASIC EDITING IN ADOBE PREMIERE 6

The following is a quick overview and tutorial for editing video in Adobe Premiere 6. I will cover inputting your video from your DV camcorder, editing and arranging scenes, adding music tracks, adding titles, adding transitions, using effects, and finally outputting back to your camcorder or to a Web-playable video format. For a more advanced overview of Premiere make sure you read Chapter 18. *A demo of Premiere is on the Program CD included with this book.*

STARTING A NEW PROJECT IN PREMIERE

After you have your camcorder powered on and set to playback mode, plug in the FireWire cable and launch Premiere. Additionally, if you are going to be using an external TV as a monitor, hook up the A/V out of your camcorder to the TV as well (see Figure 19.1).

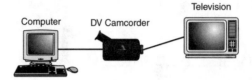

Figure 19.1

Hooking your camcorder to an external TV will enable you to preview all your video playback in Premiere on the TV.

The first thing you will see when you launch Premiere is the Load Project Settings window (see Figure 19.2). In this window you select the appropriate template for your source video and desired output. Usually this will be DV-NTSC or DV-PAL Standard 48kHz. These templates have all the correct settings for normal interlaced DV video.

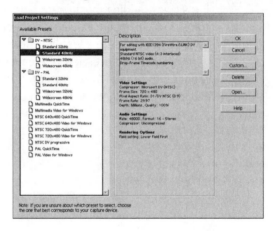

Figure 19.2

When you start a new project, the first thing you have to do is pick a template.

If you have a progressive video–capable camcorder and have shot in that mode–and want to keep your video in that mode–you will need to create your own custom template by clicking the Custom button.

Just highlight the PAL or NTSC Standard 48kHz DV template, which will enable you to start from the settings of this template. Then click Custom and select the Keyframe and Rendering option from the drop-down menu. Go to the Fields drop-down box, and select No Fields. Then select the Save button and name your new template appropriately, such as *DV Progressive* (see Figure 19.3). Whenever you want to work with progressive frame footage, use this project template.

Figure 19.3

If you are editing progressive video footage you will need to create a custom template.

CUSTOMIZING YOUR PREMIERE INTERFACE

In Premiere, everything is resizable and customizable, so set up the interface to your liking and then go to Window, Workspace, Save Workspace (see Figure 19.4). You probably will want to set up multiple workspaces to suit different editing tasks. I have one for general video editing, and another for when I am doing a lot of audio work. Using the Window drop-down menu you can open or hide all of the various elements of Premiere.

Figure 19.4

Throughout the movie building process you can change between several workspaces by going to Window, Workspace.

CAPTURING DV VIDEO IN PREMIERE

Once you have chosen a template and workspace, go to the File drop-down menu and select File, Capture, Movie Capture. A Movie Capture window will appear with a monitor, VCR-like controls, and a Logging and Settings palette (see Figure 19.5).

Premiere enables you to choose your exact model camcorder from within the Settings palette; however, the default Generic DV Device Control works fine for most camcorders, so you can often skip this step. If you have camcorder control problems, go to the Settings palette and select the Edit button under Preferences. A Preferences window will pop up. Under Device Control, click the Other button and another interface will appear, enabling you to choose your specific model DV camcorder (see Figure 19.6).

Figure 19.5

In Movie Capture mode you can easily control your camcorder and capture footage from it.

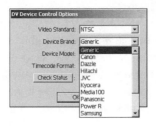

Figure 19.6

Premiere enables you to select your exact camcorder model in the Preferences, to ensure perfect camcorder control.

Capture Control Overview

The Movie Capture interface has ten camera control buttons (Keyboard Shortcuts are in parentheses): Frame Back (left arrow), Frame Forward (right arrow), Stop (S), Play ('), Slow Reverse, Slow Play, Rewind (R), Fast Forward (F), Pause, and Record (G). You will also see a Shuttle bar for controlling the camcorder. The farther you move it one way or another the faster your video will go. Above the Shuttle is a Frame Jog, a thin horizontal line strip that moves video back and forth more precisely. A time code window will display your camcorder's time code information.

Once you click Record, capture will begin on whatever you are playing in the monitor. You will see a dialog that will tally frames captured and frames dropped above the monitor (see Figure 19.7). Clicking Stop or pressing Esc will end the capture, and a File Name screen will pop up. Enter your desired file name for the newly captured clip and click OK.

All clips you capture will go into whatever Bin is highlighted on the Project window. So, if you want to capture clips to different Bin files, you will have to switch which Bin is highlighted after each capture. The Project window works like any file explorer interface, so you can always drag and drop files later on.

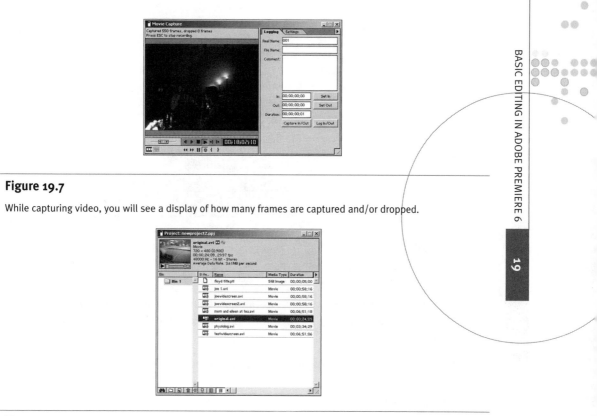

Figure 19.7

While capturing video, you will see a display of how many frames are captured and/or dropped.

Figure 19.8

The Project window is where all your movie files are organized.

Advanced Capture Control

From the Movie Capture interface, you can also perform batch captures to mark out all the scenes you want captured from your camcorder (see Figure 19.9). Make sure the Logging palette is selected and while previewing your DV video camcorder playback use the Set In and Set out buttons which are positioned right next to the Record button, or use the Set In and Set Out buttons on the Logging palette. Every time you finish marking off a clip that you want to add to the Batch Capture list, select the Log In/Out button and you will be asked to name the clip—by default each clip is timecode labeled. The Batch Capture dialog will pop up after that, and all subsequent scenes you mark off will be added to the Batch Capture list in the same way. Once you are done marking off your video, just click the red Record button at the bottom of the Batch Capture window, and the automated batch capture process will begin.

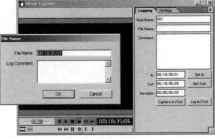

Figure 19.9

Premiere's Batch Capture control enables you to mark off all clips you want captured, and the program will import them all from your camcorder automatically.

As previously stated, Batch Capture strains your camcorder drive and is more time-consuming than capturing footage the normal way and editing out clips later. So I don't recommend using this feature.

Once you're done capturing your video, close the Movie Capture window.

Capture Caveats

If you are using Win98/WinMe or Win2k/XP with FAT32, you can only capture 4GB of video per individual file. That translates to about 20 minutes (DV takes up one gigabyte per five minutes of footage). I have never found this to be a problem whatsoever. In the rare occasion that you have to stop capture in the middle of a scene you want, reassembling that scene is, as they say, wicked easy. If you are using Win2k or XP with the NTFS file system, you have no capture size limitations. Additionally, there are no file size limits for Mac users.

QUICK USER INTERFACE OVERVIEW

In case you skipped over the previous chapter, I will briefly go over the basic Premiere user interface before we go with the editing tutorial.

Premiere has three main parts of the interface: Project window, Monitor window, and Timeline window (see Figure 19.10). The Project window is where all video, music, and image files for your project are kept. The Monitor window is where all video and/or audio from your clips or the timeline can be previewed and edited into smaller clips. The Timeline window is where you arrange all of the media elements for your movie project.

Project window   Monitor window   Timeline window

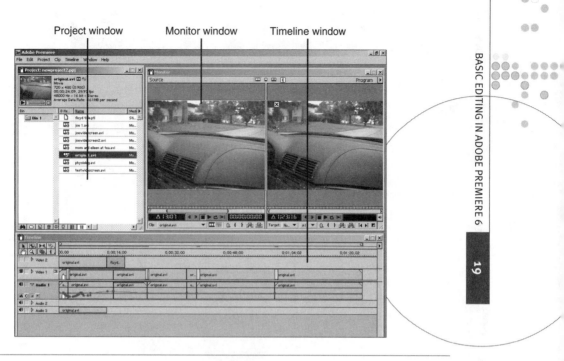

Figure 19.10

Adobe Premiere 6 has a very well-designed interface overall.

Additionally, a number of secondary interface elements—Audio Mixer, Effects palettes, Effects Controls, Navigator, History and Commands palettes—round out the Premiere interface. Each one will be covered when its use becomes relevant to this tutorial.

EDITING SCENES FROM CAPTURED VIDEO

Editing out scenes from your captured video is the heart of the editing process. Just click on whatever file you want to edit scenes from in the Project window, and it will appear in the Source monitor (see Figure 19.11). If you are in Twin View mode—recommended, just select the left double monitor icon button—the Source monitor is the left monitor. (The second monitor, the Program monitor, previews whatever you have on the timeline; in other words, your movie.)

If you are not using an external TV as a preview monitor and you find the Source monitor too small to work with, right-click on the Source monitor and select Open in Clip Window. This function will open a larger resizable monitor window with all the same controls found on the Source monitor window (see Figure 19.12). So, whichever mode you work in, all the following controls discussed will be the same.

Figure 19.11

The Monitor window allows you to preview clips and the timeline, and most clip editing takes place here.

Figure 19.12

If you find the Source monitor too small, you can select Open in Clip Window and get a larger monitor workspace.

Source Monitor Controls—Editing Clips

The Source monitor controls allow you to preview and edit your clips (see Figure 19.13). There are two main Source monitor controls for editing clips. The first is the Shuttle—the upside-down blue triangle—that you can move to quickly get around the clip. Above that is a thin striped bar which is the Frame Jog. Moving it right or left will allow you more precise movement within a few frames.

Mark In and Out Buttons

The two most important buttons are the Mark In and Mark Out buttons. These buttons enable you to precisely mark off scenes you want to add to your movie from your captured video clips. All you have to do is find the starting frame of the clip you want to create, click Mark In, and then find the desired ending frame of your clip and click Mark Out.

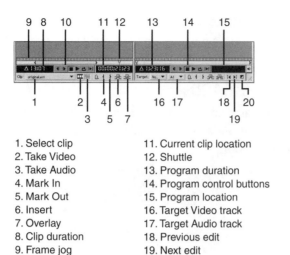

1. Select clip
2. Take Video
3. Take Audio
4. Mark In
5. Mark Out
6. Insert
7. Overlay
8. Clip duration
9. Frame jog
10. Clip control buttons
11. Current clip location
12. Shuttle
13. Program duration
14. Program control buttons
15. Program location
16. Target Video track
17. Target Audio track
18. Previous edit
19. Next edit
20. Add default transition

Figure 19.13

The easiest way to edit your clips is to use the Source monitor controls.

Then click on the monitor window, hold down, and drag your newly edited clip anywhere you want on the timeline (see Figure 19.14). If you are going to be editing a bunch of clips, and want them to follow each other on the timeline, click on the Insert button and the clip will be added to the timeline.

Figure 19.14

Once you are finished editing a clip you can drag it from the Monitor window to the Timeline.

If you want to grab another scene from the same video file, just set a new in and out point and repeat the above steps for adding it to the timeline. With this method, you can edit all your scenes from one really long file capture—or a few medium size captured files.

USING THE STORYBOARD

Another option for assembling clips into a movie is using the Storyboard. Just right-click the file area of the Project window and select New, Storyboard. A storyboard window will pop up (see Figure 19.15).

Figure 19.15

The Storyboard allows you a quick and easy way to assemble your clips.

You can then drag desired movie files from the project window into the Storyboard. If you want a bunch of scenes from one particular video file, just drag multiple instances of that file on to the Storyboard and each one will become a separate scene on the Storyboard.

Editing Scenes via the Storyboard

If you need to specify new in and out points for any of the files added to the Storyboard, just double-click on the Storyboard frame and the file will appear in the Source monitor. Use the same marking process as defined earlier, marking the in and out points.

You can also work on any one movie file in the Source monitor, edit out a clip—or multiple clips—and drag each new clip into the Storyboard as a new scene.

Adding the Storyboard to the Timeline

Once you are done editing and arranging clips on the Storyboard, the next step is to add those clips to the timeline. Premiere makes this easy with the Automate to Timeline function. Just right-click in any empty area of the Storyboard window and select Automate to Timeline (see Figure 19.16).

Figure 19.16

The Automate to Timeline function adds the contents of the Storyboard to the timeline.

A window will pop up allowing you a number of options—desired timeline placement, transition, frame overlap, and so on (see Figure 19.17). By default, Use Transition is selected. I recommend turning this off unless you want a transition between every scene. Keep in mind that most films and TV shows have few to no transitions between shots. If you disable transitions, set frame overlap to zero (so your clips will not overlap).

Figure 19.17

You can customize how you want the contents of your storyboard added to the timeline.

In addition, for some reason audio is disabled by default, so unless are making a silent movie, or some kind of Baywatch style music video montage, make sure Ignore Audio is unchecked. If your Timeline is empty, then Insert at Beginning is the correct setting.

Personally, I don't use the Storyboard feature, as I find editing in the Source monitor and adding clips to the timeline manually to be faster. If the appeal of Storyboard is being able to see individual frames of each video, you can set the Timeline window to display the first frame of each clip on the timeline by right-clicking in the Timeline window, selecting Timeline Window Options, and changing the track display preferences (see Figures 19.18 and 19.19). This feature will raise your RAM usage, so if you have 256MB or less of RAM I would recommend not doing this.

Figure 19.18

Premiere enables you to customize how your video tracks are displayed on the timeline.

Figure 19.19

These are some examples of the different ways to display your video tracks on the timeline.

OVERVIEW OF TIMELINE INTERFACE

The Timeline interface enables you to move around the sequence of your clips, add additional video and audio tracks, and add effects and transitions. The most important function on the Timeline window is the Time Zoom Level. Altering this—the pop-up menu on the lower-right corner—alters how much of your movie you see on the timeline (see Figure 19.20). If you want a broad view of the entire movie, you would set it to one minute or higher; if you want to take a close look at a small amount of the film for more precise editing, maybe one second or lower.

Getting Started on the Timeline

Once you are done editing clips in the Monitor or Storyboard, the action moves to the Timeline, where you can reorder your clips and start polishing your movie.

Figure 19.20

The Time Zoom pop-up menu enables you to quickly alter how much of your program is displayed on the timeline.

If you want to change the order of the clips, just drag and drop desired clips to new positions. If you want to re-edit any clips, just double-click them and they will show up in the Source monitor where you can alter them further. The Source monitor will only display the clip from the edited in and out point. So, if you wanted to make the clip longer, you will need to right-click in the monitor window and select Edit Original (see Figure 19.21).

Figure 19.21

When editing timeline clips in the Source monitor, you have the option of editing the original clip.

When you set a new in and out point on a clip in the timeline, a button labeled Apply will appear at the top of the Source monitor. To finalize your changes to the clip on the timeline, you need to click Apply (see Figure 19.22).

If the new clip ends up being longer, the movie will automatically lengthen to accommodate the new duration. However, if it's shorter, you will now have an empty space on the timeline and in your movie. If you are moving clips around a lot, you might end up with empty spaces, too. For the sake of this tutorial, shorten one of you clips on the timeline (you can undo it right afterwards) or create an empty space some other way.

To eliminate the empty space, you need to use the Track Selection Tool, which is the in the second button location (clockwise) on the top left corner of the Timeline window (see Figure 19.23).

Figure 19.22

When editing timeline clips in the Source monitor you need to click the Apply button to finalize your changes.

Figure 19.23

The Track selection tools allow you multiple ways of selecting your video and audio tracks.

Select the Track Selection Tool, and click on the clip that follows the empty space. You will see that all the clips on that track become highlighted. Now, just drag the selected clips over to fill the empty space. If you had multiple tracks of video and audio that you needed to move over to fill an empty space—a less common occurrence—you would use the Multitrack Select Tool. If, however, you just want to move one clip around, you would use the generic Selection Tool.

Adding Transitions

To add a transition, click the Transitions Palette, locate your desired transition, and then just drag it in between clips (see Figure 19.24). You can only add transitions to clips in the main video track—Video 1. Furthermore, if you double-click any transition, a preview settings window will pop up, giving you a general idea of how it looks. You have to render the transition before you can preview it unless you have one of the real-time effects video cards—Matrox RT2500 or Canopus DV Storm. Figure 19.25 gives you an idea of how many transitions Premiere offers you.

To alter the Transition duration, you can right-click on the transition on the timeline and select Duration from the pop-up options window; this is the easiest way. Alternatively, if you select a close zoom level—4 seconds and below—you can drag the transition larger, with the default Selection Tool, (see Figure 19.26). However, transitions are hard to drag larger unless you have the zoom level maxed out; at lower time zoom levels transitions are too thin on the timeline for the Selection tool to detect the transition edge.

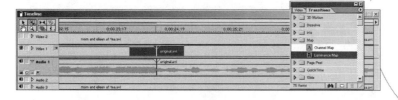

Figure 19.24

To add a transition, drag it from the Transitions palette in between any two adjacent clips.

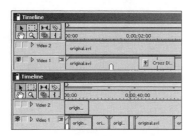

Figure 19.25

Premiere includes 75 available transitions; don't take that as an invitation to use them all.

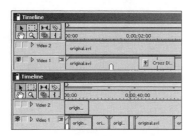

Figure 19.26

If you want to drag transitions larger you need to choose a high zoom level, otherwise the cursor does not have enough room to detect the transition edge.

If you are having trouble seeing your transitions on the timeline—which can happen if you are zoomed out too much—you might want to switch into A/B Track mode. When in A/B mode, transitions are placed on a separate line below the video track (see Figure 19.27). You can engage A/B mode by clicking the white and gray rectangle button on the right corner of the Video 1 track.

Adding Video Effects

Adding effects in Premiere is also a simple drag-and-drop affair (see Figure 19.28). And while you can't see video previews of effects—unless you have a real-time effects card—you can see still frame previews, which works well enough. Go to the Blur effects folder, and add Fast Blur to one of your clips. And check out Figure 19.29 for an idea of all the video effects to choose from.

Figure 19.27

In A/B mode transitions are placed on a separate track from your video clips.

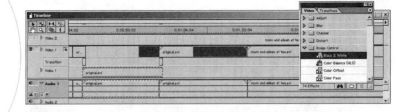

Figure 19.28

To add a video effect, simply drag it on top of any video clip in the timeline.

Figure 19.29

Premiere includes 73 video effects accessible via the Effects palette.

When adding effects, make sure you have the video track expanded. When expanded, you will see an extra rubberbanded track under your video file, with the name of the effect applied on it—in this case Fast Blur. If you apply multiple effects to a track, a downward triangle button will appear next to the primary effect name, which when clicked will open up a drop-down menu of all the other effects applied to that track (see Figure 19.30).

Effects Controls

When you add an effect to a clip, the effect will also appear on the Effects Controls palette—accessible via Window, Show Effects Controls (see Figure 19.31). The Effects Controls palette is where you can adjust video effects parameters—most effects have adjustable parameters, a few do not. For instance, if you added the Fast Blur effect to a clip, you could set blurriness by moving a triangle icon along a slider. You could also set whether you wanted horizontal fast blur (which would create the illusion of fast horizontal motion), vertical fast blur (which would create the illusion of fast vertical motion), or a horizontal and vertical fast blur (which would create the illusion that the camera man was shaking the camera every which way). Every effect has its own set of editable parameters. You can also arrange the order of effects, if you have more than one applied.

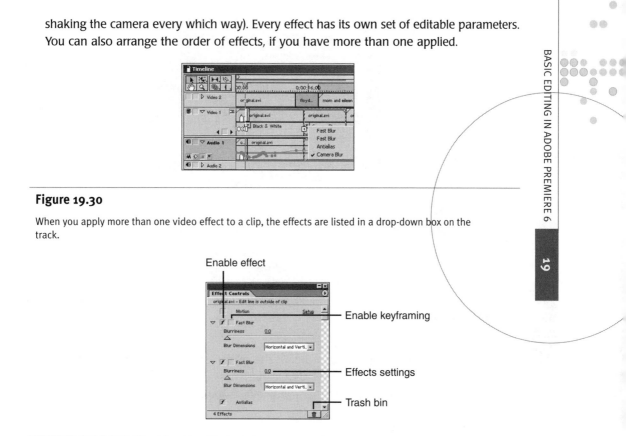

Figure 19.30

When you apply more than one video effect to a clip, the effects are listed in a drop-down box on the track.

Figure 19.31

The Effects Controls palette is where you can customize or remove added effects.

As you tweak the effect settings parameters, you can view a static preview of the effect on one frame of your movie in the Program Monitor (see Figure 19.32). The static effect preview will also output to DV, so if you are editing with an external TV you will observe a nice large-screen static preview.

Keyframing

Keyframing enables you to alter an effect at different points throughout the clip. So if you wanted to capture the effect of someone drunk, disoriented, or sleepy, you could take a subjectively shot video clip and add varying amounts of blur to it along the timeline. You can do this with keyframes.

To add keyframes, just position the edit line wherever you want the keyframe to go and then click the empty box under the Video 1 text. A diamond-shaped keyframe will appear (see Figure 19.33).

Figure 19.32

When you add a video effect you can see a static preview in the Program monitor.

Figure 19.33

Keyframing enables you to alter an effect over the duration of a clip.

Click on the keyframe and then adjust the effects parameters as desired. To add more keyframes, repeat the same steps. Using keyframes adds many effects options to your editing arsenal, and generally can make your effects look more natural.

Adding Audio Tracks

You can add all the audio tracks you want to your movie project. By default you have three; the first audio track corresponds to the audio from video files added to Video 1 track (assuming you captured your movies with audio). To add more audio tracks, just right-click on an empty part of the timeline and select Add Audio Track from the pop-up menu.

You can add most of the major sound file formats to your Premiere timeline—WAV, AIFF— and you can also add MP3 files to the timeline.

Audio Track Controls

If you want to change the levels of your audio, Premiere includes a number of easy ways; the primary methods are adjusting the audio rubberbands or using the Audio Mixer.

Audio Rubberbands

Expand the audio track you want to work on; you will then see a red rubberband track (see Figure 19.34). To adjust the volume levels for your track, click anywhere on the rubberband and a square will appear, called a handle (see Figure 19.35). Move the handle up or down to raise or lower the volume. The more precise you need your volume to be, the more handles you will have to create.

Figure 19.34

You can alter your audio levels via the audio rubbberband.

Figure 19.35

Clicking anywhere on the audio volume rubberband creates a handle, which you can then move up or down to raise or lower the volume level of that track.

If you want to change the panning of your track, click on the blue handle button, and the blue panning control rubberband will appear (see Figure 19.36).

Pan rubberband button

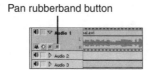

Figure 19.36

The blue rubbberband allows you to customize the panning of your audio track.

Audio Mixer

The Audio Mixer—choose Window, Audio Mixer—makes audio editing even easier than the previous approach, especially if you are working with multiple audio tracks (see Figure 19.37). All you need to do is click on the pencil icon for the track you want to edit the levels of. Then play the timeline and adjust the volume level using the slider. The levels you set will be automatically written to the audio rubberbands (see Figure 19.38). The same holds true for any panning changes you make on the mixer. You should practice with the pencil icon unselected until you get the hang of using the mixer.

Adding Audio Effects

Adding audio effects works the same way as adding video effects (see Figure 19.39). You can even keyframe your audio effects. Audio effects can among other things be helpful in eliminating motor noise. Using both the Highpass and/or Lowpass Bandpass filter effects can sometimes help minimize motor noise. After adding an effect, click the Setup link in the Effect Controls. Then click the Preview Sound box and adjust the effect to your liking (see Figure 19.40).

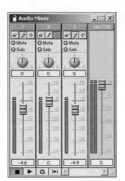

Figure 19.37

The Audio Mixer enables you to easily customize your audio levels over multiple tracks.

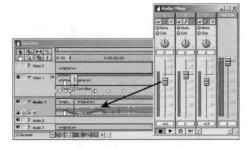

Figure 19.38

When in Write mode, any changes you make on the Audio Mixer are reflected by the audio rubberbands.

Figure 19.39

Premiere includes 21 audio effects in the Audio Effects palette.

Premiere also works with DirectX effects, technically; though, I have found the more complicated the plug-in, the less likely it will work.

Figure 19.40

You can preview your added audio effects by checking the Preview box in the Settings window.

ADDING TITLES

To add titles to your video, right-click on an empty space in the Project window and select New, Title, which will then launch the title creator (see Figure 19.41).

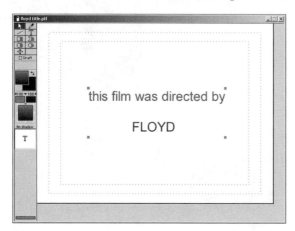

Figure 19.41

The built-in title creator offers only basic title creation capability.

The title creation interface is straightforward. All the controls are on the left of the workspace, and if you right-click in the title work area, you can access additional controls (see Figure 19.42).

Figure 19.42

Right-clicking in the title creation window will open up a pop-up menu of additional/alternate options.

You can choose your font color, including gradients (which are a combo of two colors) by customizing the color boxes. You can also create a shadow effect for your text, setting the shadow color and direction.

If you put the title on one of the secondary video tracks, the title text will automatically show over the video in the primary video track (see Figure 19.43).

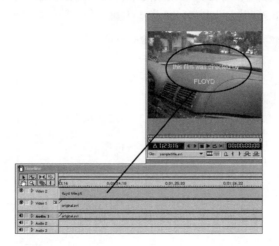

Figure 19.43

Any title added to a secondary track, Video 2, 3, 4, and so on, will be overlaid on whatever clip is on the Video 1 track.

Rolling Titles, Title Animation

To create rolling credits or other title animations, select the T icon with four arrows around it (see Figure 19.44). With this tool, drag a rectangle as big as you want your title area to be. Then fill it with text. You have to fill the entire visible area or the text won't scroll from offscreen to onscreen, so fill the box with empty spaces if you don't have enough text. If you are going to be scrolling upward, you will want to add a bunch of empty space before your text starts. Then right-click, select Rolling Title Options, and select which direction you want the title to animate (see Figure 19.45).

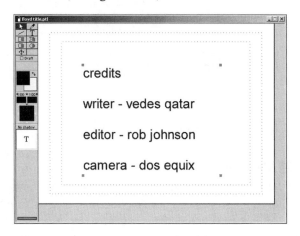

Figure 19.44

You can create rolling text animations in Premiere title creator.

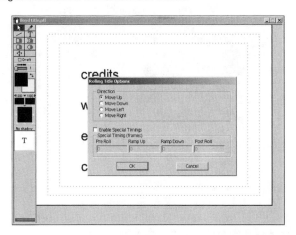

Figure 19.45

You can customize your title animations in the Rolling Title Options window.

Title Fade In and Fade Out

If you want your titles to fade in and out, you will need to apply that effect on the timeline. Just add your titles to one of the secondary video tracks. Expand the tracks so that the opacity rubberband is showing. Alter the rubberband to conform to where you want the title to fade in and out (see Figure 19.46). If you want to fade out, move the rubberband down; if you want a fade in effect, start the rubberband down and move it up—so your rubberband looks like an up ramp.

Figure 19.46

To create a text fade you will need to lower the opacity rubberband.

Advanced Title Creation

The Title creator built into Premiere is one of the weaker elements of the program. For more advanced title creation, you can use the TitleDeko plug-in, which is included on the Premiere CD (see Figure 19.47). I sometimes use a budget video editor like VideoStudio or Videowave to make titles, importing the result into my Premiere projects.

Figure 19.47

TitleDeko, a third-party text plug-in, is included on the Retail Box Premiere CD.

WORKING WITH MULTIPLE VIDEO LAYERS

Premiere enables you to add up to 99 video layers to the timeline. All secondary video layers—any video layer other than Video 1—have an opacity rubberband. The default is full opacity, which means that if you add a video clip on Video 2 it will block whatever video clip you have on Video 1. If you lower the opacity rubberband, thereby increasing the transparency, you will now see the clip in Video 1 through a transparent Video 2 clip (see Figure 19.48).

Transparency effects are useful for many different functions. You can create ghost scenes with it by shooting a room twice, once with the room empty and once with a person walking through it. Place the second clip on Video 2, increase the transparency, and you now have a ghost walking though the room. All transparency changes will have to be rendered—choose Timeline, Render Work Area—before you can preview them.

Figure 19.48

By altering opacity (transparency) you can have the clip on Video 1 show through the clip on Video 2.

OUTPUTTING YOUR VIDEOS IN PREMIERE

When you are done building your movie, you have multiple output options. First of all, if you have added any effects or transitions, you need to render the entire movie project—Timeline, Render Work Area. For reference, a ten-minute film with four five-second transitions, a ten-second title sequence, and a one-minute black and white effect took ten minutes to render on a 1GHz computer. However, some of the special effects can add up to an hour to your rendering time just for a one-minute effect. Since Premiere only renders effects and transitions, length and type of effects and transitions will determine how long rendering takes. If you don't add any effects or transitions to your movie, rendering time will be zero, no matter the length or the number of scenes of your movie.

Once everything is rendered, you are ready to output. All of your output options are available from File, Export Timeline (see Figure 19.49).

Figure 19.49

To export your movie, select File, Export Timeline, and select from one of the options.

You can output your movie in multiple ways—you don't have to choose just one. Your main options are to output back to your camcorder or to create a Web-optimized video—for playback on the Internet or to send via e-mail. For the latter, you can use the Advanced Window Media export tool, the Advanced RealMedia Export tool, or the Save For Web option, which opens the included Cleaner EZ encoder plug-in.

If you are interested in the highest quality, then outputting back to DV tape is still the best quality option available. While home DVD authoring is now possible, encoder quality has not reached archival quality (*archival quality* means you don't lose any quality). Furthermore, the best quality DVD MPEG-2 consumer encoders take longer to encode than outputting to DV tape.

If you are interested in creating MPEG-1 or MPEG-2 for VCD, SVCD, or DVD videos, you will need to buy an additional plug-in for Premiere, as Premiere does not include MPEG-1/2 capability. Use of these plug-ins will be covered in the next chapter.

Outputting Back to Your Camcorder

If you are exporting back to your DV camcorder, you would select File, Export Timeline, Export to Tape. After selecting Export to Tape, a settings window will pop up (see Figure 19.50). Check the Activate Recording Deck box, which will engage record on your camcorder, and start outputting the movie when you click the OK button.

Figure 19.50

When you select Export to Tape, this options window will appear.

If you are outputting back to tape for the first time, you should monitor things to make sure the output is working perfectly. Don't pay attention to video on the computer monitor, which will probably be stuttery during output; that's normal. However, the signal into your camcorder should have no stuttering or audio dropouts. If you experience any video or audio dropouts, consult the optimization guide below.

Premiere DV Output Optimization Guide

The following is a lengthy list of all the things to check and/or try when you run into problems outputting your video back to tape.

- Install the Premiere 6.01 update (and any other available updates) which can be downloaded from the Adobe Web site under Support, Downloads.

- Uninstall Premiere 6, reboot your computer, and then reinstall. You will be surprised by how often this fixes problems.

- When plugging the FireWire jack into your camcorder, if you get a message to overwrite any system files, always select Keep the Most Recent File. If you accidentally do otherwise then uninstall/reinstall Premiere.

- Go to Control Panel, System, click on the Device Manager tab, and then click on Disk Drives. Click on each IDE drive, and then click the Settings tab and make sure DMA is enabled.
- In Premiere, go to General project settings and click the Playback Settings button. Disable the Playback to Desktop feature when you are ready to output to camera.
- Defrag your hard drives.
- Lower your monitor resolution during the output process to 800×600. Having your monitor at a high resolution can drain CPU cycles.
- If you are running Win98/Me, then go to System Properties, Performance, Virtual Memory, and select Let Me Specify My Own Virtual Memory Settings. Then set the minimum and maximum to 192, and reboot. After that, if you get any low on system memory warnings, you'll need to raise the settings; raise both in increments of 32.
- Make sure you have the latest drivers for your motherboard.
- Make sure you flash your motherboard with the latest stable version BIOS (especially if you have an AMD CPU and motherboard, or any VIA chipset motherboard). Check your motherboard manufacturer's site for the latest BIOS. A note about flashing BIOS: If you have never done it before it can seem fairly involved, but it is not. Just follow the directions (included with the BIOS) and it will only take a few minutes.
- If you have recently upgraded motherboards and did not reformat your hard drive and reinstall everything, *DO IT*. Make sure you back up all your data to another drive before reformatting.
- Test your hard drive performance with a program like Hdtach or SiSoft Sandra (included on the Program CD). If performance is lower than expected and you have DMA enabled, you might have a bad IDE cable (or one that your motherboard just does not like). Buy one or two new ATA66 or ATA100 cables and install (ATA100 cables are not all that helpful since ATA100 drives only have bursts that approach 100MBps… a good 7200rpm drive can usually only maintain a data rate around 30MBps).
- Go into the BIOS (press the Delete key during startup). Click on Integrated Peripherals, Find HDD Block Mode and make sure it is enabled (it should be by default).
- If you have a VIA chipset (and an nVidia video card), disable 4X AGP and fast AGP writes in the BIOS.
- If you have two hard drives, run the program off one, and put all your footage and temp files on the other.
- If you add MP3 tracks to the timeline, make sure they are CBR (constant bit rate). Premiere 6 stutters more with VBR (variable bit rate) MP3s. If you are not sure if your MP3 is CBR or VBR, just play it with Winamp, and if the bit rate jumps around

it is VBR. If you must use VBR MP3s, see the following bullet (but even then I don't think Adobe renders them down very well, so stick to CBR or WAVs).

- If you have multiple audio tracks, export all your audio from the timeline to a DV audio AVI file—Export Timeline, Audio. Then delete all your audio tracks and import the newly rendered DV audio track and place it on the timeline. (I would advise creating a new copy of your project and making all the above changes on that, so you preserve your original project in case you need to make future changes.)

- If you only have a 5400rpm drive, consider upgrading to 7200rpm. If you only have one hard drive, consider adding a second.

- Go to System Properties, Performance, File System, Hard disks and set your hard drives to Network Server.

- Run SiSoft Sandra in Wizard mode—this is a good program (the basic version is free and is included on the Program CD) that checks your system for problems and gives you directions on how to fix them.

- I have had problems with #x4 RAM (this is the newest SDRAM design which is only compatible with some motherboards) causing video hiccups during FireWire transfers. So if you have a computer which uses SDRAM, I recommend only #x64 RAM in sticks of 128MB or larger. You need 128MB or more to take advantage of memory interleaving, which is kind of like RAID for RAM.

- Upgrade to 256MB of RAM.

- Get a faster processor.

Outputting Web Video: Windows Media, Real Media, or QuickTime?

If you want to put video on your Web site that people can play while at your Web site—as opposed to having to download it—you need to create a streaming video file. The three competing streaming formats are Windows Media, RealMedia, and QuickTime. All are competitive when it comes to video and sound quality; the main differences are compatibility issues.

Windows Media format has all the advantages that come with being backed by a monopolistic super power (see Figure 19.51). Most computers are PCs running Windows, and while I have often had problems getting RealPlayer to work on my various computers (possible conspiracy?), the Windows Media Player always works. Reading through the newsgroups this problem appears not altogether uncommon.

Interestingly enough, Windows Media Player is actually notoriously unstable on the Mac. As a result, if many of your users are Mac owners, then Windows Media format might not be a good idea.

QuickTime has good operability on both PCs and Macs (see Figure 19.52). However, QuickTime players are not as ubiquitous as Windows Media and RealMedia players. QuickTime streams differently as well. In fact, it really does not stream at all. With

QuickTime, the whole video file downloads to your computer—QuickTime calls this progressive download. This prevents viewing problems caused by bandwidth congestion and interruptions. Windows Media and RealMedia streaming video files never really touch your hard drive.

Figure 19.51

The Windows Media Player (thanks to monopoly power) is the most popular general video player.

Figure 19.52

The QuickTime movie player is a product of Apple.

One problem I have with QuickTime is the nag screens—pop-up messages trying to get you to upgrade to QuickTime Pro. RealNetworks is rather annoying too, as they make it really hard to find the link to the free RealMedia player on their Web site.

Many major Web sites post video in multiple formats to ensure compatibility (usually Windows Media and RealMedia), though some have all three (see Figure 19.53). QuickTime is popular for movie trailers because the progressive download feature ensures the highest uninterrupted playback quality. I would tend to recommend Windows Media first, followed by RealMedia for most Web video. For amateur filmmakers, I would consider using QuickTime. QuickTime has the longest encoding times.

Figure 19.53

Major Web sites often post streaming video in multiple formats to maximize compatibility.

Advanced Windows Media Export

If you want to output your movie as a Windows Media file, go to File, Export Timeline, Advanced Windows Media. The Windows Media Export Plug-In will appear (see Figure 19.54).

NOTE

If you don't see Advanced Windows Media as an option, reinstall Premiere and make sure you say Yes to the Windows Media install when prompted.

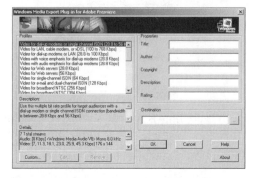

Figure 19.54

The interface of the Windows Media Export Plug-in is very straightforward.

The interface for the plug-in includes numerous profiles that fit different streaming video applications. Try to find the one that matches closest to what your audience will be. If you are creating a movie for a family Web site, and most of the family has cable modems, then one of the Video for broadband profiles would be appropriate. If encoding for the general Web audience, then you will need to select Video for Web servers (56Kbs) because most people still use 56k dial-up modems.

If you can't find a Profile that suits your needs, click the Custom button. Another window will appear called Manage Profiles. Select New, and a wizard will appear which will enable you to create a new custom template (see Figure 19.55).

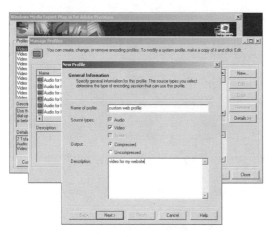

Figure 19.55

You can create your own encoding templates in the Windows Media Export Plug-in.

The first screen enables you to name the profile and select whether you want compressed or uncompressed video. You want compressed; otherwise your file size would be immense and unplayable as a Web video. On the next screen, you select the bandwidth you want the profile to have. On the next screen you select codec, audio format, and video size. Regarding the defaults, the only thing I would change are video size and audio format. Keep in mind that the higher you set the audio format, the less data is left for video. The larger you make the video screen size, the lower the video quality will be.

Advanced RealMedia Export

The RealMedia export works a little differently and has more hidden options. With the RealMedia export, you can encode one movie at more than one bitrate—called Multi-Rate Surestream (see Figure 19.56). Multi-Rate Surestream enables you to serve one movie file at different speeds depending on different user's connections. I would personally recommend just sticking with the Single-rate setting. Most encoding professionals prefer to encode a version for high-speed users and another version for low-speed users separately. If you have been to a site with streaming video, they usually have a link for low speed connections and another for high speed—also referred to as broadband.

Save for Web—Using Cleaner EZ

The Save For Web option—File, Timeline Export, Save for Web—opens up the Cleaner EZ plug-in (see Figure 19.57). This plug-in enables you to create files in Windows Media, RealMedia, QuickTime, and MPEG-1 formats.

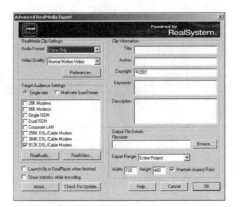

Figure 19.56

The Advanced RealMedia Export interface enables you to encode your video into a Multi-rate stream.

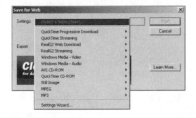

Figure 19.57

Another Premiere export option is to use the Cleaner EZ plug-in.

The Cleaner interface is very simple if you want to use one of the prefab settings. However, if you want to customize things, I prefer the other export plug-ins. Customizing encoding settings in Cleaner is not very intuitive.

I would only recommend using the Cleaner plug-in for creating MPEG-1 or QuickTime encoded video. However, the MPEG-1 encoding quality is not all that great, not to mention slow, so if you need good quality MPEG-1 you really should buy a good external plug-in.

Alternate Way of Creating QuickTime Web Video

For creating QuickTime Web video, I prefer using Premiere's normal Movie Export. Select Export Timeline, Movie. Select Settings, change the file type to QuickTime, and then select Video from the drop-down box and choose the Sorenson video codec from the Compressor drop-down box (Sorenson is the technical name for the QuickTime Web codec) (see Figure 19.58).

Figure 19.58

You can choose the QuickTime Sorenson codec from the Compressor drop-down box.

CODECS: A CONSTANT EVOLUTION

Every year, or even less, Microsoft or Real comes out with a newer codec. The newer codecs usually have better quality but they often require more CPU performance. This means that the plug-ins built into Premiere are going to be dated; nevertheless, your encoded files will still work with newer players.

The RealMedia Export plug-in includes an updater, but the Windows Media plug-in does not. If you want to use a newer codec and you can't update the included plug-in, you have options. Both Windows and Real offer free standalone encoder applications that you can download from their respective Web sites.

CHAPTER 20

ADVANCED MOVIE OUTPUT AND DISTRIBUTION OPTIONS

The technology to import and edit DV video into your computer and output back to DV camcorder tape is very mature, and, for the most part, easy to use. However, DV tape is not the most compatible format for distributing your movies to friends and family, as many people don't own DV camcorders (yet). Consequently, you will probably need to choose among several output options such as VHS, video e-mail, VCD, SVCD, and DVD. The advantages and disadvanges of all output formats will be covered in this chapter, as well as guides on utilizing each.

VIDEO AUTHORING AND DISTRIBUTION OPTIONS

Alternative output options such as video e-mail, VCD, SVCD, and DVD are all less perfect (or in some cases immature) technologies, comparatively speaking.

Video quality between your computer and DV camcorder is pretty solid and hard to screw up. However, when it comes to creating VCDs, SVCDs, DVDs, and other forms of distributable video, more variables are involved, so video quality can vary significantly. The in-between steps you take going from DV camcorder to that final DVD or CD burning can determine whether you end up with something that resembles your original DV footage, or something that is so far worse than even VHS quality. Ultimately, for many, VHS, the most technologically dated format, might still be the best distribution option. If you decide on using one of the other output formats, this chapter will outline a number of methods to achieve optimal results.

VHS

Okay, VHS is an old-school option, but until DVD writers become more affordable—and DVD players become more ubiquitous—VHS is probably the best way to distribute your movies to friends and family (see Figure 20.1). Furthermore, this process is very easy. All you have to do is output your movie back to DV tape. Then, hook your camcorder's A/V out cable to the A/V in jacks of a VCR. Set the VCR to SP mode (best quality). Set the VCR to line. Finally, press Record on your VCR and press Play on your camcorder (make sure your camcorder is in playback mode).

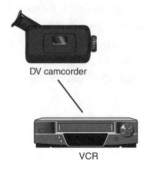

DV camcorder

VCR

Figure 20.1

The best distribution format for your DV movies for most people is still VHS.

You can also hook up a VCR to your camcorder's A/V jacks and record the FireWire movie output signal from your video editing software direct to VCR. Quality will be the same using either method.

Video E-mail

Video e-mail is basically any type of video clip you attach to an e-mail message and send out (see Figure 20.2). However, I don't recommend sending video in an e-mail unless the recipient knows you are sending it, because large attachments take forever to download and can be really annoying. Furthermore, if the user has only a 56k modem—the main net connection for most people—forget about video e-mail altogether.

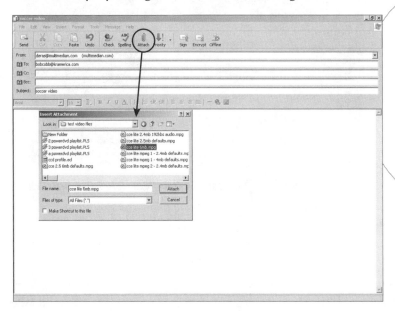

Figure 20.2

Sending video e-mail attachments at our current stage of Internet evolution is limited.

Assuming you and your recipients have broadband connections, you still should stay below 5MB file size. Many mail servers will reject mail bigger than 5MB. Limited to such a small size, video quality is going to be really unimpressive, and your movies will have to be really short (see Figure 20.3). Most video editors include video e-mail templates that you can use or you can create your own. But overall, due to current Internet speed limitations, video e-mail is not a recommended video distribution format.

Video Data CD

A *video data CD* is any video data file burned onto to CD for playback on a computer. VCDs (Video CDs), SVCDs (Super Video CDs), and DVDs (Digital Video Discs) all conform to somewhat strict format standards, so they can play back in compatible VCD, SVCD, and DVD players. However, a video data CD has no such limitations. As long as the computer has a CD-ROM drive, is fast enough to handle the bit rate and codec of the video, and has a compatible media player, it will play. Since DVD burners are still expensive, and VCDs and SVCDs only play back on some DVD players, video data CDs are a very versatile distribution format.

Figure 20.3

To achieve the small sizes necessary for video e-mail, you end up with very poor video quality.

When making a video data CD, you need to decide which codec to use. The most popular options are MPEG-1, MPEG-2, MPEG-4, DivX (modified MPEG-4), Windows Media, RealMedia, and QuickTime (Sorenson)—all of the last three are based on MPEG-4. You can expect more new codecs to be rolled out every year.

MPEG-1 Video Data CD

The most universally compatible of these formats is MPEG-1. Pretty much every home computer, whether PC or Mac, can playback MPEG-1. MPEG-1 is the least CPU intensive codec, so even slow computers down to 200MHz can play back MPEG-1. MPEG-1 has a bad reputation; this is due to shoddy encoders and does not represent the potential of MPEG-1. Using TMPGenc, Cinema Craft, or Panasonic MPEG-1 encoders, you can produce very good quality MPEG-1 videos that will play on more computers than any of the other codecs mentioned previously.

MPEG-4 Video Data CD

If you, or the users you expect to see your video, have faster computers (600MHz+) the MPEG-4–based codecs are a popular option. Windows Media, RealMedia, DivX, and Sorenson are all based on MPEG-4 and provide near-DVD quality at very low bit rates. You can fit between 1–2 hours of good-quality video on one CD using one of these codecs. However, if you want the best video quality, you're limited to less than an hour. The less video you put on one CD, the higher you can set the bit rate—resulting in better quality.

The big advantage of MPEG-4 codecs is price. Windows Media, RealMedia, DivX, and Sorenson codecs are all free and can be used to encode videos off your timeline in Premiere, as well as many budget video editors. You can also easily obtain free standalone encoder applications for these codecs.

When deciding between MPEG-4 encoders, you have to consider quality and player avail-ability. All of the codecs have pretty good video quality; sound quality tends to be the big-ger dividing line. DivX is very popular because it has great sound quality. The biggest concern should be whether the user will have the codec and player to play back the file. Based on player compatibility, Windows Media encoded video is best for PC; QuickTime encoded video is best for Mac.

One solution to codec and player incompatibility concerns is to bundle the player with your video file. If you encode in DivX, this would be a good idea, since most grandparents are not hip enough to have downloaded and installed the DivX codec.

MPEG-2 Video Data CD

MPEG-2, another encoding option, requires more CPU speed but displays fast action bet-ter. MPEG-2 video also supports interlaced encoding, which is the video format of your standard television. SVCD and DVD videos all use various forms of the MPEG-2 codec. Because MPEG-2 is much less space-efficient compared to MPEG-4 and almost as CPU intensive, MPEG-4 is a more popular data video CD encoding option. Furthermore, most computers without DVD drives can't play back MPEG-2 video files as they lack the neces-sary MPEG-2 decoder.

VCD (Video CD)

VCDs use low bit rate MPEG-1 video and playback on most DVD players. However, most MPEG-1 encoders are horrible, and as a result, most VCDs look worse than VHS. Even with the best encoder, the VCD spec has such a low data rate that, best case scenario, your footage will be near VHS video quality. If you want to produce affordable okay-quality videos that can be played back in many DVD players, then VCD might be the format for you. Otherwise forget VCD.

SVCD (Super Video CD)

SVCD—unlike VCD—is based on MPEG-2, the same codec used for DVD movies. SVCD is basically low bit rate DVD on a CD. The quality of SVCD is pretty good—with a good encoder you can achieve near SVHS quality (see Figure 20.4). You can fit about 30 min-utes of video on CD using SVCD. The problem with SVCD is that very few set top DVD play-ers support SVCD playback.

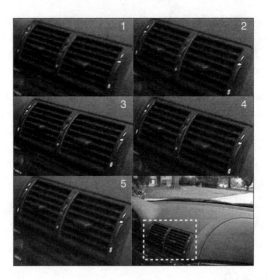

Figure 20.4

Image quality comparison: 1—VCD, 2—SVCD, 3—DivX/MPEG 4, 4—high bit rate MPEG-1, 5—high bit rate MPEG-2.

Due to these limitations, SVCD is really only a good personal display format—for playback on your own DVD player. I burn SVCD disks and play them on my Pioneer DVD player and they are great. But unless you buy your relatives and friends compatible DVD players or tell them what model to buy, then in all likelihood their DVD player won't play back your SVCDs.

DVD (Digital Versatile Disc)

When DVD players become the standard household video devices, DVD will be the ideal distribution format. The quality of DVD with the right encoding can approach your DVD original. In the fall of 2001, the first consumer DVD burners arrived on the market, capable of burning DVDs playable in standard set top DVDs. The future of DVD authoring looks to be very bright. But at the consumer level, DVD burning is still in the early stages. For instance, the first DVD-R drives appear to have playback compatibility problems with some DVD players.

DVD burners should eventually replace CD burners as the standard writeable drive of choice in home computers. But, right now, prices for drives and media still need to drop to be more accessible to the average consumer. The technology also has to mature.

MiniDVD

A few new DVD authoring programs allow you to burn a DVD to a regular CD disc. Very few set top DVD players will play these back, but most computer CD or DVD drives will play them back as long as you have DVD playback software installed on your computer.

Web Authoring Resources

Encoding and authoring is bleeding edge technology so things are always changing, and good information can be hard to find. Luckily you'll find good Web sites on the Internet that can keep you up to date on the latest encoding technology, as well as provide tutorials and other resources. The following sites also link to lots of helpful freeware tools as well as the latest video codecs:

- VCDhelp (www.vcdhelp.com) is one of the most comprehensive resources on the net for video encoding and authoring. They also have a well-trafficked message board.

- Doom9.net (www.doom9.net) provides well-regarded encoding guides and the latest news on the encoding technology.

- Flexion.org (www.flexion.org) is another great resource site with news, tutorials, and other resources devoted to MPEG video and audio.

You will find additional links to even more resources on all of the preceding sites.

A Software DVD Player Is Recommended

If you are going to be doing a lot of MPEG encoding on your computer, I strongly advise getting a Software DVD player even if you don't have a DVD drive. (If you already have a DVD drive, your computer should already have a software DVD player.)

Software DVD players will install MPEG-2 codecs necessary for playing back MPEG-2 files you create. Software DVD players will play back all types of MPEG files more smoothly than your computer's default media player. The software DVD players I recommend are PowerDVD and Cinemaster (see Figure 20.5).

Figure 20.5

Cyberlink's PowerDVD is one of the best software DVD players. PowerDVD will also play back pretty much every other video file format.

AUTHORING VIDEO DATA CDS

Video data CDs are the easiest to produce because there are no strict formats you need to stick to as with VCD, SVCD, and DVD. For this, you need to consider your audience, the speed of their computers, and what kind of media players they might have.

Authoring an MPEG-1 Video Data CD

Pretty much every video editor has some sort of MPEG-1 encoder built in that you can use, but in general the quality tends to be sorry. If you care about quality, take the time and use a good encoder.

MPEG-1 Encoding in Ulead Video Studio 5

The quality of the encoder is very mediocre in UVS5, so use this only if you don't have the time or money to explore the other options explained later in this chapter (see Figure 20.6). Since we are on the threshold of DVD authoring, I expect that consumer MPEG encoders will start improving over the next few years, but right now most are substandard.

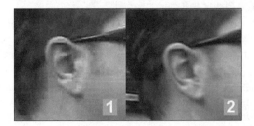

Figure 20.6

A comparison of two different caliber MPEG-1 encoders: 1—Ulead Video Studio 2Mbps, 2—Panasonic 2.4Mbps.

Follow these steps:

1. Just load your desired video files onto the UVS timeline. If you are already editing your movie on the timeline, you can skip this step.

2. Then select Finish at the top of the UVS5 interface.

3. In Finish mode, click the movie reel icon button and select from one of the prefab templates or select Custom (see Figure 20.7).

   The Custom mode enables you to adjust all the settings. Unfortunately—based on my tests—the custom settings in UVS for some reason consistently produce lower-quality encodes than those of the templates—even when using higher bit rates. So, while I usually recommend customizing most settings, my advice in UVS is stick to the templates when creating MPEG files. Keep in mind that the prefab template encoding results are not very good; they just tend to be better than custom settings.

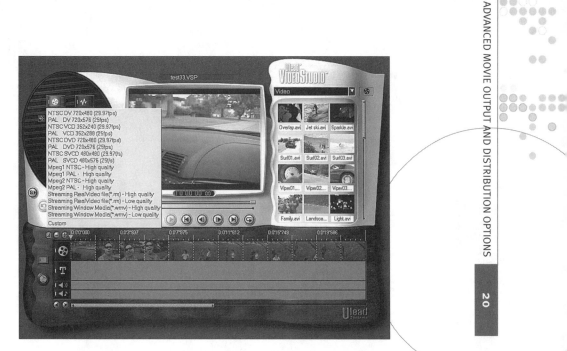

Figure 20.7

Click the movie reel icon to access your template options.

Though I have found the Custom Settings in UVS to provide quality lower than the built-in templates—an unusual phenomenon—I have still included an overview of customizing settings, as customization is sometimes necessary to fit your desired amount of video on one CD.

4. After you select Custom, a Save As window will pop up. Select Mpeg files from the Save As type drop-down box (see Figure 20.8).

5. Then click the Options button and a new tabbed window will appear where you can define all of the settings for your video file (see Figure 20.9).

6. The first tab is labeled Ulead Video Studio, and you should not have to make any changes. On the General Tab, you can set the frame rate and video size. I would recommend leaving that at the default as well, which should be 29.97fps and 720 × 480 if you are working with NTSC video—if PAL, 25fps and 704 × 576. On the Compression tab you need to set the Media Type, the Video Data Rate, and Audio Settings (see Figure 20.10).

Figure 20.8

To create a custom MPEG file you have to select MPEG Files from the Save As type drop-down box.

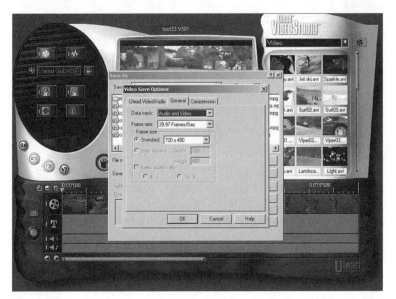

Figure 20.9

You can customize the UVS MPEG encoder settings.

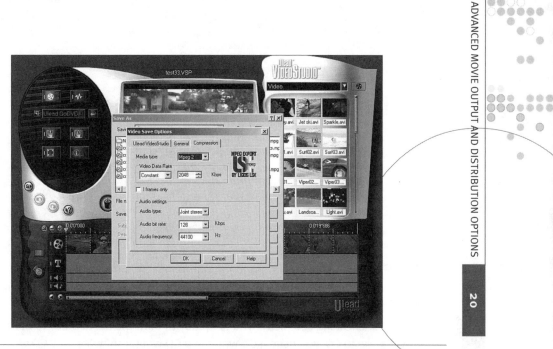

Figure 20.10

Most of the time you will only want to alter the settings under the Compression tab.

7. The Media Type should be set to Mpeg 1. The Video Data Rate should be set to Constant, and between 0–2,000Kbps. 2,000Kbps is the max UVS allows for MPEG-1. I would recommend setting the data rate to 2,000Kbps if possible. If you are feeling experimental and want to fit more footage on one CD, you can choose variable bit rate (VBR), which will encode more efficiently. But generally, at low bit rates CBR (constant bit rate encoding) is superior to VBR.

The higher you set the data rate, the higher the video quality will be; however, the file size will also be larger, resulting in less video per CD. Yet, at a data rate of 2,000Kbps, you can fit well over 30 minutes per CD. Since the UVS codec is not very good, you need every bit of that data.

8. If you need to determine how much video you can fit on a CD at different bit rates, use the bit rate calculator located on the Program CD included with this book, in the Utilities folder (see Figure 20.11).

9. Once you are done customizing settings, just click OK. Then fill in a name for the new file, and make sure to save it in a directory that you can locate later. I recommend saving things on the Desktop or a custom My Videos folder. Once you have selected the file destination, click Save and the encoding will begin.

Encoding time will vary depending on the speed of your computer. For example, on a 800MHz AMD Athlon system, encoding one minute of MPEG-1 video in UVS takes around three minutes.

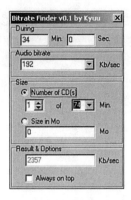

Figure 20.11

A bit rate calculator is a very useful tool which helps you figure out how high you can set the bit rate and still fit your video on a CD.

Once the encoding completes, you are ready to burn the file to a CD. To burn your MPEG-1 video file to CD, you need a CD writer and CD writing software. Any CD writer is fine; the faster the writing speed the quicker the writing process.

 The average CD burning speeds based on a 650MB CD are as follows:

- 4×—20 minutes
- 8×—10 minutes
- 12×—6 minutes
- 24×—3 minutes

Quality MPEG-1 Encoding Using Third-Party MPEG Encoding Plug-Ins

If you can afford the price, the highest quality and most convenient MPEG-1 encoding option is a third-party MPEG encoding plug-in for Adobe Premiere. Panasonic, Ligos, and Cinema Craft all make high-quality MPEG-1 encoding plug-ins for Premiere.

Panasonic MPEG Encoder   The Panasonic encoder is pretty affordable at $80, and delivers the best full screen (720×480) quality at lower MPEG-1 bit rates. At 2.4Mbps, the Panasonic encoder looks the best, with smooth playback and muted artifacting. At 4Mbps the encoding quality has very few visible signs of artifacts—though I can find some if I freeze frame. Unfortunately, the Panasonic encoder is really slow; a 25-second test clip took almost five minutes to encode on a 800MHz Athlon system.

Ligos LSX-MPEG Encoder   The Ligos LSX-MPEG encoder comes as a plug-in for Premiere—you can also get a standalone version. Overall full screen quality was okay at 2.4Mbps; obvious video artifacting was present but most of it was dispersed throughout the picture, sort of blending in.

Artifact is a term used to describe aberrant video data produced by the encoder. Typical MPEG video artifacts are visible blockiness and/or pixelation.

At 4Mbps, slight but still noticeable artifacting occurred and video quality was far better, but still very distinguishable from the original.

As a side note, the VBR mode with the LSX-MPEG Encoder never sticks to the average VBR you specify; rather, it stays closer to the maximum VBR, resulting in much larger files, effectively defeating the purpose of VBR.

The LSX encoder is expensive at $179 for the lite version, and $249 for the full version. The full version enables you to use VBR (variable bit rate) encoding. The LSX-MPEG encoder also encodes MPEG-2 video. The LSX-MPEG strong point is speed; it encodes about four times faster than the Panasonic. My 25-second test clip took just over a minute to encode. However, the quality is clearly below the Panasonic and Cinema Craft encoders.

VBR (Variable Bit Rate) or CBR (Constant Bit Rate)?

VBR encoding enables the encoder to vary the data rate in response to the complexity of the scene being encoded. In general, at high bit rates 4Mbps and above, using VBR is a good idea. Below 4Mbps it depends on the encoder, but many do better in CBR mode. At lower bit rates, I would advise encoding in both modes to see which one you prefer.

Cinema Craft Lite Encoder (CCE-Lite)   The Cinema Craft Lite (CCE-Lite) encoder delivers slightly better quality at 2.4Mbps than LSX-MPEG (see Figure 20.12). At 4Mbps, it exceeds even the Panasonic encoder, with very few visible signs of artifacting (see Figure 20.13). Best of all, Cinema Craft Lite is a speed demon, encoding the 25-second test clip in just 51 seconds. The Cinema Craft Lite encoder also encodes MPEG-2 files. At $250, the cost is high, but the speed and quality advantage really justify the price tag. Cinema Craft Lite is my preferred encoder plug-in.

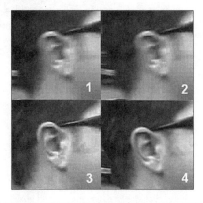

Figure 20.12

2–2.4Mbps MPEG-1 encoder quality comparison: 1—MovieFactory, 2—CCE-Lite, 3—Ulead Video Studio, 4—Panasonic.

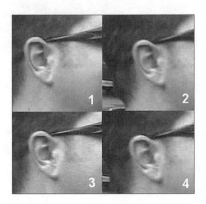

Figure 20.13

4Mbps MPEG-1 encoder quality comparison: 1—CCE-Lite, 2—Panasonic, 3—TMPGenc, 4—LSX-MPEG.

Using a Plug-In in Premiere

If you want to follow this tutorial, I recommend installing the Cinema Craft Lite plug-in from the Encoder folder on the Program CD.

If you buy any of the previous plug-ins, using them is very easy. Follow these steps:

1. Once you are done putting together your movie on the timeline, select Export Timeline, Movie. An Export Movie window will appear.

2. Click the Settings button. In the File Type drop-down box, select CinemaCraft MPEG-2/1 (or Panasonic MPEG1 or LSX MPEG-1 or MPEG-2—depending on which plug-in you installed) (see Figure 20.14).

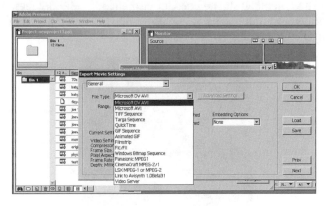

Figure 20.14

To access an MPEG plug-in in Premiere, click the File Type drop-down box, and choose CinemaCraft MPEG-2/1.

3. Then click the Advanced Settings menu, which will open the plug-in control window where you can customize the encoder. For CinemaCraft, the main settings are under the Video, Bitrate, and Audio tabs (see Figure 20.15).

Figure 20.15

Cinema Craft Lite MPEG encoder settings window.

4. Under Video, you can choose MPEG-1 or MPEG-2 (see Figure 20.16). Under Bitrate, you set how much data you want to devote to each second of video (see Figure 20.17). The higher the rate, the larger, and more system-resource-spending, your video file will be, but the video quality will be better. For MPEG-1 video, I recommend choosing a video bit rate between 2 and 4Mbps.

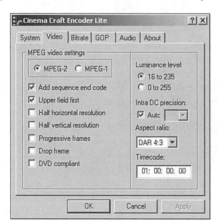

Figure 20.16

Under the CCE-Lite Video tab you can specify MPEG-1 or MPEG-2 encoding.

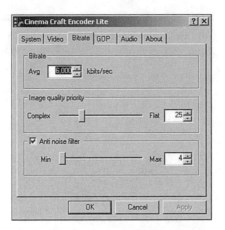

Figure 20.17

Under the Bitrate tab you can set your desired video bit rate.

5. Under Audio, you can set the audio bit rate (see Figure 20.18). MPEG-1 and MPEG-2 video use MPEG-1 layer 2 audio encoding—also known as Mp2. This audio format is different from the popular Mp3 audio format. Mp2 is less efficient at lower bit rates below 96kbps, but at higher bit rates it's more equivalent. Bottom line, depending on the audio sound system you expect to play back your video on, 128Kbps to 256Kbps is a good range.

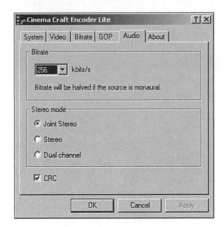

Figure 20.18

Under the Audio tab you can set the audio bit rate.

Many other settings can be tweaked as well, but I have based all my testing on the defaults—other than changing bit rate settings. Check out the guides and message boards at VCDhelp.com—one of the more popular encoding resource sites—as people exchange favorite encoder settings, or experiment yourself to find your favorite settings (see Figure 20.19).

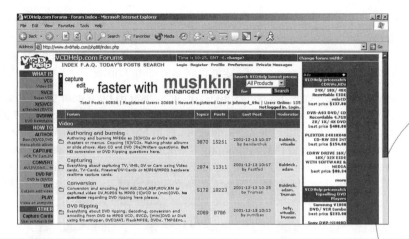

Figure 20.19

VCDhelp.com message boards are a great place to find and exchange encoding tips.

6. For testing, I recommend using a small under-30-second encoding test file that has a wide range of content—landscapes, people, fast action. My test clip is composed of filming while riding in a car, close up footage of someone talking, and footage of some people dancing in an open field.

7. Once you are done configuring your plug-in settings, select OK. Then fill in the name of your file and make sure to select a folder location you will be able to locate later. Saving the output on a secondary hard drive is not necessary, but it is the conservative, overly safe thing to do—if you have two hard drives.

8. Click Save and the encoding will begin.

An Exporting status window will display frames rendered as well as estimated time remaining (see Figure 20.20). If you expand the window by clicking on the triangle icon, you can get more stats, such as how many frames are being rendered per second.

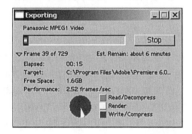

Figure 20.20

The export status window will display how many frames are rendering per second and elapsed time.

My experience with some of these export plug-ins—especially Cinema Craft—suggests sensitivity during the encoding process. Apparently, working in my word processor while the encode process was ongoing caused Cinema Craft to crash, so if this happens to you, you might want to leave your computer alone until encoding finishes.

Once the encoding process has completed, you are ready to burn your CD. Those running Windows XP have CD burning built in now, so all you have to do is to drag and drop your newly created video file onto the CD-R drive letter in My Computer or Windows Explorer. Unfortunately, I have found that XP burning is twice as slow on my machine compared to using third-party programs. So I recommend using a third-party CD burning program if you want the fastest performance. My CD writing application of choice is Nero—a trial version of it is included on the Program CD in the Utilities folder (see Figure 20.21).

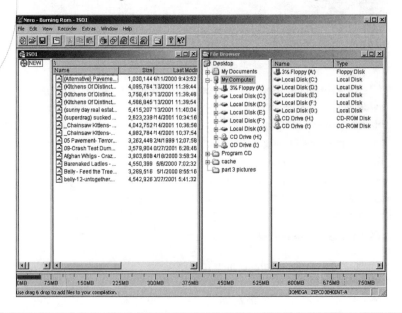

Figure 20.21

Nero Burning Rom is a very well-regarded CD-writing program.

Adding a Read Me File   You may want to add a Read Me file to your CD, describing the movie, noting credits, and giving instructions for playing the file, such as minimum system requirements. Add something to the effect of "if playback is jerky, you should reduce the size of the media player window." Also, giving optimal playback instructions might be helpful, like "Alt + Enter is the Windows Media Player keyboard shortcut for full-screen playback."

Creating a Self-Booting Video Data CD   If you want to make things really easy for your users, you can create a Video Data CD that self-boots. This means the video will start playing right after the CD is inserted. Note: The following settings will only work with Windows operating systems. However, anyone with a Mac can still view the video file; they will just have to manually start playback (by clicking on the file).

All you need to do is add two very small files—autorun.exe and autorun.inf—located in the Utilities folder on the Program CD along with your video file. Then add both files along with your video file to your CD burning program of choice and write the CD.

Now, whenever a user puts your CD in their computer—as long as they are running Windows 95/98/Me/2k/XP—the video file will start playing.

Video Data CD—Closing Thoughts

For reference, I created a 23-minute 3.5Mbps MPEG-1 video file—the audio bit rate was set to 192kbps—with the Cinema Craft Lite encoder. The encoded MPEG file was slightly under 650MB. I wrote the file to CD, and the video played back flawlessly full-screen on a Pentium II 300MHz computer with a 16x CD-ROM. Since MPEG-1 is pretty much universal, all a user needs to do is put the CD in the drive, open the drive contents, and double-click on the movie file, and the default media player should start playing the video. If you follow the self-booting tutorial above, the user does not have to do anything but put the CD into the computer.

The lower you set the bit rate, the more compatible it will be with the slowest of computers, but average computer speeds are rising, and you should use a bit rate of at least 2Mbps if you want your video quality to look nice (3–4Mbps recommended). Using a 3.7Mbps total bit rate I was able to fit a 23-minute movie on one 650MB CD-R. By lowering the total bit rate you can of course fit more video on a disc (2.7Mbps = 33 min movie).

Until DVD authoring matures and becomes more affordable, MPEG-1 video data CD authoring is an attractive alternative. Considering both quality and compatibility, MPEG-1 is a very good video distribution format. Moreover, if you buy the Cinema Craft encoder, you can encode in MPEG-1 now, and later in MPEG-2 for output to a DVD writer when they become more affordable.

Authoring an MPEG-2 Video Data CD

The advantage of MPEG-2 over MPEG-1 is that you can encode interlaced video, so if you are outputting to a standard TV, MPEG-2 is preferable—not really an advantage on computer playback. MPEG-2 also has improved motion algorithms, so it deals with fast action better. With a good encoder, quality difference between MPEG-1 and 2 is really only noticeable on fast action scenes.

The downside of MPEG-2 is that it is more CPU intensive; in other words, you need a faster computer to play it back smoothly. Furthermore, MPEG-2 needs to be licensed by software developers while MPEG-1 is free. As a result, many computers can't play back MPEG-2 video unless a software DVD player is installed.

So, if you want to create an MPEG-2 video data CD for friends and family, you need to verify that they have the hardware and software to play it back. MPEG-2 playback quality is pretty variable. Some 600MHz computers can play back an MPEG-2 file smoothly, but some will choke on it, and many don't have the necessary codecs. Common signs a computer is underpowered are out-of-sync audio and choppy video playback.

Taking into consideration all these factors, if you still want to encode an MPEG-2 video data CD, follow the same steps used in the MPEG-1 section.

Low-Cost Quality MPEG-1 and 2 Encoding Using Frame Serving and TMPGenc

Not everyone can afford Cinema Craft or LSX-MPEG. So if you are on a budget, TMPGenc is an affordable quality MPEG encoder that many discerning videophiles use (see Figure 20.22).

Figure 20.22

TMPGenc is a one of the best shareware MPEG encoders around.

TMPGenc is a high-quality shareware encoder that can encode MPEG-1 and MPEG-2 files. TMPGenc encoding speed is only average, about three times slower than Cinema Craft and LSX. You have to register after 30 days to retain the ability to encode MPEG-2 files, but MPEG-1 encoding is always free. However, TMPGenc is incompatible with DV AVI files, the file format used for capturing video from your DV camcorder. Thanks to a technique known as frame serving, you can get around this limitation, and output video from your Premiere timeline into TMPGenc.

Frame serving is a technique that creates a dummy video file which you load into TMPGenc, and then video frames are served via that dummy file into TMPGenc.

To accomplish frame serving between Premiere and TMPGenc, you need to install a few files located on the Program CD in the Utilities folder:

1. Go to the Program CD and Open the Utilites folder, and then open the Avisynth folder. All the files you need are there.

2. Place AVISYNTH.DLL in your Windows/System folder (see Figure 20.23).

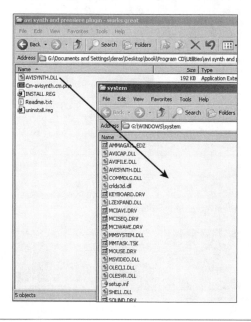

Figure 20.23

AVISYNTH.DLL goes in the Windows\System folder.

3. Click the Install.reg file. When asked whether you want to add this to the registry, click Yes (see Figure 20.24).

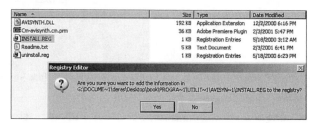

Figure 20.24

You need to click Yes when you see this window.

4. Place Cm-avisynth.cm.prm into the Plug-in directory of Premiere by choosing Program Files, Adobe, Premiere, Plug-ins (see Figure 20.25).

5. Now, whenever you want to output a Premiere timeline project, repeat the usual timeline export steps—choose Timeline Export, Movie.

6. Select Settings, and from the File Type drop-down list select Link to Avisynth 1.0Beta31 (see Figure 20.26).

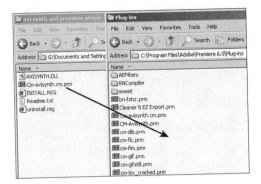

Figure 20.25

Cm-avisynth.cm goes into the Premiere plug-ins folder.

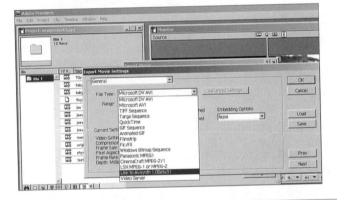

Figure 20.26

Choose Link to Avisynth 1.0Beta31.

7. Select OK, and then leave the file name as untitled and click Save. A frame serving status window will appear (see Figure 20.27).

8. Open TMPGenc and select your desired encoder settings by clicking the Setting button (see Figure 20.28).

9. Click the Browse button to set the Video Source file. Set the File types drop-down box to All files. Browse to your main hard drive—usually C—and look for a file named part0.avs. Select it (see Figure 20.29). You should now see the first frame of your video in the TMPGenc monitor.

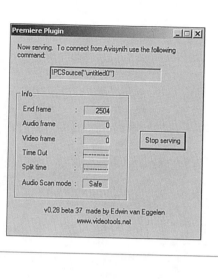

Figure 20.27

Avisynth frame serving window appears after you click Save.

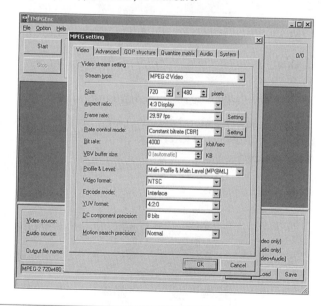

Figure 20.28

Before starting encoding, set your TMPGenc MPEG settings.

10. Make sure part0.avs is also selected for the audio source.

11. Complete Output file name location and then select the Start button and the encoding will begin. (On my 800MHz test system, a 25-second test file using default encode settings took 3 minutes.)

Figure 20.29

Browse for the parto.avs file.

Hardware MPEG Encoders, Potential Still Unfulfilled

As we all hate to wait, hardware MPEG encoders are a very attractive encoding solution, as they work in real-time. However, most of the current crop of MPEG hardware encoders (Dazzle DVC1/2 and Hauppage Win PVR), while delivering fairly good quality MPEG video, have other problems (see Figure 20.30). One of the most significant is out-of-sync audio.

Figure 20.30

The Dazzle Digital Video Creator 2 is an affordable hardware MPEG encoder.

Another issue both of these cards have is producing non-compliant DVD and SVCD streams. You can usually get around these bugs, but it can be very tricky. So if you are a novice, the annoyance curve is steep.

Eventually, we should see competent and affordable hardware MPEG encoders on the market, but not until the market for MPEG encoding grows enough to entice more manufacturers. In addition, as chip speeds increase, quality software encoders will approach or exceed real-time performance.

The ATI video cards (All In Wonder and Radeon) that advertise MPEG capture use software encoding. So unless you have a really fast chip, you can't get good quality real-time encoding. The ATI cards also produce non-compliant MPEG streams, so they won't work with SVCD or DVD without some serious hacking.

Encoding MPEG-4 Video Data CDs

MPEG-4 was created to be a more efficient file format than MPEG-1 or MPEG-2. The newest RealMedia, Windows Media, and QuickTime codecs are all based on MPEG-4. The infamous DivX format is also MPEG-4 at the core. The problem with MPEG-4 is that while video quality is better at really low data rates—1Mbps and below—above 1Mbps quality does not improve much. MPEG-4 was engineered to be an ideal low bit rate format for the Web, not to compete with MPEG-2. MPEG-4 is also more CPU-intensive than even MPEG-2, and currently no MPEG-4 hardware decoding is built in to video cards (however, many video cards include MPEG-2 decoding features).

Since most computer users have a Windows operating system, encoding videos in a Windows Media–based MPEG-4 format is probably the most convenient MPEG-4 option. RealMedia would be next in line. QuickTime has nice quality as well, but the encode times are three times longer than Windows Media and RealMedia, so I don't favor it.

Windows Media MPEG-4 Codec Options in Ulead Video Studio

Windows Media has a bunch of different codecs; the default version built in to UVS is very mediocre. The best Windows Media codec is Windows Media 8; however, it has not been integrated into any video applications as yet. An older, but still very good, codec is Microsoft's MPEG-4 v3, which the original DivX codec was an altered version of. Luckily, you can access this codec from within Video Studio and most other editing programs.

To encode in Windows Media in UVS, follow these steps:

1. Select Finish mode, and click the movie reel icon.
2. Select Custom (see Figure 20.31). A Save As window will appear. In the Save As type drop-down box, Microsoft AVI files should be selected. Then click the Options button.
3. Select the Compression tab, and scroll down the compression drop-down list until you see Microsoft MPEG-4 Video Codec V3 (see Figure 20.32). Select it.

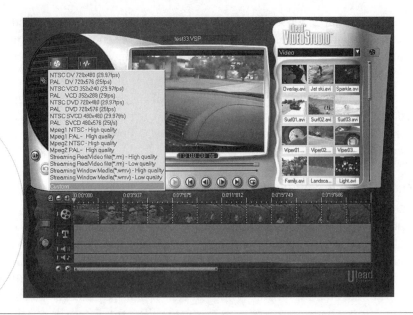

Figure 20.31

Select Custom template.

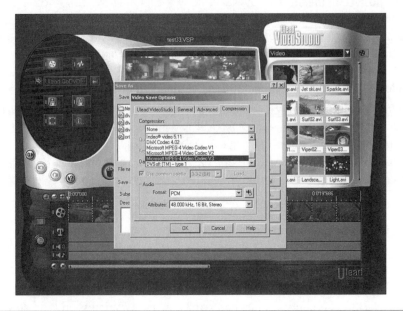

Figure 20.32

You have a number of video compression options in UVS.

4. Then click the Configure button. A Configure window will appear with two scroll-bars allowing you to set the Compression Control and the Data Rate (see Figure 20.33). I would generally recommend only changing the Data Rate; you can get good results selecting from 600 to 1600Kbps, depending on how much video you want to end up getting on a CD.

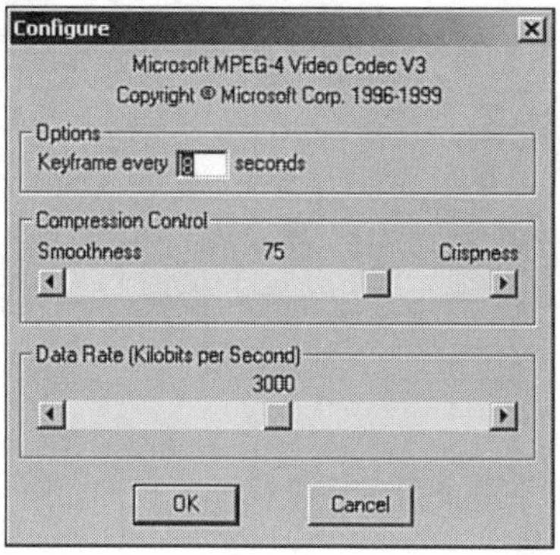

Figure 20.33

The Microsoft MPEG-4 V3 codec settings screen has only two alterable parameters.

You should experiment yourself to see what your favorite settings are. Note that the higher you set the Compression Control, the more the encoder focuses on picture sharpness; however, this can result in frame dropping. The lower you set the Compression Control bar, the smoother playback is, but picture quality is blurrier.

5. After finalizing settings, click OK, name your file, click Save, and the encoding will begin.

DivX—Open Source MPEG-4

DivX—the most popular MPEG-4 codec among video hobbyists—is often used nefariously to transcode DVD movies to DivX CDs using a program called Flask (see Figure 20.34). The DVD-to-DivX process is very time consuming (from three to ten hours on a very fast computer, depending on settings), and the quality can vary. So I personally don't see the appeal (but I am pretty lazy).

However, you can also use DivX to encode a high-quality compressed movie CD from your own home video footage. The original DivX 3.11 codec was a hacked version of Microsoft's MPEG-4 V3 codec. The newest DivX codec, version 4, is totally rewritten from scratch, making it a technically legal codec. The new DivX codec will play back older DivX files.

DivX has a lot of popular support, and the new legal codec could further its appeal and user base. DivX technology has already begun to be implemented for Video on Demand broadband content delivery. Eventually, DivX technology may find its way into TiVo-like hard drive–based VCRs.

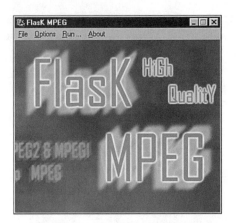

Figure 20.34

Flask is used to nefariously transcode DVD movies into highly compressed DivX movies that can fit on a CD.

Encoding with DivX   If you want to encode using DivX, you need to install the DivX codec, which can be downloaded from DivX.com (www.divx.com). You can find a copy of DivX 4.12 codec on the Program CD in the Encoder folder.

After installing the codec, you should now see DivX 4.12 as one of the compression options in all your video editing programs. To encode a DivX movie, select DivX from the compression options, then click Settings or Configure (button name will vary depending on which editing program you use). A DivX Video Codec Configuration window will pop up, allowing you to customize encoding settings (see Figure 20.35). The main settings to configure are bitrate and Variable bitrate (VBR) mode.

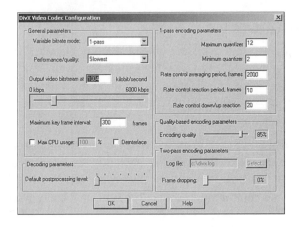

Figure 20.35

The DivX 4.12 codec has far more customizable settings than the old DivX codec.

As you get more into MPEG-2 and MPEG-4 encoding you might run into several different options for VBR mode. The main options are one pass and two pass. One pass means your video is being encoded at the same time the encoder reads the video data. Two pass means that the encoder reads through the entire video file to determine where best to devote bits and then encodes on the second pass. While two pass encoding is usually better, it can be extremely time consuming. Furthermore, the quality leap, depending on the quality of the encoder, is often not that significant or even noticeable.

I achieved pretty good quality using 1Mbps and 1-pass VBR mode. However, the bit rate settings are off with this encoder because my 1Mbps encoded test files were the same size as my MPEG-1 and MPEG-2 4Mbps encoded test files. The quality of the latter was better, too. So be forewarned, the bit rate settings are way off.

If you are interested in learning more about DivX, read through the previously mentioned resource Web sites or go to DivX.com.

Creating a Self-Booting DivX CD   A number of autorun programs are available for DivX which enable you to put a DivX file and codec files on a CD (see Figure 20.36). When a user puts the CD in their computer, an interface pops up, which enables them to install the DivX codec and then start the movie. These autorun programs make DivX a more promising distribution format.

Figure 20.36

With one of the many DivX launcher programs you can create menued self-booting DivX movies.

The problem with the autorun programs is that most of them are written for Win98/Me and often do not work in Windows 2000 and XP, which are the newest operating systems. If the user already has the DivX codec installed, you can use the self-boot method diagramed previously, which is the only autorun method I have found so far that works on every Windows operating system.

CREATING A VCD

The following sections on VCD creation cover many of the same steps you will need to go through to author an XVCD, SVCD, XSVCD, or DVD.

The VCD format uses low bit rate MPEG-1 video to achieve 74 minutes of at best near-VHS video quality. Most DVD players will play back VCDs, but not all. You can go to VCDhelp.com and check their online database, which lists playback compatibility of most DVD players (see Figure 20.37).

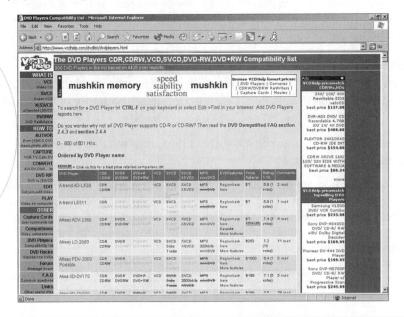

Figure 20.37

You can see if your DVD player is VCD/SVCD/XVCD/XSVCD compatible by checking the VCDhelp.com DVD database.

VCD has a pretty strict spec of what the bit rate and audio rate need to be. The video bit rate can be no greater than 1.15Kbps. The audio bit rate needs to be 224Kbps. At such a low bit rate, quality is usually compromised, so it's important to choose a high quality encoder to make the most of those limited bits.

VCDs also need to be properly written to CD-R; otherwise a VCD-compatible DVD player won't be able to read them properly. Most CD burning programs have a VCD template, which ensures a properly written VCD.

VCD-Compliant MPEG-1 Encoding in UVS

VCD video encoding in UVS is very easy; just add your desired movie files to the timeline and select Final. Click the movie reel icon and select the NTSC or PAL VCD template—NTSC for U.S., PAL for Europe (see Figure 20.38). Then, set a name for the movie file, click Save, and the encoding will begin. Be forewarned: The encoding quality is very bad.

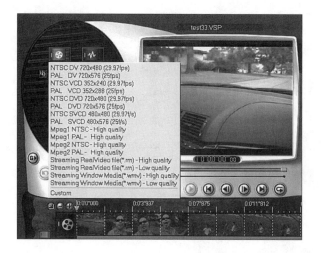

Figure 20.38

Ulead Video Studio, like most other consumer video editors, includes a VCD template.

Alternate VCD-Compliant MPEG-1 Encoding

If you want the best quality possible within the VCD spec—which is never going to be that great—use TMPGenc, LSX, Cinema Craft, or the Panasonic MPEG-1 encoder. Most of these programs have VCD templates; use them.

Authoring Your VCD

Authoring is the process of writing your video files to a readable media, in this case a CD. A number of easy options are available. You can use your preferred CD writing program (like Nero) and just follow the directions for VCD writing. Another option is to use the Ulead GoDVD plug-in for UVS.

Authoring in Nero

One way to author a VCD is with the program Nero. A demo of Nero is on the program CD included with this book. To begin, follow these steps:

1. When you start Nero, a New Compilation window will appear, which enables you to choose what type of media you want to burn (see Figure 20.39). On the left side of the window you will see a bunch of CD icons. Scroll down until you see Video-CD. Select Video-CD.

2. Select New; this will launch a track window for your new VCD.

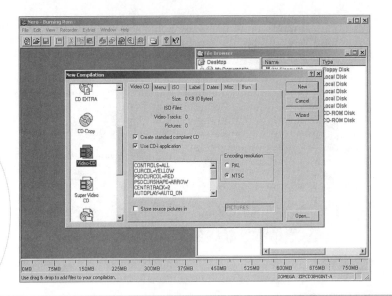

Figure 20.39

The opening screen in Nero prompts you to choose what type of CD project you want to create.

3. All you need to do is drag compliant MPEG-1 video files and then drop them in the track window (see Figure 20.40). The only advantage to creating a bunch of small MPEG-1 video files (each an increment of a larger movie) as opposed to one big MPEG-1 movie file is that users will be able to quickly fast-forward to later tracks.

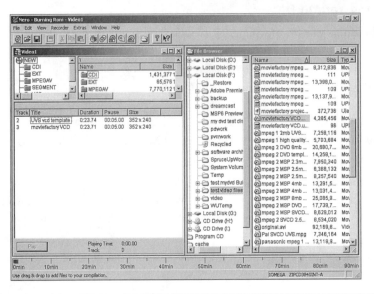

Figure 20.40

Add your VCD movie files to the Nero track window.

However, in regular play mode, a VCD with one large track or a bunch of small tracks will play exactly the same, as long as you set the pause time between tracks to zero—which can be done by double-clicking on each track (see Figure 20.41).

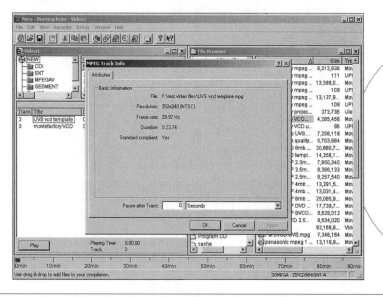

Figure 20.41

You can customize your VCD track settings, such as how much time you want between tracks.

4. Once you are done dragging files into the track window, go to File, Write CD. A tabbed Write CD window will appear where you can finalize your VCD settings (see Figure 20.42).

5. The only really important tabs are Video CD and Burn. On the Video CD tab, the important setting is the NTSC/PAL radio button (see Figure 20.43). Make sure if you are creating an NTSC VCD (for playback in U.S. DVD players) that the NTSC radio button is selected. If you are in a PAL country, select the PAL radio button. By default, this tab is set to NTSC, so NTSC users can ignore this step.

6. Click the Burn tab and make sure that all your CD-writer settings are in order. The defaults are usually correct.

7. Nero also enables you to create a menu for your VCD which lists the name of each track, optional thumbnails for each track, and a title for your VCD (see Figure 20.44). You can set the font colors, the background, and a few other style variables. You can also preview your menu by clicking the preview check box.

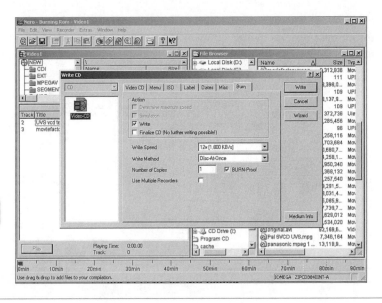

Figure 20.42

The Nero Write CD dialog is a tabbed menu full of customizable options you can alter.

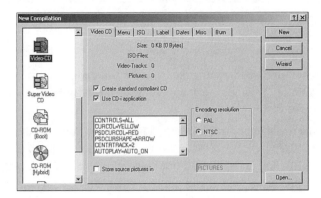

Figure 20.43

The Video CD tab is where you specify whether your VCD is PAL or NTSC.

However, testing on two different DVD players (Pioneer DV333 and APEX AD-500W), I experienced problems with VCDs (and SVCDs) that I added menus to. While all of my menuless VCDs and SVCDs played fine, when I added a menu, the CDs were either not recognized, or the menu loaded but I could not get any video to play. So I can't endorse the Nero menu system in its current form. However, Nero-created menus might work on your DVD player.

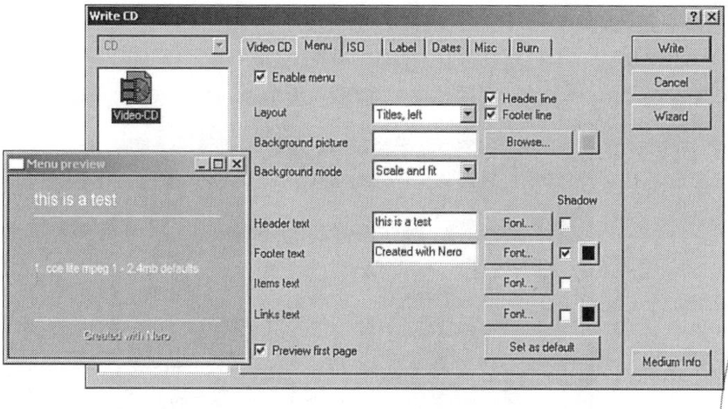

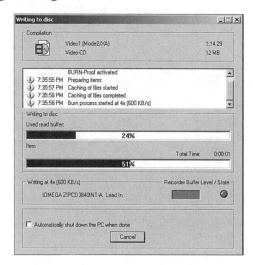

Figure 20.44

The Menu tab enables you to create a custom opening menu for your VCD.

8. Once you are finished customizing, select the Write button and the burning of your VCD will begin (see Figure 20.45).

Figure 20.45

The Writing to disc window displays the status of the VCD writing process.

Authoring with the GoDVD Plug-In in Ulead Video Studio

Ulead Video Studio has an optional GoDVD plug-in available (cost $50) which enables you to author and burn VCD, SVCD, and DVDs from within the UVS interface. This plug-in is included with Ulead Video Studio DVD edition.

The plug-in only works with one movie file, so you need to render an entire movie into one MPEG-1 compliant VCD file using the VCD template. Then, just highlight the new clip in the Video Library window—where all newly created clips are added—and then click the left arrow next to the Ulead GoDVD plug-in (see Figure 20.46). The Ulead GoDVD plug-in will launch (see Figure 20.47). The only variable you can customize is whether you want a scene selection menu. If you want one, keep the box checked; otherwise uncheck it.

Figure 20.46

To create a VCD in UVS, you need to select the GoDVD plug-in.

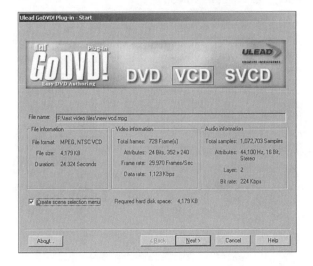

Figure 20.47

The GoDVD plug-in interface is very easy to follow.

Another window will appear enabling you to create scene selection thumbnail links that will appear on your VCD when played back in a DVD player (see Figure 20.48). This feature is the VCD equivalent of DVD chapter menu screens, where you have thumbnails that can be selected to start playing the video at that scene.

The VCR control interface enables you to move throughout the video, adding as many scene links as you want. There does not appear to be a limit on how many links you can have. I was able to add 25, but only six thumbnail scene links can be displayed per menu page. So, I am inclined to recommend sticking with just six scene links.

Figure 20.48

GoDVD enables you to select scene points that will become thumbnail buttons on the opening menu of your VCD.

Once you are done marking scenes, click Next and you will be able to select and customize the look of your scene menu. GoDVD offers over 20 template formats, most of which look bad but a few look cool (see Figure 20.49). You can enter text under each of your selected scenes by clicking under the thumbnail. You can also import your own custom background image for your menu.

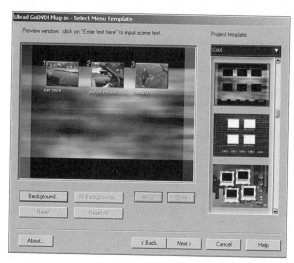

Figure 20.49

You can customize the look of your menu, choosing from a number of templates, and even adding your own background image.

Once you are done customizing the look of your menu, click Next. This will bring up the Playback Simulation window where you can simulate how your menu will work with a standard DVD player (see Figure 20.50). As you will notice, this menu works differently than most DVD menus, in that you select each scene by clicking the scene number. Most DVD menus use the arrow buttons for menu selections—so this may confuse some users. However, the play button works just like a regular DVD play button.

Figure 20.50

The GoDVD Playback Simulation window enables you to preview/test your menu as it will appear on a regular DVD player.

When you are finished simulating your VCD, click Next, which will bring up your CD writing options (see Figure 20.51). Your defaults should correspond to the optimal settings. The only option you may want to change is the Perform Writing Test Before Recording option. If you have just installed a new CD burner, I recommend test burning, otherwise you can go straight to writing the CD.

Clicking Next will bring up the final screen (see Figure 20.52). Again, the default settings should work fine, so click the Create VCD button and the writing will commence. Once the writing finishes, your CD should auto eject.

The advantage of the GoDVD plug-in is that you can create scene selections from one video file. In Nero, if you want to have multiple scenes, you have to encode your movie into several smaller MPEG-1 files.

The downside of the GoDVD plug-in is that it does not seem to work with MPEG-1 files (or MPEG-2 in the case of SVCD and DVD authoring) encoded with other programs. So, you are stuck with the substandard MPEG encoding quality of UVS. Hopefully, Ulead will fix this in a future update.

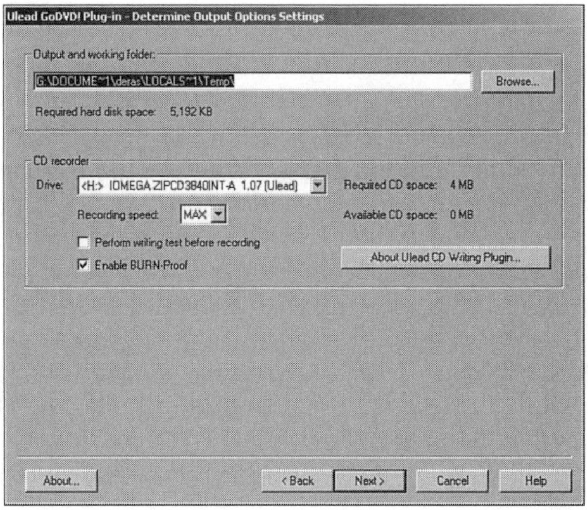

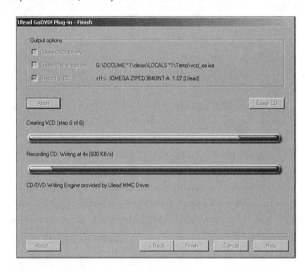

Figure 20.51

The GoDVD Output Options screen; usually all the defaults are correct.

Figure 20.52

The finish screen enables you to engage the VCD writing and monitor the status of the burn.

CREATING A SVCD

Creating an SVCD works almost identically to creating a VCD. The only difference is that you encode your files into SVCD-compliant MPEG-2. SVCD is far less compatible with set top DVD players than VCD. Again, check the VCDhelp.com DVD database to see which DVD players will play back SVCD. With limited compatibility, SVCD is really only viable for making movies to play back on your own DVD player—assuming you buy or already have a DVD player that is SVCD-compatible.

Nero and GoDVD work the same way with SVCD authoring as they do with VCD authoring.

CREATING XVCDS AND XSVCDS

The X in XVCD and XSVCD denotes that the video you are creating exceeds the specs of the VCD or SVCD format. For instance, the VCD spec calls for video to be sized at 352 × 240, the SVCD spec calls for video to be 480 × 480, and XVCD or XSVCD ideally is sized at 720 × 480, which matches the original dimensions of DV video. By avoiding resizing, you maintain higher video quality.

The bit rate of XVCD and XSVCDs is also higher, but usually not exceeding 2.6Mbps including both video and audio bit rates (though some players, like the very affordable Daewoo 5000N, play back XSVCDs up to 6Mbps!). Most players that play back SVCD will playback XVCD and XSVCD. Again, check the VCDhelp DVD database for compatible players.

If you have a player that supports XVCD and XSVCD playback, I can highly recommend using Nero to burn your XVCD and XSVCD files. Nero will issue you a warning that the file does not meet the SVCD spec—assuming you're burning a SVCD—but it will allow you to ignore the warning (see Figure 20.53). The Video Studio 5 GoDVD plug-in, however, will not author XVCD or XSVCDs.

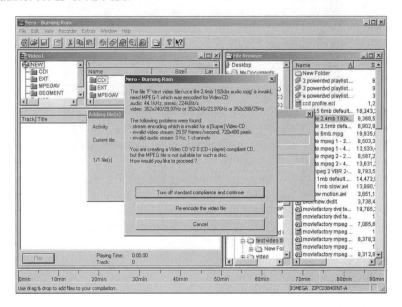

Figure 20.53

When you import out-of-spec video files in Nero, you get a warning; if you are creating an XVCD or XSVCD just click Turn Off Standard Compliance and Continue.

CREATING DVDS

Home computer users at long last have the ability to create their own DVDs. The prices are still a little high, and the hardware and software still new and immature, but eventually creating a DVD will be as easy as burning a CD.

Ulead Video Studio 5 and the GoDVD plug-in—both are sold together as Ulead Video Studio DVD edition—provide an easy, affordable, and borderline-quality DVD authoring solution. However, Ulead makes a much better product for authoring DVDs (as well as VCDs, SVCDs, and MiniDVDs) called MovieFactory.

Ulead MovieFactory

Ulead MovieFactory is the shining light among the current consumer DVD authoring options. MovieFactory enables you to capture video from your camcorder or take video files already on your hard drive, edit your video files, encode quality MPEG videos quickly, and easily author to VCD, SVCD, DVD, or miniDVD—all for $49.

MovieFactory rates very high in both video quality and speed, right behind the top-performing CCE-Lite. Taking into consideration all the other features, this software is a must have for any consumer interested in burning DVDs (as well as miniDVDs, VCDs, and SVCDs).

Overview of MovieFactory

A demo of MovieFactory is included on the program CD that came with this book. Please install it if you want to follow along with this tutorial/overview.

When you click the Movie Factory shortcut, you are faced with four options: Capture Video, Author Menus, Burn Disc Images, and Make CD Labels and Covers (see Figure 20.54).

Figure 20.54

The MovieFactory opening screen lets you choose from four options.

Capture Video and the Video ToolBox

Selecting Capture video launches the Video ToolBox. The Video ToolBox contains three modes: Capture, Edit, and Export. The Capture Mode enables you to capture video from your DV camcorder, and operates similar to most DV capture interfaces (see Figure 20.55). Connect the FireWire to your camcorder, control your camcorder with the onscreen controls, and click record to start capturing footage.

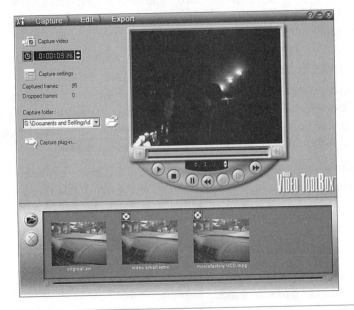

Figure 20.55

You can capture video from your DV camcorder in MovieFactory's Capture mode.

Edit mode enables you to edit video clips captured from your DV camcorder as well as other video clips you may already have on your hard drive (see Figure 20.56). The editing is very basic. You can't add effects, transitions, or titles. But, you can take one or more video files and easily put together an entire movie.

For instance, if you capture one large video file from your camcorder, go into Edit mode and highlight the clip. The clip will appear in the preview monitor. Two bars rest under the video window, a Jog bar and Mark bars. The Mark bars mark the beginning and end of a scene. Moving the Jog bar and clicking the scissors button enables you to cut your original file into additional files.

techtv tip

If you want to create multiple scenes from one large clip, just move the Jog dial anywhere into the green area and click the scissors. If you want to grab ten clips from your movie file, do this ten times. Then, just customize the mark in and out points of each clip on the Video Strip.

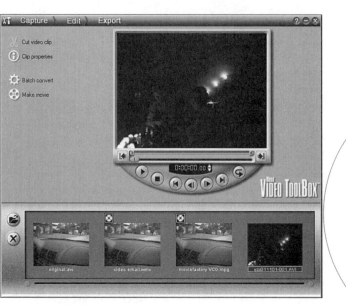

Figure 20.56

In Edit mode you can edit captured or imported video clips.

MPEG Encoding in MovieFactory

The most important function of the Video ToolBox is to encode your video into MPEG-1 or MPEG-2 video. As mentioned, the encoder built into MovieFactory puts many of the current alternatives to shame—not even taking into consideration MovieFactory's price.

You have two encoding options: Batch Convert and Make Movie. If you have multiple clips on the Video Strip, Batch Convert will convert each clip you have selected into an individual MPEG file (see Figure 20.57). Make Movie will encode all the clips into one mpeg file.

The encoding parameters for Batch Convert and Make Movie are identical. You have 15 encoding templates—though only ten of them are related to the VCD, SVCD, and DVD formats. You can also customize your own video template by selecting Custom (see Figure 20.58). Don't be confused by the similar options, look, and templates MovieFactory appears to share with Ulead Video Studio, because the MovieFactory encoder quality is a major step above UVS.

The custom MPEG encoding settings are accessible by clicking the Options button. A Video Save Options window will appear. Click Compression. The Media type drop-down box contains a number of profiles. If you are authoring DVD, SVCD, or VCD, choose one of the associative profiles—and then customize the presets from there if necessary. (Please note, MovieFactory—at least the version I tested—will not burn XSVCDs or XVCDs.) Once you complete your settings, click OK, fill in a name for your new file, specify the output directory, click Save, and the encoding will commence.

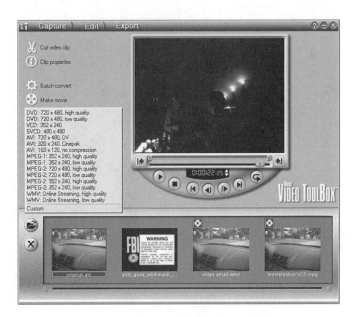

Figure 20.57

Selecting Batch Convert will launch a pop-up of encoding template options.

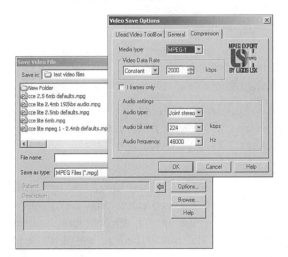

Figure 20.58

You can customize your MPEG settings in MovieFactory if you to don't like any of the templates.

Once you are done encoding your movie or movie files into MPEG, you can click Export and proceed to your DVD/SVCD/VCD authoring options. However, I found it is easier to exit, reopen MovieFactory, and select Author Menus from the opening menu.

DVD Authoring in MovieFactory

A menu wizard will appear, enabling you to choose your authoring format (see Figure 20.59). Assuming you are burning a DVD or miniDVD, select the DVD radio button and click Next.

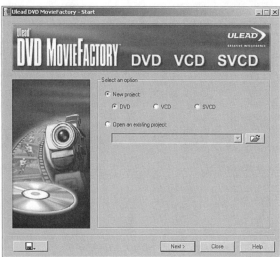

Figure 20.59

MovieFactory's authoring start screen allows you to choose between DVD, SVCD, and VCD.

The next screen of the wizard allows you to add all the MPEG files you want to your DVD (see Figure 20.60). This gives MovieFactory another advantage over Ulead Video Studio and the GoDVD plug-in (as well as Media Studio Pro and its DVD Plug-in) because with those applications you can only author one movie file to a DVD/SVCD/VCD. Your only limitation is media size. If you are using a DVD-R writer, you can write up to 4.7GB on each DVD-R disc.

If you create a DVD with multiple movie files, you can create DVDs with two levels of thumbnail menus, a main menu with thumbnail links to each movie file and submenus for scene links within each movie file. If you don't add scene links for your authored DVD, you will just have a main menu.

If you want to add multiple movie files from one folder, hold down the Ctrl key and click each file that you want to add to your DVD (see Figure 20.61). Then click Open and all the highlighted files will be added.

If you want a custom DVD menu, click Next. If not, uncheck the Create Scene Selection Menu checkbox and click Next.

Figure 20.60

MovieFactory enables you to import multiple movie files for your DVD projects.

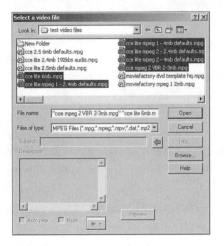

Figure 20.61

If you hold down the Ctrl key you can select (left-click) multiple video files.

Creating a Scene Menu

The Add Scene window enables you to add an endless amount of thumbnail links to any part of your video files (see Figure 20.62). Keep in mind that the menu templates only allow a maximum of six links to be displayed per menu page. So, if you create 12 scene links, you will end up with a two-page menu.

Figure 20.62

You can select multiple scene points from each movie file.

Selecting scene links is pretty obvious; just navigate the preview bar to a desired spot in your video and click Add. You should only select I frames as your scene links because all other Mpeg frames are missing image data (so they have lower still image quality).

MPEG video saves data space by only encoding the video information that changes from frame to frame on most of your video; however, a certain percentage of your frames called *I frames* are completely rendered. As long as you have the Locate scene frames box checked, you will only be able to choose I frames as thumbnail buttons (recommended).

As already mentioned, if your DVD is composed of multiple movie files, you will have a main menu, with a link to each file. If you add any scene links, they will exist on secondary menus that will be activated when you click on one of the main menu links.

If you check the Add introduction video file box, you will be able to add an introductory video that will play prior to the appearance of your menu (see Figure 20.63).

After you finish picking your scenes and appropriately setting the check boxes, click Next. If you chose to add an introductory file, this will bring up the Add Introductory Video File screen. Browse for your file and click Open, then click Next. Any file you import will play from beginning to end on your DVD, so you may want to edit down your introductory video in MovieFactory's video editor or another editor before you reach this step. Once you have selected your intro movie, click Next.

Figure 20.63

MovieFactory allows you to choose an introductory movie to play before your menu appears.

The Select Menu Template enables you to create the look of your menu or menus. If you double-click on any thumbnail button, you can change the frame displayed; however, the original scene link will remain the same. You can choose a different template for each menu, if you have more than one. Use the drop-down box to access submenus. You can add your own custom background image as well as background music for each menu (see Figure 20.64).

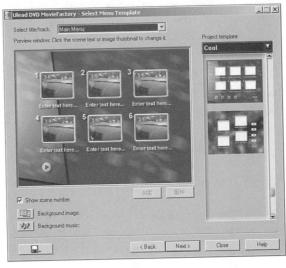

Figure 20.64

MovieFactory enables you to customize the look of your main menu and submenus, as well as add background music for each.

Take note that DVDs use a different type of MPEG audio file, so MP3s or any other audio file you add as menu background music will need to be transcoded into MP2 during the authoring process, adding to processing time. (If you add a five-minute song, expect the authoring process to take around five extra minutes on an 800MHz computer.) Once you are finished with menu settings, click Next.

DVD Playback Simulation

The Playback Simulation screen enables you to test drive your authored DVD, and should exactly resemble how your DVD will appear on a regular DVD player—assuming everything is compatible (see Figure 20.65). Once you are done simulating, click Next.

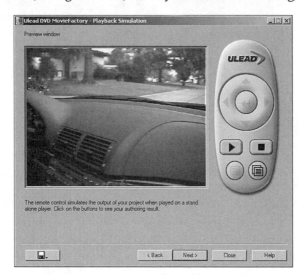

Figure 20.65

The Playback Simulation window enables you to test/preview how your authored movie will appear on a DVD player.

Finalizing Your DVD

The Determine Output Options screen works just like the GoDVD plug-in version already covered. The defaults are usually perfect. If you have a DVD writer and a CD writer installed on your computer, make sure you select your DVD drive from the Drive drop-down box (unless you are burning a MiniDVD, in which case you would choose the CD writer). Clicking Next will bring up the Finish screen, where you can click Create DVD to start the authoring process (see Figure 20.66). If you did not add any music, the disc writing process will start up after the menus are quickly rendered. If you are writing a full 4.7GB DVD-R, the process will take around thirty minutes.

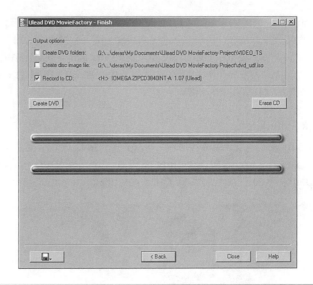

Figure 20.66

Once you are ready to start writing, click Create DVD, and you will be able to view the status of the writing process.

Putting DVD on a CD

Two other distribution options are miniDVD and cDVD. MiniDVD is basically a DVD written on a CD. So, you obtain DVD quality and DVD menus on a twenty-five–cent disc. Due to size limitations, you can only fit between 10 and 20 minutes of video on a disc, enough for a short home movie.

However, most set top DVD players won't play back miniDVDs. The reason is a DVD player has to spin a CD much faster than a DVD to read the same amount of video, because 10 minutes of high-quality video can take up an entire CD. However 10 minutes of video on a DVD is only about 10% of the disc—much less physical space for the DVD reading head to cover.

Fortunately, most computer DVD players will play back miniDVDs, as will most CD-ROMs if you have an MPEG-2 codec on your computer. To get an MPEG-2 codec on your computer, you need to have a DVD software player such as PowerDVD or Cinemaster installed.

As with the other video formats, VCDhelp.com lists which set top DVD players will playback miniDVD. The most affordable competent DVD player which plays miniDVD appears to be the Sampo 620—priced at $150.

Unfortunately, miniDVD is the least compatible of the previously listed formats in regard to set top DVD players.

Both GoDVD and MovieFactory will author miniDVDs.

cDVD

cDVD is a proprietary format from the makers of MyDVD and DVDit (Sonic). A cDVD is basically a miniDVD with a player included, so even if the user has no DVD playback software, they theoretically can play back the cDVD in their computer's CD drive.

Presently, only Sonic DVD authoring software—MyDVD and DVDit—can create cDVDs. A lot of users, however, have reported problems playing back cDVDs on their computers. My attempts to author a cDVD failed as neither MyDVD nor DVDit would recognize my CD burner. Since I have a common CD burner, which most programs recognize—including GoDVD and MovieFactory—I am inclined to fault the software.

OTHER DVD AUTHORING SOLUTIONS

Until the consumer DVD writer market grows, and software makers can devote more resources to software development, consumers will have limited choices. The GoDVD plug-in, while not delivering the best quality or customizability, is very easy to use. Ulead MovieFactory sports ease of use, advanced features, and a quality encoder. Two other prominent authoring alternatives currently on the market are Sonic MyDVD and Ulead Media Studio Pro.

Sonic MyDVD

Sonic MyDVD is included with most of the new DVD burners, both the DVD-R/RW and DVD+R/RW variety (see Figure 20.67). The program is basically a limited version of DVDit, allowing a maximum of ten video tracks for any DVD you can create.

The program enables you to customize buttons and backdrops, and link those buttons to your video files for somewhat professional-looking DVD menus.

While the program interface is easy to navigate, MyDVD has a lot of compatibility problems (in regards to what MPEG-2 files it will accept). I would be reluctant to even consider it unless it comes bundled with your DVD writing drive, or you can verify compatibility with your DVD or CD drive.

MyDVD includes an MPEG encoder, but it is so slow you will cry, longer than any encoder I have observed. So, if you use MyDVD you should use a separate video encoder. This failing is probably reason enough to dump the program, as it eliminates the simplicity of the program, which is all MyDVD has going for it. MyDVD will likely improve in future editions, but currently I would recommend looking elsewhere.

Ulead Media Studio Pro Director's Cut

Ulead Media Studio Pro 6.5 (MSP) is a well-regarded prosumer video editor and a demo copy is included on this book's CD (see Figure 20.68). For reasons already covered, I think it is inferior to Premiere in some ways when it comes to basic DV video editing. However, unlike Premiere, it comes with very good MPEG-1 and MPEG-2 video encoders, as well as a DVD authoring plug-in.

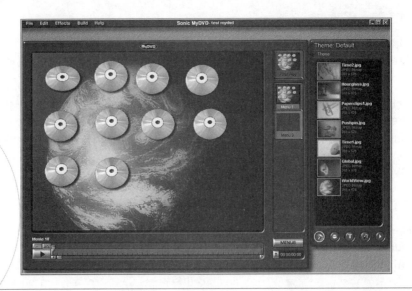

Figure 20.67

Sonic MyDVD has a nice looking interface, but I had problems with the performance and compatibility.

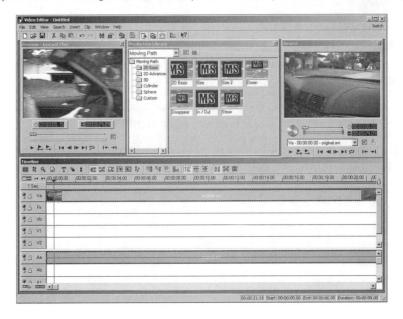

Figure 20.68

Ulead Media Studio Pro is a full-featured prosumer video editor that includes a great MPEG encoder.

The DVD Plug-in has the same easy-to-use interface as the GoDVD plug-in available for Ulead Video Studio. Unlike the GoDVD plug-in, it works with any MPEG file you throw at it for DVD authoring. (One caveat: You can only create XVCDs and XSVCDs with files you encode in MSP.)

The MPEG encoding quality built in to MSP is so good most users probably don't need to use an external encoder, but you have that option. In addition, like the GoDVD plug-in, MSP's DVD Plug-in can author miniDVD, VCD, SVCD, XVCD, and XSVCD, and of course DVD.

Now for the best part: While MSP costs $499, a more stripped down version—called Media Studio Pro Director's Cut (MSPDC)—which includes the quality MPEG encoder and the DVD plug-in costs $199. MSPDC packs the highly desirable combination of quality plus ease of use, making it a highly recommended DVD authoring solution. If you can do without instant timeline editing, not only will MSPDC make a great DVD authoring solution, it will also work great as a video editor. Though MSP lacks Adobe Premiere's instant timeline playback and superior sound controls, MSP previews all effects of your timeline playback in real-time. The faster your processor is, the higher quality the preview.

Creating a DVD with Media Studio Pro

The following steps to create a DVD with Media Studio Pro also apply to creating a miniDVD, SVCD, XSCD, VCD, XVCD:

1. Encode your video into an MPEG video file (if you have already done this, skip to the next step).

2. Once you have finished putting together your movie on the timeline, go to File, Create, Video File.

3. A Create Video File window will appear. Select MPEG files from the Save As Type drop-down box. Then click Options.

4. A Video Save Options window will appear. Select the Compression tab. The Compression tab displays all of the encoder options.

5. Select media type. The Media type drop-down box includes a number of setting profiles. Each profile just alters the settings to fit that selection. For creating a DVD, you can select either NTSC DVD (preferred) or Mpeg 2 (or PAL if that is the television standard of your audience) (see Figure 20.69). For creating VCD and SVCD, choose the included VCD and SVCD profiles. For creating XVCD and XSVCD, you will need to select Mpeg 1 or Mpeg 2 and set your own audio and video bit rate. For XSVCD and XVCD, I recommend staying under 2.6Mbps total, 2.4Mbps for video, 192Kbps for audio (unless you have a player that supports higher bit rates).

6. If the default DVD NTSC profile settings are acceptable to you, click OK, fill in a name for your file, choose the output directory, click Save, and the encoding will begin. The encoder built in to MSP is about three times slower than the CCE-Lite encoder, but the quality is about the same. Furthermore, you can't use the CCE-Lite encoder off the MSP timeline.

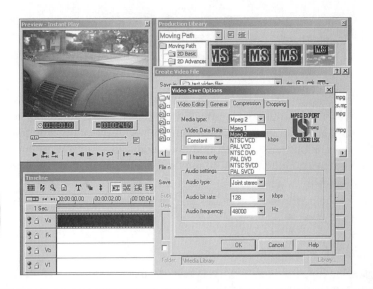

Figure 20.69

For encoding MPEG-2 for DVD, NTSC DVD is a good choice, or you can customize your own settings.

If you want to use CCE-Lite–encoded files with MSP's DVD plug-in, you will need to render out to an AVI file and encode it with the standalone version of CCE-Lite. When you buy CCE-Lite you get both the standalone version and the Premiere plug-in. If you have Premiere, you can edit your movie on the Premiere timeline and use the CCE-Lite plug-in, and then import the MPEG into the MSP DVD Plug-in later.

Authoring Your DVD with the MSP DVD Plug-In

Once you have your movie encoded into an MPEG file, follow these steps:

1. Choose File, Export, Ulead DVD Plug-in (see Figure 20.70).
2. A Select File window will appear. Navigate to the folder where you placed your MPEG file and select the file. Then click Open (see Figure 20.71). (If you are authoring an XSVCD or XVCD, you will get a message about exceeding spec, inquiring whether you want to create an XVCD or XSVCD; answer Yes.)

The interface of the DVD-Plug-in is identical to the GoDVD plug-in, so refer to the GoDVD section of the VCD creation tutorial. The only amended note to that tutorial is that all DVD menus—including those authored by the MSP DVD Plug-in and the GoDVD plug-in—work with the arrow buttons on a DVD remote control, whereas VCD and SVCD menus work with the number buttons.

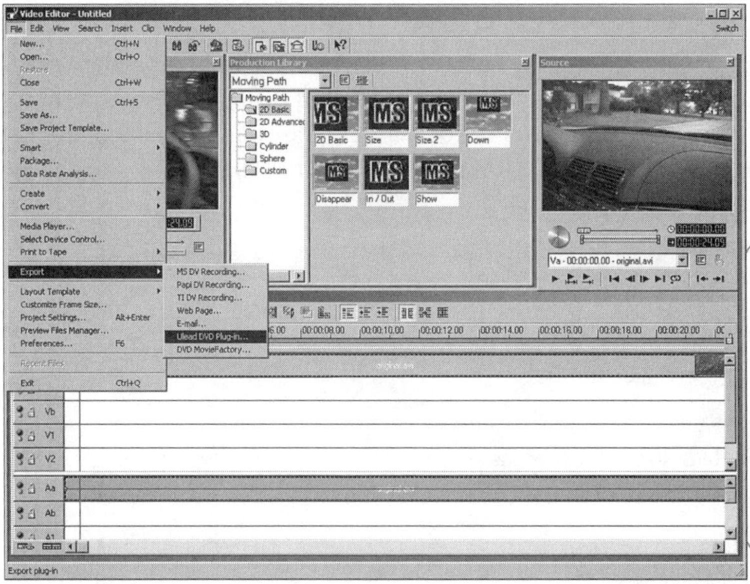

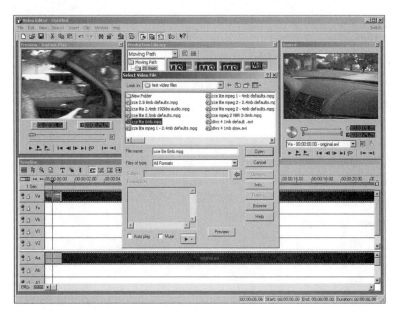

Figure 20.70

When you are ready to author to DVD, select File, Export, Ulead DVD Plug-In.

Figure 20.71

You can only author one movie file with the Ulead DVD Plug-In.

OVERVIEW OF ENCODER QUALITY

The following table rates the quality of several of the most prominent encoders currently available (all of which have been covered in this book). A 25-second DV AVI multi-scene test file was used as the source for the test. The computer performing the test was an 800MHz Athlon with 384MB RAM and two 7200rmp IBM 60GXP hard drives. Each encode file was rated on a scale from one to ten.

TABLE 20.1 AN ENCODER QUALITY TEST

Encoder	Quality	Speed
DV original	10	—
CCE-Lite MPEG-2 6Mbps	9	54s
MSP MPEG-2 8Mbps	9	169s
MovieFactory DVD HQ template 6Mbps	8.75	85s
CCE-Lite MPEG-2 4Mbps	8.5	54s
Panasonic MPEG-1 4Mbps	8.5	365s
TMPGenc MPEg-2 4Mbps	8.5	242s
CCE-Lite MPEG-1 4Mbps	8.25	51s
MovieFactory MPEG-2 4Mbps VBR	8.25	85s
TMPGenc MPEG-1 4Mbps	8.25	233s
MSP MPEG-2 4Mbps	8	164s
DivX 4.02 4Mbps	8	74s
LSX MPEG-2 4Mbps	8	78s
LSX MPEG-1 4Mbps	8	77s
UVS DVD HQ template 4Mbps	7.75	105s
Panasonic MPEG-1 2.4Mbps	7.75	361s
MSP SVCD template 2.5Mbps	7.5	165s
MSP MPEG-2 2.5Mbps	7.25	167s
TMPGenc MPEG-1 2.4Mbps	7.25	238s
MovieFactory MPEG-2 2.4Mbsps	7	85s
UVS SVCD template 2.4Mbps	6.75	103s
LSX MPEG-2 2.4Mbps	6.25	78s
UVS VCD template 1.3Mbps	4.75	101s

CHAPTER 21

ADVANCED VIDEO AND SOUND EDITING TECHNIQUES

They have yet to create a program that covers every possible need an average digital video producer (that's you) might have, so it is very likely you will need to resort occasionally to external applications beyond your trusty video editor for some tasks. This chapter covers the following:

- How to capture still images from your video and properly process them so they can be used on Web pages or e-mailed to friends and family. Every second of video is composed of 30 potential still images, but you need to change the aspect ratio, and sometimes deinterlace before your video stills will be usable.

- How to eliminate motor noise from your digital video audio. As you might already know, many DV camcorders have a problem with this, but it can be overcome by using special audio editing software.

- How to rip tracks from audio CDs and encode them into the MP3 audio format. Unfortunately, you usually can't just grab a file of an audio CD and import it into your video editing program.

GRABBING STILL IMAGES FROM YOUR VIDEO

More and more camcorders are including separate still image picture taking capability. But as I already covered, the quality is not that great, and you need to use a separate transfer method to download the stills to your computer (usually serial or USB). Consequently, for many users who just want pictures for a Web site or e-mail use, grabbing stills from your video files is often a more convenient option. And considering every second of video is composed of 30 frames, you have a huge amount of potential stills even in just a few minutes of video (see Figure 21.1).

Figure 21.1

Every second of video is potentially 30 still images you can grab for use on a Web site or to e-mail.

If your camcorder includes a progressive video mode then as long as you shoot in that mode, all you need to do is capture any still within your video editing program of choice, and you now have a 720×480 full resolution still.

The final step, which is not absolutely necessary (but recommended), is to change the aspect ratio to 4:3. DV video records footage in 3:2 aspect ratio, but when you play it back on your TV it conforms to the 4:3 aspect ratio of your TV (similar to SVCD, whose 1:1 aspect ratio conforms to 4:3 aspect when played back on a TV). However, on a computer, DV stills when in the original 720×480 3:2 aspect appear wider and fatter (see Figure 21.2). The only way to correct this is to change the aspect ratio of each still to 4:3, resulting in a 640×480 still. Any image editing program (Photoshop, Paint Shop Pro, Photo Impact) will do this very easily.

Figure 21.2

Stills captured from DV video need to be resized to 640×480 so that they don't appear horizontally elongated.

Most users have interlaced video camcorders, which means each frame of captured video is composed to two separate fields of video taken 1/60 of a second apart (1/50 of a second for PAL), interlaced together. As long as the video frame has little or no motion in it, you can extract the entire interlaced frame just like you would if it was a progressive video frame, because the fields are so identical that it will resemble a progressive video frame. However, if there is too much movement in between that 1/60 second interval then you will get an odd-looking still that resembles two different images spliced together (see Figure 21.3). The only way to fix this is to deinterlace. Deinterlacing usually discards one of the fields and then fills in the empty space of the lost field by doubling the remaining field or by interpolation.

JARGON

Interpolation refers to a technique whereby the software takes the current image information and uses that to guess what image data should fill the empty image space.

Consequently, image resolution is affected. Theoretically, you should end up with half the original resolution, as you are dumping one of two fields; however, the effect is usually not that dramatic. In any case, you should only use deinterlacing when necessary.

Capturing Stills in Adobe Premiere

You can capture stills two different ways in Premiere: from an individual clip or from the timeline. If you are capturing from a clip, navigate to the frame you want in the Clip monitor and select File, Export Clip, Frame. If you are capturing from the timeline, navigate to the frame you want in the Program monitor and select File, Export Timeline, Frame (see Figure 21.4). An Export Still Frame window will pop up, enabling you to name and choose a destination for the still image file.

Figure 21.3

If there is too much movement between the capture of each interlaced frame, exported stills will exhibit what is known as the combing effect.

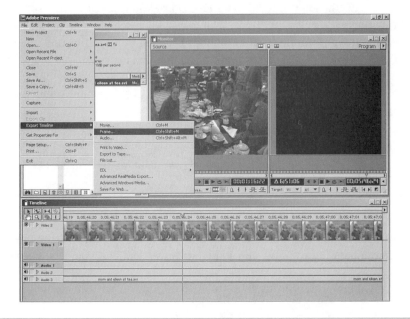

Figure 21.4

You can grab still images from any clip, or from anywhere on the timeline in Premiere.

The default file format for stills in Premiere is Bitmap (BMP). You can change to a different format by clicking Settings, but I recommend sticking with BMP. You can change to a more efficient file format (like JPEG) in your imaging application of choice later. Once you have typed in a file name and selected a destination, click Save.

Deinterlacing Still Images in Paint Shop Pro 7

In Paint Shop Pro (PSP) select File, Open and navigate to the captured still file, click on it, and select Open. Select Effects, Enhance Photo, Deinterlace; a Deinterlace menu will appear (see Figure 21.5). You have just two options: to retain the Odd or the Even field. You can preview both options to decide which one you like better by clicking the eye button. Once you are happy with your settings, select OK.

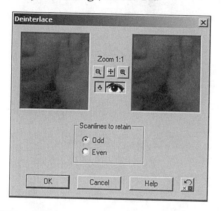

Figure 21.5

If your still has a lot of movement in it, you can use Paint Shop Pro 7's deinterlace filter to drop one of the frames, which will usually clear up the image.

To change the aspect ratio, open any DV-captured still and select Image, Resize. A Resize dialog will appear (see Figure 21.6). First, at the bottom of the menu, uncheck Maintain aspect ratio. Then select the Pixel size radio button,1 change the Width to 640, and keep the Height at 480. Click OK and you now have a still with the correct aspect ratio for viewing on a computer. (Remember though if you are going to add stills to a movie, they still need to be in the 720×480 3:2 format.)

Deinterlacing Still Images in Photoshop

Open your DV still and then select Filter, Video, Deinterlace. Unlike PSP where you choose the field you want to keep, in Photoshop you select the field you want to eliminate (see Figure 21.7). You also have to select how you want to fill the empty space of the eliminated field. I usually prefer interpolation, but you may want to experiment on a picture by picture basis. Photoshop lacks any preview for the deinterlace filter, but using the Edit, Undo command enables you to reverse any changes and try other settings.

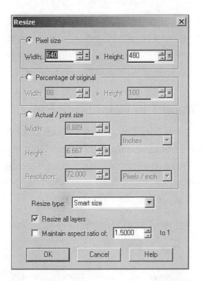

Figure 21.6

Changing the aspect ratio is recommended for all stills grabbed from DV video.

Figure 21.7

Photoshop's deinterlace filter gives you the option of interpolation or duplication to fill in the lost field's image data.

To change the aspect ratio, open any DV-captured still and select Image, Image Size. An Image Size dialog will appear (see Figure 21.8). First, uncheck Constrain Proportions. Then in the Pixel Dimensions area, set the Width to 640 and leave the Height at 480. Click OK and you are done.

Photoshop enables you to create a Batch command which will apply certain changes or filters to multiple files. This can come in handy when you need to change the aspect ratio of a large number of DV stills.

To create a new Batch function, go to the Actions palette and click the Create New Action button (see Figure 21.9). Give your new action a name ("resize"), and then make any changes you want to make to one of your DV stills, in this case resizing it to 640×480. Then click the Stop button and your new action is ready to use.

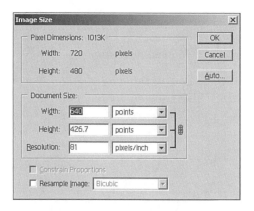

Figure 21.8

If you don't correct the aspect ratio, all your DV stills will look abnormally wide (so instead of adding 15 pounds it will add 30 pounds to everybody).

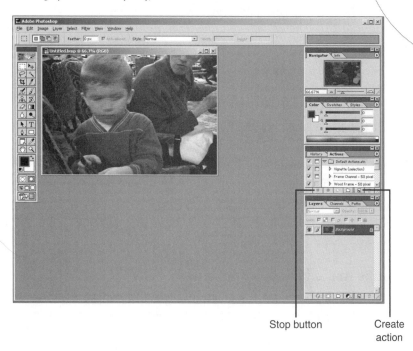

Stop button   Create action

Figure 21.9

Creating an Action in Photoshop enables you to apply the same changes (in this case resizing) to a large number of image files easily.

To apply your new actions to multiple files, select File, Automate, Batch. A Batch dialog will appear, enabling you to select your newly created action (or an action you have previously created). You can set the Source folder or files, the Destination folder, and whether you want to overwrite the old files with the newly changed files (see Figure 21.10).

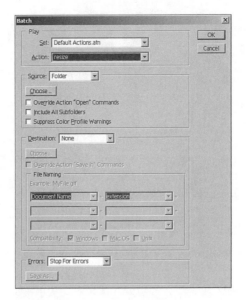

Figure 21.10

The Batch menu gives you numerous options in implementing your Batch Action.

REMOVING MOTOR DRIVE NOISE FROM YOUR AUDIO

If you are unhappy with motor noise your microphone is picking up from your camcorder's tape drive, you have options besides using an external microphone. You can use software to screen out a certain degree of the motor noise, ideally without affecting the rest of the sound on the tape.

First, you need to export the audio track from your movie project. Many consumer video editors like Ulead Video Studio 5 do not allow this; however, most prosumer video editors do.

Exporting Audio in Adobe Premiere

(In an ideal world you would use a DirectX plug-in to remove noise, but in my tests all noise reduction plug-ins I have tried were inoperable in the most recent version of Premiere.)

You can export your audio from Premiere in a number of ways. If you have a large number of clips, the easiest and fastest method is to assemble a finished movie on the timeline first and then export the audio track from the entire movie.

If you have already added music files to your movie, lock those tracks so the music does not get exported. Otherwise, wait until you have applied noise reduction to your movies' main audio tracks before adding music.

To export audio from the entire timeline project go to File, Export Timeline, Audio (see Figure 21.11). An Export Audio window will appear. The default export format is a DV AVI audio file. Most audio programs don't recognize this format, so you need to change the export format. Click the Settings button, and a new window will appear. From the File type drop-down box, select Windows Waveform and click OK. Name the file, select a destination folder, and click Save.

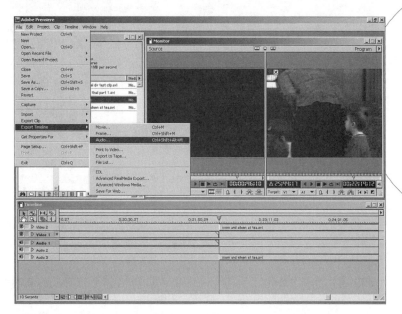

Figure 21.11

To get the motor noise out of you audio you will have to export it from Premiere so you can work on it in another audio editing program.

Now that you have the raw audio track, a number of programs are available that enable you to remove most motor noise. Considering both price and performance you really can't beat Cool Edit 2000. Cool Edit 2000 is a shareware audio editor which has one of the best noise reduction filters you will find. Cool Edit 2k is free for thirty days; after that it costs $69 to register.

Removing Motor Noise in Cool Edit 2000

A demo of Cool Edit 2000 is included on the Program CD.

Open the audio file you exported from Premiere in Cool Edit. Find a quiet portion of the recording where only the motor drive can be heard. Zoom into that area by clicking the magnifying glass button. Highlight a small area by left-clicking on the waveform and dragging slightly to the right (see Figure 21.12).

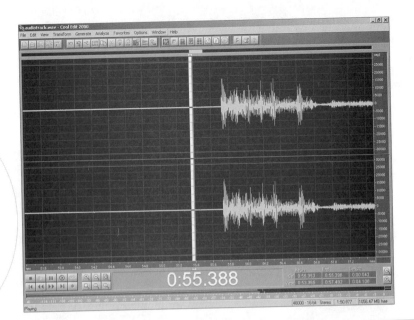

Figure 21.12

Make sure you zoom in enough so that you can select a very small segment of your audio track, which only contains motor noise.

You want to capture as little as possible, as this will serve as a sound profile of what Cool Edit will filter out of the entire audio track. Because motor drive is a redundant sound, you should make sure the waveform area you highlight is totally flat (no peaks or valleys). Click the Loop button (the infinity symbol) to make sure the sample you selected contains only the motor drive.

Then select Transform, Noise Reduction. A Noise Reduction interface will appear (see Figure 21.13). Click the Get Profile from Selection button. Then click Save Profile, name your profile, and click Save.

techtv tip

If the highlighted selection is too small, the Get Profile button will not activate. To activate the button, lower the FFT size in the Noise Reduction settings and/or increase the size of the selection.

Click the Close button and select Edit, Select Entire Wave. Again select Transform, Noise Reduction. Click Load Profile, find the profile you just saved, and click Open.

Click the Preview button and you will now hear your audio track after removing the selected noise profile. Adjust the Noise Reduction Level slider to your own preference. While setting it at 100 will totally eliminate motor drive noise, you often lose ambient room tone and some portion of the frequency spectrum, which can affect overall sound quality. I find a setting somewhere between 70 and 85 is the best compromise between eliminating motor noise and keeping the rest of the audio intact. Once you find a setting you like, click OK and the filter will be applied.

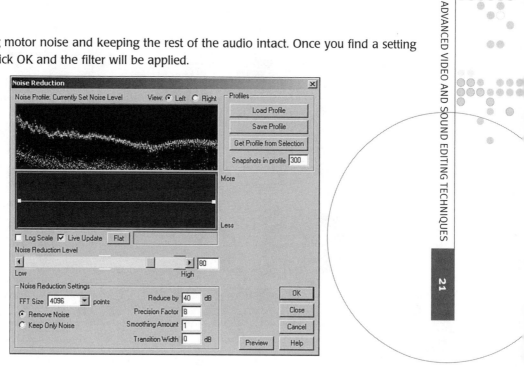

Figure 21.13

Cool Edit 2000's noise reduction plug-in is one of the best tools to remove motor noise from your DV audio track.

If you need optimal quality, you will need to apply noise reduction on a section-by-section basis, because motor drive noise can vary depending on how high or low the camcorder's auto audio gain control is set. Before resorting to this, try applying the effect to the entire track length and see if it sounds good enough. You can always undo any changes in Cool Edit and start over.

Adding the Altered Audio Track Back to Premiere

Reopen your Premiere project. First unlink your main audio track from your video track using the unlink tool, or by right-clicking on the audio track and selecting Unlink Audio and Video. Then use the Select Track Tool and click on the audio track (or tracks) you output earlier. Once selected, go to Edit, Clear and the tracks will be eliminated (see Figure 21.14).

Right-click the Project window and select Import, File. Locate the audio track file that you just edited in Cool Edit, highlight it, and click Open. Drag that file from the Project window into the Timeline and you now have motor-drive-free (or at least reduced) audio (see Figure 21.15).

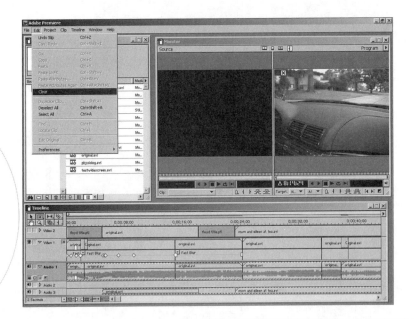

Figure 21.14

Before you add the newly cleaned audio track, you will need to delete your old audio tracks.

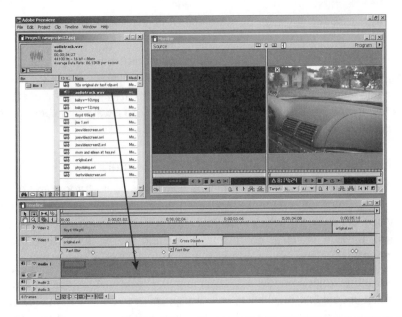

Figure 21.15

After dragging your new audio track into the timeline, you will now have a motor-noise-free movie.

Other Programs for Reducing Motor Drive Noise

Sonic Foundry Sound Forge, Steinberg Wavelab, and a few other programs can achieve similar results, but most of them cost far more and don't work any better.

GETTING MUSIC FROM A CD INTO A COMPUTER

Adding music is a great feature available in every video editor mentioned in this book. However, you need to extract the music from your audio CDs into your computer in order to add them to your movies. In the original Audio CD form, you can't access your song files with most video editing software. You will need to use a program called a ripper to extract your audio files to common readable WAV files. This is the same tool used in the MP3 creation process.

Several audio rippers are available. My personal favorite is Audiocatalyst (cost $30), but Musicmatch is by far the most popular program (probably because it is free) (see Figure 21.16). So I will conduct the following tutorial using it. RealOne Player and Sonic Foundry Siren are two other free CD-ripping and MP3 creation options.

Figure 21.16

Musicmatch is a pretty good encoder/ripper application, but the main reason for its popularity is the price.

Ripping To WAV with Musicmatch 7.0

Ripping to WAV ensures that you maintain 100% quality of your original CD. Audio CDs are basically in WAV format to begin with, so when you rip an audio CD you are just transferring the file to your computer hard drive. The downside of ripping to WAV is that files sizes are large. A full 74-minute audio CD is 650MB.

If you decide to rip to WAV, go to Options, Recorder, Settings and select the WAV format radio button in the CD Quality section (see Figure 21.17).

Then click the Track Directory button and specify where you want the ripped WAV files to go on your hard drive. After you have made those changes, click OK. Then select Options, Quality and make sure WAV is marked. Select Options, Source and make sure the drive where you loaded the audio CD is selected. Then click the red Record button on the Musicmatch player. The Recorder module will launch; click the red Record button and the ripping will begin (see Figure 21.18).

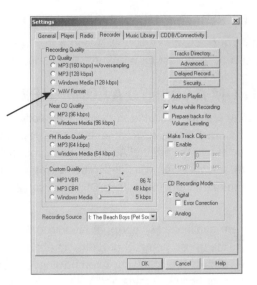

Figure 21.17

To rip your files to WAV, you will need to set the Musicmatch Recorder appropriately.

Figure 21.18

The Recorder module in Musicmatch is where you specify which audio CD tracks you want ripped and/or encoded.

On my 48x CD-ROM, Musicmatch ripped at 7.8X speed, which is identical to the ripping speed I achieved in Audiocatalyst (so a three-minute song took about 23 seconds). Ripping speed depends greatly on how fast your CD-ROM can do DAE (Digital Audio Extraction). DAE speed varies among CD-ROMs and usually has no relation to the data speed rating of a drive. To check the DAE speed of your drive, check out the Web site CD SPEED (www.cdspeed2000.com). They feature software that can test the DAE of your drive, and they also maintain a list of CD-ROMs with the fastest DAE.

Ripping to MP3 with Musicmatch 7.0

If you are short on disk space or just want to encode straight to MP3 (most video editors are MP3-compatible), Musicmatch enables you to go straight from audio CD to MP3. All you have to decide is what bit rate you want your MP3s to be.

MP3 quality at 128Kb/s is indistinguishable from WAV on the average television or computer speaker setup, and takes just 1/12th the space of the original audio CD. On a high-fidelity home theater system, 256Kb/s is considered indistinguishable from the CD original and takes 1/6th the space. 160Kb/s or the VBR (variable bit rate) equivalent is considered to be the best compromise between quality and space.

To encode to MP3, go to Options, Recorder, Settings and select your preferred bit rate in the Custom Quality box (see Figure 21.19). Then repeat the same steps as above.

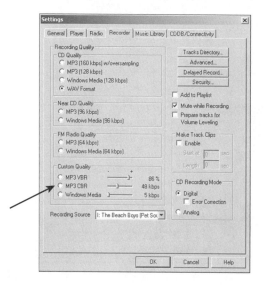

Figure 21.19

Musicmatch has a confusing number of different MP3 settings. I recommend using the custom VBR mode at around 75%.

Ripping and Encoding Options for Audio Snobs and Perfectionists

This header, of course, refers to me when I have the time or extreme need, but usually I go for the middle approach, which I think Audiocatalyst represents—that is, a good combo of speed and quality (see Figure 21.20).

If, however, you want to ensure a perfectly ripped CD, I recommend using a program called Exact Audio Copy (see Figure 21.21). That is not to say you can't get a perfect rip with Musicmatch or many other programs. Indeed, if your CDs are clean, most of the time you should. However, Exact Audio Copy (EAC) has numerous methods to ensure no pops or glitches during the extraction process. The cost for this quality assurance is time; EAC is slow.

As important as a quality rip is the MP3 encoding quality. Just as with MPEG video encoding, the quality of the encoding engine is everything. If you want to encode into MP3 at the highest possible quality, I recommend using the Lame MP3 codec, which is free and can be obtained online. I have included both of these on the Program CD. You can configure EAC to work with the Lame codec; otherwise you will need a frontend for Lame.

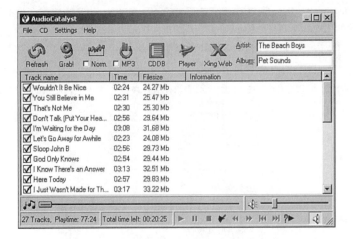

Figure 21.20

If you have $30 to spend, I prefer the quality, speed, and ease of use delivered by Audiocatalyst for my audio CD-ripping and MP3-encoding needs.

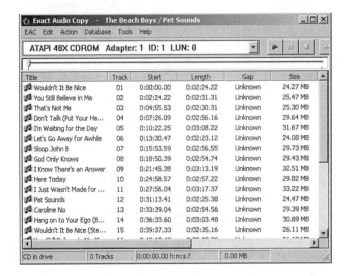

Figure 21.21

Exact Audio Copy is a good ripper option on those occasions when you need to guarantee error-free ripping.

A *frontend* is a user interface that works with a raw encoding engine. Many freeware encoders need frontends to work.

Using EAC and Lame is slower than most other ripper/encoder combos, but you can ensure perfect quality on the rip, and superior quality on the MP3 encode. So if you have a lot of CDs to rip and encode into MP3, I would not recommend this route. However, if you just have a handful of songs and you need perfect quality, and you are willing to use slightly more complicated software, this is a good option. You can of course use Lame separate from EAC (if you find EAC unbearably slow). If you have a good DAE on your CD-ROM and clean audio CDs, using EAC is probably not necessary. But you can still use the Lame encoder to get the best quality MP3 encoding.

CHAPTER 22

ADVANCED SPECIAL EFFECTS

If you want to create the illusion of flying through the sky, or scaling Mount Rushmore, you no longer need a Hollywood movie contract to do it. A few consumer video editors and all prosumer video editors give you the capability to construct these fictional scenarios, and the learning curve is very reasonable.

The ultimate quality depends a lot on your own imagination and skill, but the software tools to insert yourself into a scene from Star Wars are in many video editors. The main effects used to do this are known as blue-screen effects and video compositing.

One of the big differences between consumer and prosumer video editors is special effect features like these. However, a few affordable consumer programs offer some of these advanced special effect capabilities. Videowave 4, which costs around $100, includes very basic blue screen and video compositing effects that are extremely easy to use. Prosumer applications like Premiere and Media Studio Pro offer far more extensive blue screen and compositing features.

BLUE SCREEN EFFECTS

If you want to superimpose yourself into a scene from the film *Gladiator*, or just in front of a picture of the Eiffel tower, you can do this with what is called the blue screen effect.

Blue screen effects derive their name from a blue background screen, which is used during special effects filming sequences. The blue screen part of the video is later replaced with a special background. In the case of an outer space movie, the background might be the hull of a space ship, or some creepy planet landscape. The color of the background does not have to be blue. (In fact, filmmakers often use green screens these days.)

The important thing is that the background screen or backdrop is a uniform color, as this entire color will eventually be replaced with your desired background. Of secondary importance is that the background color be an unnatural color not representative of whatever you are filming in front of it. So if you have a yellow sheet and someone in front of it is wearing a yellow shirt, their torso is going to be removed when you eliminate the background.

If you have seen a blue screen or green screen before, they are neonish colors, colors you don't see in the real world. Consequently, when the background color is removed, whatever you shot in the foreground is unaffected. The blue screen process is technically referred to as *Chroma Keying* (or just keying) because you select a key color, which is then removed.

DIY Blue Screen

You have several options when creating your own blue screen. You can use a uniform color bed sheet against a wall (easiest and cheapest method) (see Figure 22.1). You can go to the fabric store and find something similar. You can try to find a wall that would work. Finally, you can paint a wall or buy some cheap sheets of plywood and paint them. Lighting will be very important because shadows on the screen can create problems when you try to remove the background in software. Refer to the lighting section of this book to minimize shadows (Chapter 13, "A Primer on Lighting"). The easiest option is to film outside, but again, avoid shadows as much as you can on the screen.

Whether you are inserting a moving or stationary background, you should shoot your video with a tripod as you do not want any camera movement, because this can potentially make the background effect look less realistic.

Applying Blue Screen Effects in MGI Videowave 4

Videowave has very basic blue screen effect capability. In general, it is hard to get the effect perfect, as I found it difficult to eliminate all of the blue screen without losing a little bit of the edges of whatever I had filmed in front of the screen.

To apply the effect, open your video and background files in Videowave by right-clicking in the Library window and selecting Add Files. Add the background file to the storyboard. Click the Video Mixer button (see Figure 22.2).

Figure 22.1

When you are shooting blue screen effects, your screen needs to cover the entire background of your shot.

Video Mixer button

Figure 22.2

Videowave makes it easy to pull off a blue screen effect, but the effect quality tends to look amateur.

You will see at the bottom of the screen two overlayed frames labeled background and foreground (see Figure 22.3). Drag the blue screen video you recorded onto the foreground frame. Set the Size slider to 100%, click the Finish tab, and set the Size again to 100%. Click the Start bar.

Figure 22.3

The blue screen effect interface in Videowave is very straightforward.

Click the Remove Color check box and click the Color button that appears (see Figure 22.4). A menu will appear; click the Pick a Color button and click whatever you used as a blue screen. Then click OK.

Figure 22.4

The Remove Color bar menu enables you to select the color of your blue screen so that you can then remove it.

The final step is to adjust the Tolerance slider. Adjusting the Tolerance slider increases the range of colors that are removed from the foreground. Once you are happy with the effect, click Apply.

Applying Blue Screen Effects in Adobe Premiere

Premiere has a blue screen option similar to Videowave, where you pick a color and then adjust for "similarity" (Premiere's term for tolerance); however, it also includes thirteen additional blue screen methods in case those results prove inadequate. The results are better than Videowave. In Premiere, you can achieve a realistic-looking blue screen effect. The only problem with the Premiere blue screen interface is that you have a thimble-sized preview screen to work with, which can make it somewhat tricky to figure out if you have removed the entire blue screen (see Figure 22.5).

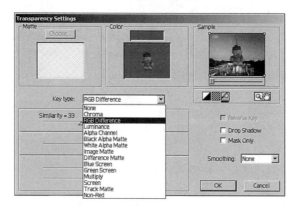

Figure 22.5

Premiere's blue screen interface has puny preview windows to work with; however the quality of the blue screen effects are very convincing.

To apply the effect, you need to place the background clip on Video track 1 and the blue screen clip on Video track 2. Then right-click Video 2 and select Video Options, Transparency (see Figure 22.6).

A Transparency Settings window will appear. Select RGB Difference from the Key type drop-down box (see Figure 22.7). Then click anywhere on your blue screen in the preview window in the Color box. Adjust the Similarity slider so that your screen is entirely removed. You can use the Sample screen along with the magnifying tool to make sure. You can also navigate through your altered clip in the Sample window. Once you are satisfied, click OK. You will have to render the timeline (or at least that part of the timeline) before you can preview the effect in the Program monitor. If you don't like the results obtained with RGB Difference, try one of the other keying options.

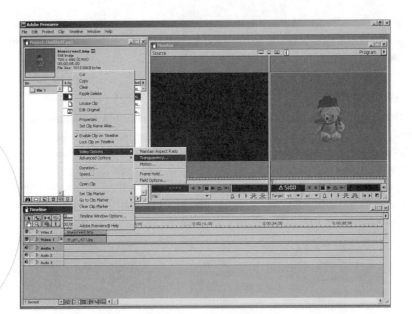

Figure 22.6

After placing your clips on Video 1 and Video 2, you will then access the transparency controls of the blue screen clip (on Video 2).

Figure 22.7

Premiere allows you a number of ways to remove your blue screen. The easiest method is to use RGB Difference.

VIDEO COMPOSITING

Video compositing is a cross between animation and video editing. Video compositing enables you to animate static images (or video files) such as a jet, or a planet, across another static image backdrop or a moving video background. Using video compositing, you can create the illusion of a person flying or levitating. Professional video compositing usually involves countless layers of animation in the same scene, such as a space ship flying through an asteroid field.

Used adroitly, you can create some amazing visual effects that would be impossible, or prohibitively expensive, to film in the real world. The king of video composition programs is Adobe After Effects. However, priced at $649 for the Standard version and $1499 for the Professional version, After Effects is too steep for most of us. The learning curve for After Effects is definitely a step up too, so it is not for everyone. Videowave and Adobe Premiere include some basic 2D compositing controls that enable you to do some interesting things, and the difficulty level is low.

Video Compositing in Videowave 4

Videowave has pretty limited compositing capability. You can specify the starting point of an image animation, middle point, and ending point.

In the following compositing example, I created the illusion of levitation. First, I videotape a teddy bear in front of a blue screen. (If you reproduce this example, remember, the camera needs to be on a tripod while recording.) Then I recorded a background for the levitation to take place.

In Videowave, I add the background clip to the storyboard. Then I go into the Video Mixer module, just as in the blue screen tutorial. I drag the blue screen clip onto the foreground frame, and go through the steps to remove the blue screen color.

Then I set the beginning, middle, and final positions of the levitator by clicking on the Start, Hold, and Finish buttons and setting my desired location (see Figure 22.8). I make sure the size is 100% in each stage, though you can always change the size if your animation calls for it. Click Apply, and the levitation effect is in the can. Since you only have nine possible animation start and stop points, you can't really do anything elaborate. However, Videowave at least provides a glimpse (though small) of what you can do in more advanced compositing programs.

Video Compositing in Premiere 6

Adobe Premiere 6 is definitely a step up from Videowave in the compositing department. Premiere enables you to compose video animations with an endless amount of direction changes and includes some control over the speed of the animation.

To create a composite animation in Premiere, take clips similar to the levitation ones and load them on separate video tracks. The background clip needs to go on Video 1, and the blue screen track goes on Video 2. Perform the blue screen removal as described earlier. Then right-click on the track and select Video Options, Motion (see Figure 22.9). You can also click on the Motion link in the Effect Controls template.

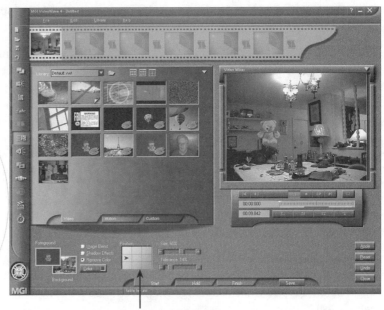

Start, middle, and end animation positions

Figure 22.8

In Videowave, you can set beginning, middle, and end positions of a video or still for a very simple animation effect.

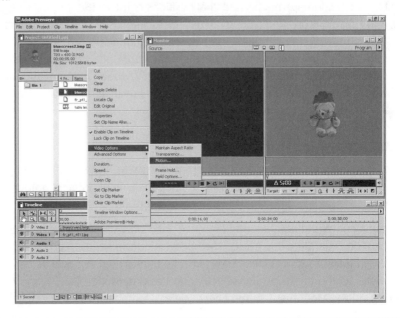

Figure 22.9

To access the video compositing features of Premiere, right-click the track you want to animate and select
Video Options, Motion.

The Motion Settings window will appear (see Figure 22.10). In this window you can set all your controls for your video animation. The left screen previews what your animation will look like, and the right screen is where you can define the animation path. You can also control Rotation, Zoom, and Delay, as well as choose from three different motion settings. Besides interesting blue screen effect animations, you can do all sorts of other animations with video clips and even still images.

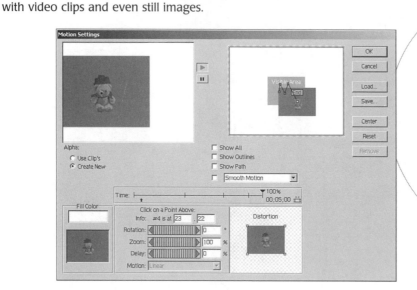

Figure 22.10

Premiere's compositing control menu enables you to set any type of motion path for your video, as well as alter numerous other parameters.

ON BEING A FILMMAKER

Digital video is becoming increasingly popular among amateur and even some professional filmmakers. USC film school (alma mater of George Lucas and Steven Spielberg) has even started to integrate digital video into their curriculum. While film is still clearly superior to digital video in terms of image quality, that gap will continue to close and film will eventually be replaced.

In the meantime, digital video is a more appropriate format for many amateur filmmakers, both because of cost and because digital video represents the future of filmmaking.

The chances of becoming a successful filmmaker are very low; moreover, making even a short film costs at least $10,000. Digital video offers a sane middle road where wannabe filmmakers can pursue their ambitions without bankrupting themselves and/or their families. Almost every film festival now screens some digital video films, and there are an increasing number of digital-only festivals. In addition, online film sites where filmmakers can submit their work are becoming increasingly popular.

DV AS AN ALTERNATIVE TO FILM

With a good DV camcorder (Sony VX2000 is one of the best) you can record high-quality video footage, but it still in all honesty won't match 16mm image quality (and not even close to 35mm). However, DV with a good camcorder is close enough to 16mm that it can be taken seriously. Films like Spike Lee's *Bamboozled* and *The Original Kings of Comedy* were shot almost entirely with DV camcorders.

Video Look Versus Film Look

One thing many film professionals are saying in this debate is that video, regardless of the quality, does not look like film. In fact, video and film do generally have a different look because the formats are significantly different. Film is composed of 24 progressive frames a second and resolves images based on a photochemical reaction, while most video is 30 interlaced frames per second and resolves images digitally. As covered earlier, 30 interlaced frames (60 half fields) resolves twice the action (good for sports), but 30 progressive frames (30 whole fields) resolves twice the image quality (good for romantic comedies).

However, in the last few years they have started to engineer special video cameras to emulate the film look. In *Star Wars Episode II: Attack of the Clones*, George Lucas is using a special HD (high definition) camera that shoots at the same progressive frame rate as a film camera (24p). You can expect that film emulation will only improve as digital video technology evolves.

Still, most consumer video camcorders shoot solely in 30fps interlaced mode. So the average camcorder owner is just not well equipped to achieve a film look.

Progressive Video Versus Interlaced Video

As we covered in Chapter 4, "Digital Camcorder Basics," interlaced video is composed of alternating half picture fields. The advantage of interlaced video is that you can record twice as much action by just capturing alternating half fields (as opposed to whole fields) in the same amount of data space. So the only real advantage interlaced video offers is bandwidth efficiency, not quality, and when interlaced video was adopted as the NTSC TV standard, bandwidth was limited.

Progressive video is similar to film, wherein each frame of video is a complete picture (or in video terms, a whole field). Computer displays are progressive. High definition televisions (HDTVs) are capable of displaying both progressive and interlaced video. Progressive video may eventually replace interlaced video, but for now interlaced video is still the most common video format.

If you are going for the film look, a camcorder capable of shooting in progressive video mode should be considered. Keep in mind that progressive video is less suited for capturing fast action such as sports. Fortunately, every camcorder that features progressive video mode also has interlaced video mode so you can shoot both ways. Unfortunately, almost none of the newest consumer camcorders in 2002 featured the progressive video mode option. A few camcorder models still exist with progressive video mode, but fewer than in previous years. If you are using interlaced mode, dropping the shutter speed can help give you more of film look.

PAL Camcorders Versus NTSC Camcorders

NTSC is the television format in the U.S. (and the rest of North America), and PAL is the television format in Europe and a number of other countries around the world. NTSC video is 30 interlaced frames per second. PAL is 25 interlaced frames a second. PAL has slightly higher resolution to compensate for the fact that is has fewer frames per second.

Based on the numbers, PAL comes closer to film than NTSC. Consequently, amateur filmmakers should consider shooting with a PAL camcorder, ideally a PAL camcorder with progressive video mode. While a PAL camcorder will not play back directly on an NTSC television, it will work with any FireWire card or video editing software. Furthermore, many DVD players sold in NTSC markets will play back PAL DVDs. So as DVD writers become more common, you will be able to author your movies to DVD for playback. If a DVD player is SVCD-capable, it will most likely play back PAL SVCDs as well.

If you are certain that your digital video will at some point be transferred to film (a very expensive process costing $100–1000 a minute), you should definitely consider shooting with a PAL camcorder that has progressive video mode (for example the Canon XL1) (see Figure 23.1). (For documentary films, an interlaced camcorder is acceptable.) If you shoot with an NTSC camcorder, even with a progressive video NTSC camcorder, you will lose six frames of video a second when transferring to film–30 NTSC frames to 24 film frame. Obviously, this will negatively affect image quality.

Figure 23.1

The Canon XL1's progressive CCD and professional quality make it ideal for professional films shot on DV.

Most PAL-to-Film transfers are transferred frame to frame, meaning 25 PAL video frames become 25 film frames. This enables you to maintain all your original video quality. But you end up with an extra film frame every second. As a result, your movie plays 4% slower. Fortunately, this is a small enough margin that the human eye and ear won't notice it. To get an idea of what this altered playback rate is like, open a normal DV video clip in Premiere and change the playback speed to 96% (see Figure 23.2). When transferring to film this way, you will also need to pitch correct your sound track so that it sounds normal when played slower.

Figure 23.2

By altering the playback rate of a clip in Premiere, you can get an idea of what a slowed down PAL-to-Film transfer would look and sound like.

PAL camcorders cost about the same as their NTSC counterparts, though they often have different model names. Many reputable online camcorder stores like Profeel (www.profeel.com) sell both NTSC and PAL camcorders.

Anamorphic Lens Adapters

Most digital video formats have the 4:3 aspect ratio of the common household television. If you want to shoot a widescreen production on DV (like a real movie), you have two options (short of buying a $10,000 DV camera): Use the letterbox mode built in to your camcorder or use an anamorphic lens. The first option causes you to lose significant horizontal resolution because you are only recording on the middle part of your CCD. Using an anamorphic lens, however, enables you to take advantage of all your CCD's resolution by optically squeezing a wide screen picture onto your 4:3 CCD (see Figure 23.3).

Figure 23.3

This figure illustrates the difference between shooting regular DV, digital widescreen DV, and DV with anamorphic adapter (courtesy of Century Optics).

Adobe Premiere 6 includes built-in widescreen template settings that enable you to edit your anamorphic footage in 16:9 mode without having to change anything. Furthermore, many MPEG-2 authoring programs will allow you to specify 16:9 playback for your authored discs, so your movie will play back letterboxed on 4:3 televisions. Or you can leave your anamorphic video as is and it will play back properly on a widescreen HDTV television (see Figure 23.4).

Figure 23.4

Widescreen 16:9 HDTV televisions are not too practical (as there is very little or no HDTV programming in most areas, and they are expensive), but they are good for watching widescreen DVDs.

If you plan on doing a 35mm film transfer at some point, shooting with an anamorphic lens is highly recommended (but remember, close to zero amateur films ever make it to even general art house movie theater distribution, so be realistic). However, distributing your movie as a widescreen DVD is becoming an increasingly realistic option as consumer DVD writers become more common.

The cheapest DV camera with 16:9 CCDs is the JVC GY-DV700WU ($10,000). Top-of-the-line HD camcorders ($100,000+) also feature 16:9 widescreen CCDs, and as HDTV becomes more dominant, we may eventually see consumer priced camcorders with 16:9 CCDs. However, HDTV does not become the new TV standard till 2006, so we may have a long wait. Until then, the best way to shoot widescreen with a DV camcorder is to use an anamorphic lens (see Figure 23.5). However, they are rather cost prohibitive, running around $800 (for a well regarded model by Optex or Century Optics). You will also have to adjust your perspective while filming, as your LCD and viewfinder will reflect a 16:9 video frame squeezed into 4:3, so everything will look narrower.

Figure 23.5

Century Optics (www.centuryoptics.com) makes a very good anamorphic lens adapter that will fit on most DV camcorders.

Moderately priced widescreen LCDs which should enable you to monitor your filming in full widescreen mode are becoming more common. Pioneer makes a 6.5″ model that sells for around $500 (see Figure 23.6). You should be able to connect one of these to a home-made Steadicam, or maybe even mount it on top of a larger DV camcorder.

Figure 23.6

The Pioneer AVD-W6000 6.5" widescreen LCD might work well as a field monitor if you are using an anamorphic lens adapter on your DV camcorder.

Final Thoughts on Camcorder Selection for Filmmakers

Progressive video mode will give you a more film-like look; unfortunately, the best camcorder for the money, the Sony VX2000, has no progressive mode (and many other very good camcorders do not either). As of the spring of 2002, the only high-end progressive CCD–equipped camera is the Canon XL1s (which replaced the almost identical XL1). Both the XL1 and XL1s are bigger and pricier than the VX2000 (and arguably do not produce better image quality). Nonetheless, they are both great camcorders and are very popular among DV filmmakers.

If you want progressive mode and can't afford the XL1/XL1s, then the only alternatives—as of spring 2002—I would recommend are the Canon Optura Pi and JVC 9800u. While they are both very good cams, they have lower video resolution and don't have the low-light performance of the VX2000 or XL1/XL1s. The Optura Pi and 9800u are also no longer being produced, so you will probably have to buy a used one off eBay.

With so few progressive video–equipped camcorders currently on the market, an interlaced-only model may be what you end up settling for. For documentary work, interlaced video works quite well. In fact, many professional documentaries have been shot on video. Personally, I shoot with a Sony VX2000 for documentary work, and for my amateur films I use a JVC 9500u (precursor to the 9800u). If you are just beginning the filmmaking hobby, avoid the temptation to overbuy; you can always upgrade later if you get hooked. As I have come to learn, the most common shortcoming in filmmaking is creative talent, not hardware quality.

RECORDING SOUND SEPARATELY (DAT, MINIDISC)

The film world records sound and video with separate hardware. Amateur filmmakers may find similar success by doing the same. Traditionally, DAT recorders are used for recording audio, but you could also use another camcorder or a MiniDisc. MiniDisc recorders offer very good quality sound, solid battery life, and portability, all at an extremely low price point (see Figure 23.7). The top model SoundBlaster Live! and Audigy from Creative Labs (and a few other sound cards) include an optical input jack which will enable you to digitally transfer your recording into your computer. Otherwise you can use the analog line-in jack.

Figure 23.7

A MiniDisc recorder can make a competent and highly portable sound recorder for DV film projects.

Recording sound separately is a more involved process, but it affords you a lot of options.

GETTING YOUR FILMS TO THE PUBLIC

Film festivals used to be the only possible route for amateur filmmakers to get their films viewed. And while they are still a great venue, thanks to the Internet you now have a growing number of online film sites that offer even more opportunities than ever before to get your movies seen.

Film Festivals

The film festival is the most traditional way to get your movie seen. In the past, film festivals shunned films shot on digital video. But the trend is moving toward acceptance, as most festivals screen at least some digital video productions and the door to digital video is only getting wider.

A great resource for digital filmmakers, 2-pop (www.2pop.com), has a list online of the major film festivals; those which accept DV submissions are noted.

Online Film Sites

Online film sites provide the most convenient and accessible display medium for film-makers of all types. The vaunted Sundance film festival is even running an online film festival during their regular festival composed of many films shot on DV. However, make sure to read the fine print on any site you post your film to. For instance, as of the writing of this book, if you submit a movie to Ifilm (www.ifilm.com), you grant them a "perpetual, unrevocable" non-exclusive license to do whatever they want with your movie. This means they could sell your movie if they wanted to (and someone was willing to pay) with no remittance to you.

If you decide to submit to Ifilm, I recommend sending them a low-quality version of your film. They accept QuickTime 320×240 format, which would be commercially worthless, but still would allow people to see your film online.

Besides Ifilm, other online film sites include AtomFilms (www.atomfilms.com) and Dfilm (www.dfilm.com).

P R O J E C T **9**

CONTROLLING YOUR CAMCORDER VIA YOUR COMPUTER

Provided your computer has a FireWire connection, you can connect your camcorder to your computer to transfer your DV videos. (If your computer did not come with FireWire, you can buy a FireWire add-on card for under $50.)

Follow these steps:

1. Hook your camcorder up to the computer with a FireWire cable.

2. Open your video editor and try controlling your camcorder with the software program's controls.

3. Try capturing some footage from the tape using the software.

4. Preview the captured video clip on your computer.

P R O J E C T **10**

MAKING A SHORT MOVIE

Experience is the best teacher, so it is time to take what you have learned and start making movies.

Take at least one hour of footage and make a 10-minute film with it, adding

- Opening title and closing credits.
- At least one instance of background music.
- Transition effects between some scenes.
- At least one video filter.

ENCODING A MOVIE IN MULTIPLE FORMATS

Digital video affords you innumerable output options. If you want to create a DVD or send an e-mail video, you will need to output your video in a specific format.

Take a finished movie and encode it into several different video formats (feel free to experiment with custom settings):

- VCD, SVCD, or DVD
- Video e-mail
- Web Video (Windows Media or RealMedia)

APPENDIX **A**

A TOUR OF TECHTV

TechTV is the only 24-hour cable television network dedicated to showcasing the impact technology has on our everyday lives and the world at large. By creating and delivering entertaining and insightful programming regarding today's and tomorrow's technology news, events, products, and people, TechTV enables viewers to stay current and connected with all things related to technology.

Offering more than a cable television channel, TechTV delivers a fully integrated Web site. TechTV.com enhances the TV viewing experience with compelling companion content and interactivity.

TechTV is owned by Vulcan Inc.

AUDIENCE

TechTV appeals to people who are excited by and curious about the many aspects of technology. By using technology as the backdrop, TechTV entertains, amazes and provides its viewers with insight into how technology enriches our lifestyles and the world around us.

WEB SITE

TechTV.com allows viewers to participate in programming, provide feedback, interact with hosts, send video emails, and further explore the latest tech content featured on the television cable network. In addition, TechTV.com has one of the Web's most extensive technology-specific video-on-demand (VOD) features, offering users immediate access to more than 5,000 videos, as well as expanded tech content of more than 2,000 in-depth articles.

INTERNATIONAL

TechTV is the world's largest producer and distributor of television programming about technology. TechTV delivers a 24-hour international version via satellite that reaches all of Asia, the Pacific, and the Middle East. TechTV Canada is a "must-carry" digital channel that launched in September 2001.

NETWORK PROGRAM GUIDE

Big Thinkers

βιg 𝒯h÷ιnKeRʃ

www.techtv.com/bigthinkers

Explore the future of technology through insightful and down-to-earth interviews with the industry's most influential thinkers and innovators of our time.

Call For Help

www.techtv.com/callforhelp

Host Chris Pirillo translates technical jargon into plain English, provides computing tips, answers live viewer questions, and interviews guests who help demystify technology. It's interactive, informative, and above all, fun.

CyberCrime

www.techtv.com/cybercrime

Hosts Alex Wellen and Jennifer London take an inside look at fraud, hacking, viruses, identity theft, and invasions of privacy, to keep users secure and aware of the potential dangers on the Internet.

Extended Play

www.techtv.com/extendedplay

Host Adam Sessler provides comprehensive reviews of the hottest new games on the market, and previews of games in development and tips on how to score the biggest thrills and avoid the worst spills in gaming.

Eye Drops

www.techtv.com/eyedrops

Breathtaking, beautiful, compelling, insightful, and sometimes even a little scary, but always entertaining, *Eye Drops* has something for everyone. *Eye Drops* showcases today's best computer-generated animated short subjects.

Fresh Gear

www.techtv.com/freshgear

Host Sumi Das takes an in-depth look at the coolest new products out there from color PDAs to ultra-light notebooks, digital cameras to PVRs, virtual operating rooms to wearable computers. Catch reviews of the latest products, get advice on what to buy and what to bypass, and explore the technologies of tomorrow.

Future Fighting Machines

www.techtv.com/futurefightingmachines

Future Fighting Machines takes a look at the latest in military hardware and gadgets, from electromagnetic energy weapons, to high-tech soldiers' uniforms with built-in mine detectors, to flying spying micro-robots.

Max Headroom

www.techtv.com/maxheadroom

In a cyberpunk future where television is the fabric that binds society, Max Headroom is a computer-generated TV host at Network 23.

The Screen Savers

www.techtv.com/screensaver

TechTV's daily live variety show hosted by Leo Laporte and Patrick Norton features guest interviews and celebrities, remote field pieces, product advice and demos, and software reviews.

The Tech Of...

www.techtv.com/thetechof

From the food we eat, to the sports we play, to buildings where we work, technology has a profound impact on the way we live. *The Tech Of…* is an engaging series that goes behind the scenes of modern life and shows you the technology that makes things tick.

Tech Live

www.techtv.com/news

Tech Live focuses on the technology world's most important people, companies, products, and issues and how they affect consumers, investors, and the industry through interviews, product reviews, advice, and technology analysis.

Technogames

www.techtv.com/technogames

Homemade machines, robots, and electronic devices face off in a high-tech international competition from London's Millennium Dome. Innovation and technical excellence are tested as robots compete at cycling, swimming, high jump, rope climb, solar-powered marathon, and shot put.

TechTV's Titans of Tech

www.techtv.com/titansoftech

Through insightful interviews and in-depth profiles, *Titans of Tech* offer viewers an informed look at where the new economy is headed. These specials profile technology's most important movers and shakers—the CEOs, entrepreneurs, and visionaries driving today's tech economy.

Tomorrow's World

www.techtv.com/tomorrowsworld

The BBC's *Tomorrow's World* takes a look at the latest innovation and discovery in medicine, space, entertainment, sports, transportation, and law enforcement. Featuring reports from every corner of the globe, *Tomorrow's World* is a fascinating, informed, and fact-based view of the future of technology.

APPENDIX **CD**

WHAT'S ON THE CD-ROM

On the *TechTV's Digital Video 101* CD-ROM you will find Web resources along with a wealth of other trial applications and utilities.

SOFTWARE

- **AVISynth** by Videotools
- **Cinemacraft Encoder Lite** by Cinemacraft
- **DivX** by DivXNetworks
- **MediaStudio Pro** by ULead Software
- **DVD MovieFactory** by ULead
- **Nero** by Ahead Software
- **Paint Shop Pro** by Jasc Software
- **Premiere** by Adobe
- **Sandra** by SiSoftware
- **VideoStudio Pro** by ULead
- **VideoFactory** by Sonic Foundry

ABOUT THE SOFTWARE

Please read all documentation associated with third-party products (usually contained in files named readme.txt or license.txt) and follow all guidelines.

I N D E X

INDEX   COLORED GELS

FILMMAKERS

INDEX

MOTHERBOARDS

INDEX

SOFTWARE PATCHES

INDEX

TIME ZOOM TOOL

INDEX

VIDEO

INDEX

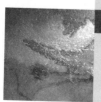

INSTALLATION INSTRUCTIONS
WINDOWS 95/98/2000/XP/NT

1. Insert the CD-ROM into your CD-ROM drive (see NOTE at bottom).

2. From the Windows desktop, double-click the My Computer icon.

3. Double-click the icon representing your CD-ROM drive.

4. Double-click the icon titled START.EXE to run the multimedia user interface.

NOTE: If Windows 95/NT 4.0 is installed on your computer and you have the AutoPlay feature enabled, the Start.exe program starts automatically whenever you insert the disc into your CD-ROM drive.

By opening this package, you are agreeing to be bound by the following agreement:

You may not copy or redistribute the entire CD-ROM as a whole. Copying and redistribution of individual software program on the CD-ROM is governed by terms set by individual copyright holders.

The installer and code from the author(s) are copyrighted by the publisher and the author(s). Individual programs and othe items on the CD-ROM are copyrighted or are under GNU license by their various authors or other copyright holders.

This software is sold as-is without warranty of any kind, either expressed or implied, including but not limited to the implie warranties of merchantability and fitness for a particular purpose. Neither the publisher nor its dealers or distributors assum any liability for any alleged or actual damages arising from the use of this program. (Some states do not allow for the exclu sion of implied warranties, so the exclusion may not apply to you.)

NOTE: This CD-ROM uses long and mixed-case filenames requiring the use of a protected-mode CD-ROM driver.